Equality of Opportunity in Irish Schools

Equality of Opportunity in Irish Schools

A longitudinal study of 500 students

Vincent Greaney and Thomas Kellaghan

Educational Research Centre
St Patrick's College, Dublin

THE EDUCATIONAL COMPANY

First published 1984

The Educational Company of Ireland Limited
incorporating
Longman Browne and Nolan Ltd.
Ballymount Road
Walkinstown
Dublin 12

ISBN 0 86167 051 5

Printed in the Republic of Ireland by
Iona Print Limited, Dublin

Contents

Preface

Today, a vast literature exists which has been prompted by an interest in and concern about inequality in the educational system. The literature comes from all over the world, East and West, developed and developing countries. Much of it focusses on inequality related to social class or socio-economic group membership, though gender has also received a good deal of attention.

The first major set of empirical data on the inequality issue for the Irish system of education appeared in the *Investment in education* report (1966). Since that time, and particularly in more recent years, several other studies have appeared. These studies share two characteristics with the *Investment in education* report. Firstly, they were based on cross-sectional data and secondly, analyses were confined to an examination of the presumed educational effects of class membership.

The study reported in this book shares neither of these characteristics with previous studies. Firstly, it is longitudinal rather than cross-sectional in nature and describes the educational progress of a sample of students from the time they were eleven years of age in 1967 until the time they left school and entered their first occupation. Secondly, while information on the socio-economic background, gender, and location of students was included in analyses, the analyses were not limited to consideration of scholastic progress in terms of these variables. Since considerable variance in school-related characteristics, such as ability, exists among the members of any class, whether the class is based on socio-economic criteria, gender, or geographical location, analyses which do not recognize such variation are inevitably limited in the amount of information they can provide.

Having considered in Chapter 1 policy and research relating to equality of opportunity, particularly in the Irish system of education, we proceed in Chapter 2 to a description of the kind of data used in our study and the procedures which we used to obtain the data.

Chapter 3 describes what happened to students in our study at the first major juncture in the Irish educational system — the transfer from primary to post-primary school. Differences between students who went to secondary school, those who went to vocational school, and those who terminated their education at this point are described. This is followed by a description of the educational progress of students who went to secondary schools (Chapter 4) and of those who went to vocational schools (Chapter 5). Chapter 6 is devoted to a description of the characteristics of students who terminated their formal education at varying points — at the end of primary school, in the early years of post-primary education before they have taken a public examination, on the completion of a junior cycle in a post-primary school, and during the course of a senior cycle. The performance of students on major public examinations (Intermediate and Leaving Certificate) is described in Chapter 7.

By the end of the post-primary period of education, the vast majority of students had terminated their formal education. In Chapter 8, the characteristics of the minority who proceeded to a third-level institution are described. The criteria used to admit students to third-level institutions are also examined as well as the relationship between student achievement on leaving post-primary school and subsequent academic performance.

In Chapter 9, an attempt is made to examine the progress of students through the system from a meritocratic point of view. In particular, the perseverance of 'more able' students in the system is examined and the question is asked whether that perseverance is a function of students' socio-economic background or gender.

In Chapter 10, the relationship between the amount of education (i.e., the highest point reached within the educational system) and students' subsequent occupational status is examined. So are the relationships between information obtained about students when they were at primary or post-primary school and future occupational status.

The final chapter contains a summary of the results of the study and discusses the extent of inequality in Irish schools.

A visual summary of the progression of the sample of 500 students through the educational system is provided inside the back cover of the book. As an aid to the reader, a glossary of terms used in the text is also provided. This glossary includes brief descriptions of variables and statistical concepts used in the study. More detailed descriptions of statistical treatments are provided in footnotes at the end of each chapter.

Longitudinal studies of their nature require institutional commitment and the support of many people over a lengthy period of time. We are grateful to the many students, school principals, guidance counsellors, teachers, and college and university registrars who responded to our numerous queries throughout the life of this project. Much of the responsibility for data collection fell at different times on the shoulders of Joan Baker, Elizabeth Neuman, and Jane O'Reilly, to whom we are very indebted for the persistence and care with which they conducted this most important aspect of the study. We are pleased to place on record our thanks to John Byrne, Demetria Collia, Mary Hegarty, Paul Kelly, and Ronan Reilly for their assistance with computer programming and analysis and to Adrian Raftery of Trinity College Dublin for carrying out a number of analyses reported in Chapter 10.

Our thanks are also due to Sandra Ryan, for preparing tables, references and indexes, to Eithne Mansfield and Caroline St. John for their help in the preparation of the indexes and to Eddie Lynch for his assistance with proofreading. We are grateful to George Madaus, Brendan Hester, Michael Martin, Owen Egan, John Macnamara, and Paul Andrews for their counsel at various stages and to Mary Rohan, Deirdre Stuart, Mairead Byrne, Catherine O'Donoghue, Gerry Smith, and the late Brian O'Reilly for assistance with data collection. The support and advice of Daniel Stufflebeam, Robert Rodosky, Mary Ann Bunda, and David Nevo while the first-named author was a Visiting Fulbright Scholar at the Evaluation Center, Western Michigan University, are gratefully acknowledged.

So many people typed questionnaires, follow-up letters, and manuscript drafts that we cannot hope to thank them all. We are particularly indebted to Nuala Flynn and Carol Marie Hitchcock, and also to Teresa Bell, Aedeen MacCaffrey, and Carol McGuinness. Finally, we wish to express our appreciation to Ursula Ní Dhálaigh of the Educational Company of Ireland for her constructive comments in the preparation of the manuscript and to Seán O'Neill and Jim Darker for type-styling and layout.

1 Irish Education and Equality of Opportunity

Every year, approximately 70,000 children in Ireland enrol in school at the age of four or five years to commence their careers in the educational system. We know in general terms what happens to those children. All will spend about eight years in a primary school after which they will transfer to a post-primary school. As the statutory minimum school-leaving age is fifteen, we may assume that most students will attend school until that age. Apart from that, the educational experiences of students will vary greatly. Some will attend small rural schools, others will go to large urban ones. Some, on leaving primary school, will proceed to a secondary school, others to a vocational school, and others to a comprehensive or community school. Some will take one or more public examinations, others will leave school without taking any. Some will attend a third-level institution, while others begin to work. Some students may spend as many as twenty years in educational institutions; the participation of others will be much shorter.

One might hope that the over-riding consideration determining the experiences of individual children, the length of time they stay at school, the type of curricula they are exposed to, and the examinations they take, would be what the primary-school curriculum has termed 'the optimum personal fulfilment' of each child (Ireland: Department of Education, 1971, p. 12) or, if that is over-ambitious, at least the optimum educational development of each child. We cannot hope to establish to what extent that is true since there is no way of assessing optimum fulfilment or development, either personal or educational; however, we can monitor the actual progress of students through the educational system and in doing this, we can also attempt to determine the relative influence of various factors on that progress. That is what the study described in this book set out to do. A group of eleven-year-old children attending primary school was identified in 1967 and the subsequent educational and early vocational careers of the children were monitored. Further, these careers were related to a variety of variables, personal, social, and educational, in an attempt to identify factors which influence the distribution of educational benefits.

Of particular interest in examining the factors related to the children's educational progress was the principle of equality of educational opportunity, a principle to which many educational reforms in the past in many countries have been attributed. It was explicitly put forward in Ireland in the 1960s as a basis for government policy and for a number of educational reforms. The principle is one which arises in the context of the distribution of educational benefits and is one which, at first sight, would seem to enshrine every child's right to educational provision and optimum educational development. In its present form, it is usually traced back to the Enlightenment era (cf. Sjöstrand, 1973); since then, it has appeared in a variety of forms in the history of the development of mass education. Frequently, inequalities related to social class were the focus of reform (cf. for example, Tawney, 1922, 1931; Young, 1947). The liberal reformers of the last two centuries, in their vision of the progressive improvement of society, had seen lack of education as preventing children from poorer classes from adequately participating in an industrialized society. It was argued that if such children were provided with adequate educational facilities, they would become more competent and satisfied members of society. While the major thrust of Jeremy Bentham's scheme for Irish education, written in 1801, was towards the emerging middle class, it also envisaged education for the 'labouring classes', who were as worthy of Benthamite happiness as anyone else. Besides, education, and particularly the ability to read, would, it was argued, guard people against 'mischievous error and imposition of every kind' while at the same time facilitating 'the intercourse of government with them' (cf. Taylor, 1980).

While educational reforms are open to a variety of interpretations,[1] we accept the position that the reforms of the 1960s in Ireland were carried out with the intention of promoting equality in the system. However, the intention to achieve an objective does not necessarily result in its attainment. Any policy, whether it involves a particular reform, rule, or incentive system, sets out to alter the behaviour of individuals and institutions. But this may not be easy to do. One is faced with the problem that educational systems as they become more sophisticated and self-conscious also become more autonomous (Archer, 1982; Musgrove, 1979). They may move away from the original ideas which brought them into existence and are likely to resist efforts to change them, whether these efforts are directed towards making them more responsive to the perceived needs of society or of students. Some characteristics of an educational system, which might be the result of economic and social conditions, past and present, may hinder rather than facilitate the implementation of a policy (cf. Archer, 1979). If, for example, as it has been argued, the educational system selects and distributes individuals across strata on the basis of characteristics which bear a non-essential relationship to scholastic progress (cf. Parsons, 1959; Sorokin, 1927), then it is important, in the context of policy implementation, to consider aspects of a particular system which might exacerbate this problem. In the Irish context, one thinks immediately of the possible effects of the structure of the post-primary system of education on the implementation of a policy of equality of opportunity; in this system students separate into different kinds of school on the basis of ability and social class (Greaney, 1973; Kellaghan & Greaney, 1970; Rottman, Hannan, Hardiman, & Wiley, 1982). Does such separation affect students' educational and later vocational chances? For example, are a student's chances of survival and of obtaining educational qualifications better in one type of school than in another?

Factors outside the educational system may also impede the realization of policy objectives. The conclusion of the *Equality of educational opportunity* report (Coleman, Campbell, Hobson, McPartland, Mood, Weinfeld, & York, 1966) that most surprised people in the United States in the 1960s was that schooling could not be regarded as a powerful equalizer in American society. The report's conclusion that school characteristics and resources, such as per-student expenditure, teacher experience, curricular differences, and library facilities, appeared to make little difference to students' levels of achievement, was taken to imply that the school's potential in this area was extremely limited. It would appear that what mattered most was the influence of students' home background, not the kind of formal education they received. While details of the conclusion of the *Equality of educational opportunity* survey can be challenged on methodological and other grounds (Airasian, Kellaghan, & Madaus, 1979; Madaus, Airasian, & Kellaghan, 1980), there is a considerable amount of other evidence to indicate that material, cultural, and psychological factors in a child's family impinge on the child's scholastic development (Ainsworth & Batten, 1974; Bloom, 1964; Cullen, 1969; Fraser, 1959; Kellaghan, 1977a; Marjoribanks, 1974, 1979) and subsequent occupational attainments (Jencks, Smith, Acland, Bane, Cohen, Gintis, Heyns, & Michelson, 1972; Sewell & Hauser, 1976, 1980; Sewell, Hauser, & Featherman, 1976). There is also evidence that if home factors negatively affect a child's progress, attempts at educational intervention to counteract the influence of these factors are limited in what they can achieve (Kellaghan, 1977b). Besides, the question of choice and preference in relation to participation in scholastic activities is one which seems important though relatively little is known about it. When policy decisions of a central authority are put in the context of these factors, we should not be too surprised if we find that the decisions do not always have a widespread and immediate impact.

In the remainder of this chapter we consider contemporary definitions of equality of educational opportunity. We then provide a brief description of the Irish system of education. In doing this, we consider the findings of empirical research which throw light on the attainment of equality in the system. We follow this with a brief review of the findings of research on the attainment of equality in other educational systems. After that, we consider the circumstances under which the central government developed a role in the formulation of educational policy in Ireland in the 1960s and, in particular, declared equality of opportunity as a goal of the educational system. The final section of the chapter contains an outline of our empirical study, which set out to examine the extent to which equality of opportunity operated for the sample of students whose educational careers we studied.

Defining Equality of Educational Opportunity

While ideas relating to equality of opportunity have been implied, if not always explicitly stated, in the context of many educational reforms in western countries over the last hundred years, the concept achieved a high level of prominence and visibility in the last two decades. The concept has been the subject of close scrutiny by commentators, leading to a variety of interpretations and definitions (e.g., Boudon, 1974; Coleman, 1968, 1973, 1975; Halsey, 1972, 1975; Jencks *et al.*, 1972; Mosteller & Moynihan, 1972). At this point, we will pay some attention to the meanings attached to the term 'equality of opportunity' since it is often used in a vague sense or in a way that makes it difficult or impossible to ascertain whether or not a policy designed to promote equality is successful. For example, a publication of the Department of Education of the Irish government asserted that 'our most urgent social and educational objective' is 'equality of opportunity'. 'Every child, without exception' the same publication states 'will receive the best possible education suited to his or her individual talents' (Ireland: Department of Education, 1969, p. 1). While one might find it difficult to disagree with such sentiments, one would find it equally difficult to ascertain whether in fact children were receiving 'the best possible education' suited to their 'individual talents'.

Traditionally, equality of opportunity has been interpreted to mean that all children — irrespective of characteristics such as race, creed, social class, gender, financial resources, place of residence, or other irrelevant criteria — should have equal *access* to educational facilities. This principle is based on the premise that social and occupational roles should be allocated on the basis of 'achievement' rather than 'ascription' (Linton, 1936). That is, roles, and education to the extent that it contributes to the achievement of such roles, should be left open to choice, individual effort, and competition, rather than being assigned on the basis of characteristics, such as gender and social class, over which the individual has no control (Foner, 1979). In its most pristine form, then, the principle of equality of opportunity implies that there should be no legal barrier to prevent a child from entering any form of education. The definition may be extended beyond this to take account of inequalities of circumstances, especially financial ones. If one accepts this definition, the implementation of equality of opportunity would involve the elimination of financial barriers, through, for example, the provision of scholarships, school transport, free education, and university grants (cf. Halsey, Heath, & Ridge, 1980; O'Donoghue, 1971). It is important to note that the emphasis in this definition is on uniformity of educational treatment for all children. This is done by making education available and free and by ensuring that a uniform curriculum and similar resources (e.g., per-pupil expenditure, science facilities, teacher qualifications) exist in all schools (Coleman, 1968).

A more radical approach to defining equality of educational opportunity is to use *participation* rather than access as the criterion. Equality in this sense is achieved only when there is a correspondence between the composition of the student body at any given point in the educational system and that of the social structure in general. The adoption of this definition has led to the use of the concepts of 'over-representation' and 'under-representation', concepts which are now deeply entrenched in the equality debate (Musgrove, 1979). To meet the participation criterion of equality, members of different groups (e.g., gender, social class) should be equally represented at each stage in the educational system. In support of this position, the assumption may be made that educationally relevant characteristics (e.g., ability, motivation) are distributed equally among members of different groups. Even if this assumption is not made, the principle of equality of participation may be put forward on the basis that participation should not be contingent on achievement. Acceptance of participation as the criterion of equality involves shifting the emphasis in equality from the achievements and qualifications of the individual, the corner-stone of equality defined as access, to an ascriptive principle of corporate identity (Bell, 1973).

The criterion of participation has the advantage that it provides a more objective and concrete yardstick than does access for assessing the extent to which equality exists. For example, the extension of compulsory schooling to the age of fifteen years and the provision of 'some' post-primary education for all students imply a criterion of participation. With a little effort, it is possible to determine whether in fact all children stay in school until they reach the age of fifteen or whether all children receive 'some' post-primary education.

A further definition of equality of opportunity uses *achievement* as the criterion. According to this definition, not only should there be equality of access and participation, there should also be equality of outcome, in proportion to their numbers in the population, between the genders, between children from different social classes, and between children in different parts of the country (Coleman, 1968; Sussman, 1967). This last definition is the most radical of all and the procedures used to achieve it may require not uniformity of treatment (as when access is the criterion of equality) but positive discrimination in the form of additional educational resources in favour of certain groups of children (O'Donoghue, 1971; Shipman, 1980). While a policy designed to achieve equality of achievement may complement one designed to achieve equality of access, it may also be antagonistic to it. Attempts to achieve equality of achievement, or even of participation, can lead to procedures which would actually reduce equality of access for some students. This can happen if use is made of a quota system, by which members of groups (for example, women or members of a minority linguistic group) which are under-represented in educational institutions or in particular types of employment are given priority in recruitment to such institutions or employment (cf. Musgrove, 1979).

Many attempts have been made to examine the extent of inequalities in educational systems (e.g., Coleman *et al.*, 1966; Floud, Halsey, & Martin, 1956; Halsey, Sheehan, & Vaizey, 1972; Jencks *et al.*, 1972). Evidence to assess inequality may use as its criterion access, participation, or achievement, in accordance with the three definitions of equality we outlined above. Most empirical studies have focused on participation, though increasingly in recent years achievement is being taken as a criterion. Access is more difficult to measure empirically except where facilities are clearly not available; inferences about access are sometimes drawn on the basis of evidence relating to participation. There has also been a number of attempts designed to help overcome inequalities, particularly inequalities in achievement. The most notable projects which undertook this task were Project Head Start and similar programmes in the United States (Lazar & Darlington, 1982; Westinghouse Learning Corporation/Ohio University, 1969) and programmes in Educational Priority Areas in Britain (Halsey, 1972). All of these involved the idea of positive discrimination. While most of the work relating to equality was carried out in the United States and in Great Britain, the Irish educational system did not remain untouched (cf. Holland, 1979; Kellaghan, 1977b).

The Irish System of Education

The Irish system of education is a complex one, reflecting the rather haphazard way in which it developed through the last century and into the present one. It has been said that it is highly decentralized (Vaizey, 1967) and that it is highly centralized (Atkinson, 1964; Barrington, 1980). Both statements are true. Individual schools exercise considerable autonomy in general management and in the appointment of staff and, at the post-primary level, in deciding what curricular options they will offer. (This situation is somewhat modified by the fact that many secondary schools are run by religious congregations and orders which may have general policies regarding the running of their schools.) Local autonomy has its roots in history. Much of the development of the system, particularly at the post-primary level, was laissez faire, the result of local initiative, with limited over-all planning in the distribution of resources (cf. McElligott, 1981; Ó Raifeartaigh, 1954). There are also centralized aspects to the system, however (cf. Hopper, 1977).[2] The Department of Education of the national civil service exercises control over the content of school syllabi at both primary and post-primary levels. At the primary level, assessment of the work of pupils (and by implication, that of teachers) is carried out by inspectors of the Department. Through its control of public examinations at the post-primary level, the Department contributes to the curricular monotony of such schools.

The system is organized horizontally into three levels.[3] The primary level is fairly homogeneous; most children are enrolled in state-funded schools. Second-level or post-primary education is more varied; at this level, there are five types of school: secondary, vocational, 'secondary tops', comprehensive, and community. Over 90% of second-level students are enrolled in the first two types. While 'secondary tops' (the secondary department of a primary school) are disappearing from the educational scene, comprehensive and community schools only appeared since 1966. Third-level education is provided in universities, technological colleges, colleges of education, and a number of other institutions which provide courses in areas such as art, music, commerce, and theology.

Primary education

All children between six and fifteen years of age (fourteen years up to 1972) are required to receive an education. Parents have the option of providing this education in their homes or of sending their children to private schools or to schools funded by the state. The vast majority of children (almost 97%) up to the age of twelve years are enrolled in state-funded schools, called national schools, in which fees are not charged. All such schools follow a similar curriculum (Ireland: Department of Education 1971) and are provided with similar facilities and resources. There is also some evidence that similarities in organization and in teaching style exist across classrooms catering for different socio-economic groups (O'Sullivan, 1980). To the extent that the vast majority of children at the primary stage are exposed to similar educational conditions, equality of opportunity, defined in terms of equality of access, may be said to exist. There are some exceptions to this. About 3% of the population do not attend national schools but go instead to private non-aided schools (Ireland: Department of Education, 1981) which do not receive any financial aid from the state and in which fees are charged. For the most part, non-aided schools are attended by children from higher socio-economic backgrounds. Virtually all such schools are in the larger urban areas and are usually junior departments of secondary schools. A further group of children attend national school but are not exposed to the common curriculum and facilities of such schools. These are children in special schools and special classes (less than 2% of primary-school students) and children in some disadvantaged areas, towards whom a policy of positive discrimination is operated and who attend schools to which additional resources (e.g., remedial teachers, smaller classes) have been allocated.

Teachers in national schools are expected to provide a minimum of four hours secular instruction each day. A further half-hour is generally devoted to religious instruction. For over forty years prior to 1971, national schools throughout the country followed a relatively narrow curriculum which placed heavy emphasis on the Three Rs. The curriculum, which was determined by the Department of Education, included Irish, English, Mathematics, History, Geography, Needlework (for girls), and Manual Instruction (for boys) (Ireland: Department of Education, 1965). It was estimated that Irish, English, and Mathematics accounted for two-thirds of the average weekly timetable (*Investment in education,* 1966). More time was devoted to the teaching of Irish than to the teaching of English (Macnamara, 1966); more recently, the imbalance in favour of Irish seems to have decreased (Ó Domhnalláin, 1978). In 1971, after students in the present study had completed their primary education, a new child-centred curriculum was introduced to replace the subject-centred one. The new curriculum was generally perceived by teachers to have had a positive impact on both teachers and students (Conference of Convent Primary Schools in Ireland, 1975; Fontes & Kellaghan, 1977b; Irish National Teachers Organisation: Education Committee, 1976). A study in which objective measures of student achievement were employed, however, failed to establish the superiority of the more informal methods of teaching associated with the new curriculum (Egan, 1982).

National schools differ in terms of their size, their locality (urban and rural), their management (Protestant, which are always administered by a lay principal, and Catholic, which may be administered by a lay or religious principal), and the gender of students who attend them (all boys, all girls, or mixed). Any of these factors might be associated with differences in resources and opportunities which might affect a child's educational progress. If such differences do exist, our earlier statement that equality of access exists at the primary level would have to be modified. Little evidence is available which might clarify the issue. In the *Investment in education* (1966) report, it was argued that children were at a disadvantage because of the limited facilities which could be offered in small schools. In the report, it was noted that there was a slower rate of progression through grade levels among children in smaller schools than among children attending larger schools and that the number of scholarships to post-primary schools won by pupils in smaller schools was not commensurate with their share of pupils. However, in a more recent study, which was carried out when a policy of amalgamating small schools had been in operation for several years and in which standardized tests of achievement were used, the relationship between school size and reading achievement (in both Irish and English) was found to be somewhat more complicated; pupils in large and small schools did better than pupils in schools of intermediate size (Martin & Kellaghan, 1977). Following the *Investment in education* (1966) report, a policy of amalgamating small schools was intensified, with the result that between 1964–65 and 1971–72 the number of schools in the country fell from 4,847 to 3,879 (Ireland: Department of Education, 1966, 1974); in 1979–80, the number was 3,415 (Ireland: Department of Education, 1981). While this policy was no doubt motivated by considerations of greater efficiency, though it may not have been very effective in this regard (McDonagh, 1977), it was also presented as being in the interest of improving school facilities and 'of affording improved educational opportunity' (Ireland, 1980, p. 41). However, the general public did not seem to accept this view; in a survey of public opinion in 1974, the number of respondents who thought the closing of small schools was a change for the worse was slightly greater than the number who thought it was a change for the better (Kellaghan, Madaus, Airasian, & Fontes, 1981).

Small schools, as one would expect, are almost all located in rural areas. Practically all of them are lay administered. Religious schools, on the other hand, tend to be large and to be located in urban areas. They also tend to cater for only one gender of pupil. There is some evidence that type of administration, location, and gender composition of school are related to achievement, though the relationships are slight (Martin & Kellaghan, 1977). One advantage in attending primary schools run by religious is that such schools are often adjacent to a secondary school which is run by the same religious body and students in these primary schools are more likely than ones in lay-administered ones to gain admission to the secondary school (cf. Rudd, 1972).

On completion of primary education, practically all students nowadays proceed to a second-level school. However, this was not always the case. When Dr Hillery, Minister for Education, introduced his proposals for comprehensive schools in 1963, a third of children were not receiving any post-primary education (OECD, 1969, p. 121). At the time the students in our study left primary school, about 7% did not transfer to a post-primary school. To the extent that future occupational and social status depend on educational credentials, those who terminated their education at the primary-school level were at an obvious disadvantage.[4] A number of empirical investigations has established that those who left school at the minimum statutory age, which would include many who did not proceed to second-level education, came predominantly from lower socio-economic backgrounds (Craft, 1974; Greaney, 1973; *Investment in education*, 1966; Kellaghan & Greaney, 1970; Roseingrave, 1971; Rudd, 1972; Ryan, 1967).

There has been a general improvement in the level of educational attainment of the Irish population since the beginning of this century (Geary & Henry, 1979; Hutchinson, 1969; MacGréil, 1974). In the most comprehensive analysis of data relating to this issue, Geary & Henry's (1979) examination of census statistics revealed that the more recently a person was educated, the more likely he or she was to have received education beyond the primary level. For example, among 20 to 24-year-old males in the country in 1971, 46% had received only a primary education, while over 80% of those aged 60 to 64 years had attained only this level of education. The position of females was slightly better but not very dissimilar. While 38% of 20 to 24-year-olds had received only a primary education, the figure for 60 to 64-year-olds was 76 per cent. The trend in improvement in educational level applied to all socio-economic groups.

While educational attainments, defined as the highest level in the educational system which is reached by a student, have been improving and virtually all students now receive at least some post-primary education, it does not follow that educational achievements, defined in terms of students' level of mastery of knowledge and skills, have also been improving.[5] We do not have any detailed information on students' levels of achievements in the system over any long period of time. We do know, however, that differences in achievement have been found to exist between students from different socio-economic backgrounds in the primary school (Fontes & Kellaghan, 1977a; Kellaghan & Greaney, 1970; Martin, 1979) and that differences between boys and girls, generally favouring the former, have been found in the mathematical achievements of students on the point of entry to post-primary school (Kellaghan, Madaus, Airasian, & Fontes, 1976).

Second-level education

Second-level education is provided in secondary schools, in 'secondary tops' in primary schools, in vocational, in comprehensive, and in community schools. Secondary schools emphasize an academic education and provide the traditional avenue to third-level education and to a variety of white-collar occupations (Andrews, 1979; Crooks, 1977). Until the 1960s, state support for such schools was limited to a small capitation grant for students and a portion of teachers' salaries (McDonagh, 1977). Other costs were met through tuition fees, which were small, and through the contributions of religious orders and congregations which established and owned the schools. Given this state of financing, it is not surprising that in 1966–67, out of a total of 586 recognized secondary schools, 485 were conducted by religious (O'Connor, 1968).

Prior to 1966, the Department of Education required that each secondary school set an entrance examination. The purpose of the examination was to show that the pupil was 'sufficiently advanced in knowledge and in intelligence to follow with reasonable success a course of secondary education' (Ireland: Department of Education, 1960, p. 70). In the past, the low standard required of examinees in these achievement tests has merited some criticism (Ó Catháin, 1958). In 1966, the entrance examination requirement was removed and was in fact discouraged by the Department (*ICE report*, 1975). Many schools, however, persisted with the practice of requiring potential entrants to sit for an examination. Passing or admission standards varied greatly from school to school. Failure to obtain a pass in one school's entrance examination did not prevent a pupil from sitting for entrance examinations in other schools.

Secondary schools attract the majority of post-primary students. This means that the proportion of students in academic as compared to non-academic schools is much greater in Ireland than in most other European countries (OECD, 1969). For example, in the 1960s, less than a quarter of the relevant population attended grammar schools in Britain (Baron, 1965; Morton-Williams & Finch, 1968), while over 70% attended secondary schools in Ireland. The Irish preference for an academic secondary education may be because this form of education has been perceived as a means of advancing to higher social and economic status; in a country which traditionally has been more agricultural than industrial, skilled manual labour may be undervalued (O'Leary, 1962).

In 1968, almost 40% of secondary schools accepted boarders. The number of boarding students amounted to approximately 18% of the total secondary-school population.[6] Fees for boarding vary considerably from school to school (cf. Murphy, 1980).

While the number of secondary schools has decreased over the last ten years — from 600 in 1969–70 (Ireland: Department of Education, 1974) to 527 in 1979–80 (Ireland: Department of Education, 1981) the number of students attending such schools has increased from 144,425 to 199,193.

Secondary education has traditionally been provided in a small number of primary schools in a department known as a 'secondary top'. These departments, most of which were in convent national schools, were sanctioned to teach the secondary-school programme. While enrolment figures for secondary and vocational schools have spiralled in recent years, the secondary tops have experienced a severe drop in numbers. In 1971, secondary tops accounted for approximately 1.6% of the total number of students receiving full-time second-level education (Ireland: Department of Education, 1974).[7]

An alternative form of second-level education is provided in vocational schools; these schools have traditionally focused on practical subjects and the preparation of students for trades, business, and agriculture. In recent years, students enrolling in such schools have consistently amounted to approximately one quarter of the total number of students enrolling in full-time post-primary education. Unlike their secondary counterparts, most vocational schools are co-educational.

The present system of vocational education dates from the Vocational Education Act of 1930. The Act introduced a system of public education by providing schools which were funded by local and central government and managed by local committees which are selected by local authorities. The schools provide 'continuation' and 'technical' education. Under the terms of the 1930 Act, continuation education is 'education to continue and supplement education provided in elementary schools and includes general and practical training in preparation for employment in trades, manufacturers, agriculture, commerce and other industrial pursuits, and also general and practical training for the improvement of young persons in the early stages of such employment'. The term 'technical education' was somewhat more restricted and was described as 'education in or pertaining to trades, manufacturers, commerce and other industrial pursuits' (Ireland, 1930). Initially, vocational schools were precluded from offering academic courses (Coolahan, 1981; Whyte, 1971).

In 1979–80, there were 246 vocational and technical schools in the country providing second-level education; 67,762 students attended these schools (Ireland: Department of Education, 1981). Figures which are exactly comparable were not consistently provided in Department of Education reports in the past; however, as in the case of secondary schools, the number of students attending vocational schools has increased over time.

Comprehensive and community schools, though they differ from each other in some respects, particularly in the way they are managed and in the way they are funded, are similar in many ways. Comprehensive schools were built between 1966 and 1974 in an attempt to construct a unified second-level educational system (OECD, 1969; Spelman, 1970). As their name implies, they were designed to provide a wide range of curricular options. Community schools, the first of which was built in 1972, represent a development of the comprehensive concept; in addition to being comprehensive in curriculum, it was envisaged they would become involved in further educational activities and that their facilities would be available to the local community. A number of community schools have evolved from existing schools, sometimes through the amalgamation of a secondary and a vocational school.

An examination of participation by social class in second-level education in the *Investment in education* (1966) report showed that in the early 1960s, participation rates of children from semi-skilled and unskilled homes became progressively lower as one proceeded through post-primary and on to higher education. Disparities in the participation rates of students in the non-compulsory sector (aged 15 to 19) and at the point of the Leaving Certificate Examination have also been reported for the early 1970s (Rottman *et al.*, 1982). Differences in participation rate related to location and gender were also noted in the *Investment in education* report. There were marked differences between counties at second level, those with the highest participation rate having 50% more students in full-time education than counties with the lowest participation rate. The authors of the report failed in their efforts to find an explanation, in terms of social-class background or income, for the differences between counties. The female rate of participation was found to be higher than the male rate.

While differences in participation in any kind of full-time education are of interest, so too are differences in participation in different types of school. Traditionally, the student entering a secondary school had an advantage over one entering a vocational school if he or she wished to proceed to the Leaving Certificate Examination, to third-level education, or even to a white-collar job (Arundel, 1977). We would expect that variation between second-level institutions in prestige, in facilities, in the courses they offer, and in the qualifications which they confer, would lead to selectivity among the institutions. If such selectivity is related to social class membership, gender, or the part of the country in which a student lives, then it has obvious implications for equality of opportunity.

The *Investment in education* (1966) report found differences in socio-economic background between students in secondary and vocational schools. This finding was confirmed in early analyses of the data used in the study reported in this book (Greaney, 1973; Kellaghan & Greaney, 1970).[8] That secondary schools also attracted more able students was clear when the performance of entrants to secondary and vocational schools on the now defunct Primary-school Certificate Examination was considered (*Investment in education*, 1966).[9] A similar inference emerges from more recent studies in which the performance of students on standardized tests was examined (Greaney, 1973; Greaney & Kelly, 1977; Kellaghan & Greaney, 1970; Swan, 1978). Differences in favour of secondary-school students have also been noted for level of students' educational aspirations (Raven, Handy, Benson, Hannon, & Henry, n.d.) and the interest of their parents as perceived by teachers (Kellaghan & Greaney, 1970). Comprehensive/community schools, in their early days at any rate, seem to have been more like secondary than vocational schools as far as the characteristics of students were concerned (Kellaghan & Greaney, 1970), while an examination of the courses pursued by students revealed a strong emphasis on traditional academic subjects (*ICE report*, 1975).[10]

The findings of the *Investment in education* (1966) report regarding participation by county in secondary as opposed to vocational school are even more striking than that report's findings on over-all participation in second-level education. The participation rate in secondary education of the counties with the highest proportions of students attending secondary schools was found to be almost twice that of the counties with the lowest participation rates.

There is also evidence of differences in participation in post-primary education which are associated with gender. From the age of 14 to 18, female participation exceeds male participation. In 1981, for example, the participation rates for males and females at age 15 were 84.5% and 89.3% respectively. At age 18, the respective rates were 23.9% and 31.1% (National Economic and Social Council, 1983, Table 3.17). Further, girls are over-represented in secondary schools and under-represented in vocational schools.[11] In 1979–80, for example, almost 74% of girls attending second-level schools were enrolled in a secondary school as against just under 61% of boys; while just over 29% of boys went to a vocational school, less than 17% of girls did (Ireland: Department of Education, 1981). Given the higher participation rate of girls in second-level education, and particularly in secondary schools, it is not surprising that more girls than boys sit for the Intermediate and Leaving Certificate Examinations.

When one looks at subjects studied, one finds further differences between the genders. While the numbers of secondary schools offering courses in mathematics (higher and lower) and in the sciences for the Intermediate Certificate Examination were similar in recent years for both boys and girls, thus indicating equality of access, more boys than girls took examinations in higher mathematics and science, indicating inequality in participation and achievement. At the Leaving Certificate level, girls are not as well served as boys in having courses in science and applied mathematics available to them. It should be noted, however, that the number of girls taking mathematics and science, particularly at the Leaving Certificate level, has increased considerably over the past decade (Kellaghan, in press a). Differential provision for boys and girls is reinforced by the fact that many post-primary schools cater for only one gender.

Third-level education

Traditionally most third-level education in Ireland was provided in universities and colleges of education. Participation was relatively low by comparison with other European countries (O'Connor, 1979). For example, in 1976/77, the 14.1% of 19–20 year-old persons who were enrolled in an educational institution in Ireland was lower than the figure for any other E.E.C. country. The figures for other countries varied between 14.6% in the United Kingdom and 32.6% in Belgium (E.E.C.: Statistical Office of the European Communities, 1980). In recent years, there has been an expansion of technical and technological education at third level in Ireland and several new institutions have been established. More recent estimates of enrolment at third-level put the figure at about 20% of an age cohort (Barlow, 1981; Clancy, 1982; Rottman *et al.*, 1982).

Of those students receiving full-time education in third-level institutions in 1979/80, 62% were in university, 22% in technical/technological colleges, under 7% in colleges of education, and under 10% in other institutions (Ireland: Higher Education Authority, 1981).

The inequalities in participation relating to social origin and location, which we noted in second-level education, persist at third level. Inequality relating to gender is also found in higher education, though it does not take the same form as at the lower level.

The *Investment in education* (1966) study reported a strong association between entrance to university and social group. Among entrants in 1963, 65% came from the families of professional, managerial, and intermediate non-manual workers (clerks, etc.), while 6% came from skilled-manual backgrounds and only 2% from semi-skilled and unskilled homes. The over-representation of the higher social-class groupings and the under-representation of lower groupings is clear when one considers that only 20% of the population in the 1961 census were categorized as professional, managerial, and intermediate non-manual workers, while 15% were classified as skilled manual, and 25% as semi-skilled or unskilled.

Other studies of participation in third-level education provide similar findings. While the number of students enrolled at this level has more than doubled over the past two decades, there are still marked differences in the representation of students from different social classes (Clancy, 1982; Clancy & Benson, 1979; Ireland: Higher Education Authority, 1980, 1981, 1982a, 1982b; MacHale, 1979; Nevin, 1967/68; Rottman & O'Connell, 1982; Ryan, 1966).[12] This is particularly true in the university sector. All social classes benefited from the expansion; indeed, the representation of students from lower socio-economic backgrounds may have improved slightly relative to the representation of students from higher socio-economic backgrounds; however, the improvement has not been sufficient to alter the over-all picture of participation.[13] Students from lower socio-economic backgrounds seem to fare better in the non-university sector of third-level education, much of which has developed over the past fifteen years (cf. Clancy, 1982).[14]

While we saw that a greater proportion of girls than of boys participate in second-level education, there is a fall-off in female participation at third level. In 1981, 53.7% of university students were male and 46.3% were female. The proportion of males in third-level education generally was even greater: 56.5% as against 43.5% for females (Ireland: Higher Education Authority, 1982b). These figures are perhaps surprising given the figures for second-level education and particularly the over-representation of females in secondary schools which provide the main avenue to third-level education.

As we have seen, location was identified in the *Investment in education* (1966) report as a correlate of participation in second-level education. Participation in both secondary and vocational education was found to vary from county to county. In more recent studies, considerable differences in participation in third-level education were found to exist between counties; this was true both for the university (Clancy, 1982; Kellaghan & Fontes, 1980) and non-university sectors (Clancy, 1982). For example, the difference between the counties with the highest and lowest participation rates attending university was of the order of 3 to 1 (Kellaghan & Fontes, 1980). There were considerable differences within some counties in the participation rates of the genders, indicating an interaction between location and gender in either facilitating or hindering university attendance. The counties with low university participation rates tended also to have relatively low rates of participation in secondary education and to be located at some distance from a university town.

After school

So far we have considered the educational system in general and research relating to equality of opportunity in the system. We will consider one further index of equality of opportunity in society, that is social mobility, which may or may not be related to equality in the educational system. Social mobility can be defined as the movement of individuals between social positions. In practice, movement on an occupational dimension is usually taken as the index of such mobility (MacDonald & Ridge, 1972). The topic has received little attention in Ireland. Only one published study is available and that was carried out in 1968 (before many of the educational reforms we have considered were initiated) and was confined to males living in the urban area of county Dublin (Hutchinson, 1969).[15] In the study, social mobility was considered to have occurred when an informant's occupational status at the time of interview differed from his father's status. It was found that 40% of respondents had retained their inherited status, 26% had fallen below it, and 34% had moved to a higher status.

Conclusion

The provision of free education at the primary level throughout the country may be taken as indicating that equality of access exists at this level. Such equality, however, does not exist universally at higher levels. Certain areas of the country are less well served than others at second-level, while distance from a third-level institution also seems to be a factor in determining whether or not a student continues formal education at this level. Given the situation regarding access, it is not surprising that disparities in participation relating to location have also been found at both second and third levels.

Inequalities in participation related to gender and social class are apparent in the system after primary schooling. All educational systems are characterized by some degree of internal differentiation and specialization, but they vary in the age at which differentiation occurs and in the number of specialization routes provided. As in many European systems, the traditional structure of the Irish system has dictated differentiation and specialization at the relatively early point of transfer to second-level schools. Such an approach is often associated with an elitist ideology of education: those who appear destined for elite positions and who are most likely to contribute to economic productivity are separated at an early stage from those who appear bound for lower positions (cf. Hopper, 1977).[16] The selective nature of the system in Ireland, however, is modified somewhat by the fact that the majority of students attend the academic sector of the post-primary system.

The characteristics of students in the two main tracks of the post-primary system reflect differences in gender and socio-economic class.

Girls, compared to boys, as well as being over-represented in second-level education in general, are also over-represented in secondary schools. Students from higher socio-economic backgrounds are over-represented in secondary schools and under-represented in vocational schools, while the opposite is the case for students from lower socio-economic backgrounds.

At third level, male participation exceeds female participation while social-class differences in participation, which became apparent at the point of the minimum statutory age for leaving school, become even more obvious.

Evidence on Equality of Opportunity in Other Countries

Information from other countries indicates that these findings regarding inequalities of participation in the Irish educational system are not untypical of contemporary educational systems. Direct comparisons between countries are difficult because of variations in social and educational systems and in the investigative procedures on which data are based. However, the findings of studies from a variety of countries, particularly studies relating to social class, show a remarkable similarity in their general thrust, and sometimes even in their detail.

The first general point that emerges is that in countries which operate different types of second-level schools, major selection in terms of social class operates at the point of transfer from primary to second-level education. A marked tendency is found for children from higher socio-economic backgrounds to transfer from primary school to an academic post-primary school, which will lead to third-level education, while the tendency for children from lower socio-economic backgrounds is either not to proceed to second-level education at all or to go to technical, vocational, 'short-cycle', or general educational establishments. This has been documented in Britain, France, the Netherlands, and Poland (Adamski, 1982; Adamski & Bialecki, 1981; Douglas, Ross & Simpson, 1968; Floud & Halsey, 1961; Girard, 1961; Girard & Clerc, 1964; Gray, McPherson, & Raffe, 1983; Great Britain: Ministry of Education, 1954; Halsey *et al.*, 1980; Karstanje, 1981; Paul, 1981; Westergaard & Little, 1967).

Secondly, beyond the point of transfer to second-level education, retention in the educational system is also related to social class. Children from higher social-class groups are more likely to remain at school through the secondary cycle, while children from lower social-class groups are more likely to leave on reaching the minimum school-leaving age. Again, support for these statements may be found in studies carried out in a variety of countries — Britain, Luxembourg, Poland, Sweden, and the United States (Adamski, 1982; Adamski & Bialecki, 1981; Bamberg, Dickes, & Schaber, 1977; Douglas *et al.*, 1968; Gray *et al.*, 1983; Great Britain: Ministry of Education, 1954; Halsey *et al.*, 1980; Husén, 1969; Jencks *et al.*, 1972; Westergaard & Little, 1967). While children from lower social-class groups tend to perform less well at school than ones from higher social-class groups, drop-out is not confined to students with poor scholastic ability. The loss of students from low social-class backgrounds during the course of secondary schooling includes children of high ability. For example, Douglas *et al.* (1968) found that in Britain nearly half the students from lower manual working-class backgrounds who were in the top 16% of the population in terms of their ability test performance had left school before they were 16½ years old; in contrast, only 10% of students from upper social-class backgrounds of this level of ability had left school by this age.

The effect of these differential drop-outs by students from different social-class backgrounds means that the social-class composition of schools changes the further one proceeds upwards in the system. By the time one reaches third-level education, students from higher social-status groups are over-represented, while those from lower groups are seriously under-represented (Gray *et al.*, 1983; Great Britain: Ministry of Education, 1959; Halsey *et al.*, 1980; Husén, 1969; Shattock, 1981; Westergaard & Little, 1967). For those who survive to the point of entry to third-level education, however, inequalities of further participation are reduced, though not eliminated (Halsey *et al.*, 1980; Westergaard & Little, 1967). While the discrepancies in participation appear worst at third level, inequalities actually operate from a much earlier stage in the system. Indeed, most of the 'damage' seems to have been done well before third level (Halsey *et al.*, 1980).

The studies on which we have based the preceding comments were based on data obtained at varying times during the course of this century. Given that many countries have attempted through a variety of procedures to improve the participation of children from low social-class backgrounds during that time, one might expect that an improvement in the participation of such children should be evident if one compares more recent with earlier data. While there are difficulties in such comparisons, the available evidence does not suggest that this has happened, at any rate not to any marked degree. Major changes in the relative participation rates of the social-class groups have not been reported for any country. For example, a review of studies carried out in

England from early in the century up to the mid-1960s, Westergaard & Little (1967) found evidence of an overall expansion of educational facilities for all social classes, but did not find evidence of a great deal of redistribution of opportunities. There was evidence of a small reduction in social inequalities in access to selective secondary education, but access to university was found to have remained more or less unaffected, and 'this despite expansion, maintenance grants for students, and the changes which have occurred in secondary school provision' (p. 224). A more recent assessment modifies this statement, but only slightly; Halsey *et al.* (1980) note that 'though the fastest *rates* of growth almost always accrue to the working class, the greatest absolute increments of opportunity go to the service class' (p. 188). There is evidence to suggest that equalization of participation between social classes occurs only when participation of the top occupational strata is approaching 100 per cent (Green, 1980; Sussman, 1967).

Inequalities in participation related to gender (cf. Bamberg *et al.*, 1977; Byrne, 1979; Great Britain: Ministry of Education, 1954; Sewell, 1971) and geographical location (cf. Shattock, 1981) have also been found to exist in countries other than Ireland. There is also evidence that there may be an interaction between social class and gender. For example, it has been reported that in the United States, talented females from lower social-class backgrounds are particularly vulnerable in the competition for schooling (Sewell, 1971). On the other hand, Bamberg *et al.* (1977) found that the combination of being female, of low ability, and from a low social-class background was associated with early drop-out in Luxembourg. In general, the evidence on gender is less consistent than that on social class. Data relating to geographical location are often described in terms of local conditions and so are not readily generalizable to other situations.

A comparison of the Irish data on social mobility with data obtained in Britain (Goldthorpe, 1980) led Rottman *et al.* (1982) to conclude that boundaries to mobility are more rigid in Ireland than in Britain. This conclusion should be interpreted in the light of difficulties in making cross-national comparisons of social mobility; for example, occupational categories may not be comparable from country to country and occupations may be grouped in a variety of ways. Thus, different analyses may lead to different conclusions. While some analyses have shown that social mobility differs in different countries (Raftery, in press), a number of commentators have been struck by the similarities, rather than the differences, that exist between countries in such mobility. This is surprising when one considers differences between societies in their levels of educational development and in the apparent rigidity of their stratification systems (cf. Boudon, 1974; Lipset & Bendix, 1959; Meyer & Hannan, 1979).

Equality of Opportunity as a Goal of the Irish System of Education

We have seen that the development of the Irish system of education owed much to local initiative. While the government Department of Education was active in the control of curricula in return for the partial financial support it provided for post-primary schools, it was relatively passive in matters of over-all planning and in the establishment of educational priorities. That changed in the 1960s, at which point, education became a key concern of government policy. This happened at a time when there was evidence of a greater consciousness of the part government should play in social and economic development; this consciousness was reflected in an increase in the state's activity in defining educational priorities.

This is not to say that in the 1960s the country was presented with a coherent national educational policy. Some government statements about policy were made and a series of reforms was proposed. However, an over-all policy or plan was never clearly articulated and one has to search fairly carefully and make a number of guesses and inferences in attempting to discover the motivations and purposes of the quantitative and qualitative changes that occurred in the educational system in the 1960s and 1970s (cf. Mulcahy, 1981). As in the case of most educational reforms, it is not obvious whether social or economic motives predominated in these changes. Neither is it clear whether the changes should be interpreted as primarily a response to conditions within the country or to international influences.[17] It would seem that both internal and external factors played a role and these factors had both social and economic aspects.

The role of factors within the country can be inferred from a consideration of the conflict that existed in Irish society in the 1950s and 1960s between old patterns of socialization and emerging new patterns of work and social relations, a situation which is frequently associated with educational reform (cf. Levin, 1976). Such conflict was a feature of many western countries in the post-World War II period. It was most obvious in Britain immediately after the war when that country was faced with the reconstruction, physical and social, of many of its institutions and buildings (cf. Halsey, 1978; Zweig, 1976). One of the major changes in Britain at the time has been described as a transformation of the economy from a laissez-faire to a corporate form of capitalism. Given this change, alterations were also required in the educational system 'to make education do certain kinds of work for a relatively new capitalism: the capitalism of large-scale production, high technology and the mass market' (Hall, 1981, p. 11). Aspects of this problem had already been attended to in the United States. Earlier in the century, a major purpose of public schooling was perceived to be to increase efficiency of industrial society by the proper selection and channelling of national manpower resources (Spring, 1976). Both these examples indicate that change was motivated by economic concerns. But social factors were also operating. By the 1960s, the United States had become the centre of powerful social movements, triggered first by blacks in the civil rights movement and joined later by a variety of groups who felt they had been excluded from influence in educational politics, particularly women, ethnic groups, and the handicapped (Tyack, Kirst, & Hansot, 1980). Several educational reforms in the United States have been identified as responses to the pressures exerted by these groups.

Though Ireland was much less well developed economically than either Britain or the United States, it would seem that similar forces were operating to bring about change. While Ireland did not have experience of laissez-faire capitalism to the same extent as her two neighbours, it too was caught up in the 1950s in problems of scientific and technological development and in the need for new technologies and skills. As in other corporate capitalist systems, the state was becoming more active and interventionist, not only in economic affairs, but also in social welfare, health, and education (cf. Litton, 1982).

It would appear that the role of economic factors in bringing about changes in the Irish system of education in the 1960s has sometimes been under-estimated. For example, Sean O'Connor (1968), who was then an Assistant Secretary in the Department of Education, in his review of these changes, beginning with the proposals of the Minister for Education, Dr. P. J. Hillery in May 1963, emphasized two fundamental purposes as the basis of the changes: 'equality of educational opportunity for all and the fashioning of education so that it is responsive to the aptitudes and interests of the individual pupil'. This would place the emphasis in reform on social and personal goals rather than on economic ones. However, Dr Hillery also pointed out that technical education

> would give the country a systematic supply of youth with a sufficient technical education to become at a later stage the technicians and higher technicians the country is, as we must all hope, going to need (OECD, 1969, p. 126).

Thus, it is clear the reforms were also directed towards the manpower needs of industrial expansion.

Evidence for the importance attached to economic factors in proposing educational reform is to be found in other documents emanating from government sources. The publication by the Department of Finance in 1958 of its study of economic development, which formed the basis for the first government programme on economic expansion, indicated that 'the emphasis must be on productive investment, though not, of course, to the exclusion of all social investment' (Ireland: Department of Finance, 1958, p. 3). Later in its *Second programme for economic expansion* (Ireland, 1964), which paid particular attention to education, the government expressed the belief that expenditure on education is 'an investment in the fuller use of the country's primary resource — its people — which can be expected to yield increasing returns in terms of economic progress' (p. 193). At the same time, the government believed that improved and extended educational facilities would also help 'to equalise opportunities by enabling an increasing proportion of the community to develop their potentialities and raise their personal standards of living' (p. 193). Thus we see in the planned changes a variety of motivations, economic, social, and egalitarian (cf. Craft, 1970; *Investment in education*, 1966; Kennedy, 1975; OECD, 1969), all founded on an unquestioning belief in education as both a social and economic investment.

While the case can be made that forces within the country contributed to the series of educational changes in Ireland in the 1960s, there can be little doubt that ideas and practices in other countries were also influential. These, to some extent, were mediated informally as, for example, through the increasing number of contacts of officials of the Department of Education with systems in other countries (cf. Ó Raifeartaigh, 1961). There were also more obvious and formal pressures on the Irish government to change its economic policy from one of protectionism to one of trade liberalization in the belief that this would help to remedy social and economic problems in the country (Wickham, 1980); these pressures emanated from international organizations, particularly the Organisation for European Economic Co-operation (OEEC), later to become the Organisation for Economic Co-operation and Development (OECD). The case as presented indicated that planning for economic growth had implications for manpower planning, which in turn placed an onus on the educational system to prepare students for the labour market. Other international bodies, including UNESCO and the World Bank, also exerted influence. The latter, for example, in providing financial resources for new developments in education stressed that educational opportunities should be equalized as fully as possible 'in the interest of both increased productivity and social equity' (World Bank, 1974).

While the emphasis on economic development is clear when one considers the educational changes of the 1960s, the attainment of social equity, as we saw, was also mentioned as a reason for the changes. In particular, equality of opportunity was stressed, not only because it was regarded as important to tap the whole 'pool of talent' in the country in the interest of providing a better labour force[18] but because the implementation of this principle was perceived as an important step in achieving greater equity in the distribution of educational and economic benefits.

The principle of equality of opportunity was enunciated in several policy statements by government ministers. Often these statements were very general and did not state clearly what was meant by equality. For example, Dr Patrick Hillery, Minister for Education, in an *Irish Press* interview, stated that his immediate aim was 'to press on with all possible speed towards my goal of equal educational opportunity for all our children' (cf. Randles, 1975, p. 172). He also spoke (in May 1963) of 'a move in the direction of equality of opportunity' (OECD, 1969, p. 126), while a statement of the Department of Education in October 1970 spoke only of providing '*reasonable* equality of educational opportunity for all our children' (emphasis added) (Randles, 1975, p. 347). Mr George Colley, however, who succeeded Dr Hillery as Minister for Education, had already spoken in January 1966, without qualification, of achieving 'equality of educational opportunity for all' (OECD, 1969, p. 127).

Besides these general statements, reference was made to specific areas of inequality relating to social class and gender. For example, Dr Hillery stated that free education was necessary so that children from poor homes would not be excluded from the system (Randles, 1975, p. 65), while a Department of Education statement recognized the need for providing equality whatever the means of children's parents or the area of the country in which they resided (Randles, 1975, p. 347). In considering problems of inequality related to location, Dr Hillery recognized that in areas where facilities for post-primary education did not exist, 'some new kind of approach' would be needed (Randles, 1975, p. 332). There was less emphasis on gender than on social class and location as sources of educational inequality, even though, as we have seen, the male rate of participation in non-compulsory second-level education fell below the female rate, while the position was reversed at third level.

There was little debate in the country on equality of opportunity at the time these statements were made. Indeed there was very little by way of comment on the topic at that time or more recently. Thus ministerial statements about equality escaped any detailed scrutiny and their possible implications have not been explored in any systematic way. While criteria of both access and participation are implied in the ministerial statements, empirical studies of inequality in the system have usually accepted participation as the criterion.

Another aspect of ministerial statements which is not clear is the extent to which a meritocratic ideal of equality was accepted. In the meritocratic view, those who achieve would become the new elite, replacing the old inherited succession (Bell, 1973).[19] An important component of achievement was considered to be ability, frequently interpreted as intelligence, a belief that influenced educational policy decisions, particularly in Britain. The influence of this belief can be seen in the operation of scholarship systems in this country and in Britain during the first half of the present century. These systems were designed to ensure that children of high ability would not be denied educational opportunities because of lack of financial resources.[20]

Despite the development of the educational system over the past 150 years and despite recent attempts to promote equality of opportunity, it is doubtful if educational participation and achievement, and ultimately occupational roles, are determined solely by 'merit'. However, here, as in other countries (cf. Duncan, Featherman, & Duncan, 1972), the extent to which status achievement depends on factors other than an individual's competence and inclination is not entirely clear. In meritocratic terms, if a system is successfully implementing a policy of equality of opportunity, final school achievement and occupation should be based on personal factors. The proponents of equality are not quite clear what these personal factors should be; mention is sometimes made of individual choice, ability, effort, and motivation, factors which might be construed to constitute 'merit'. What they are clear about is that school achievement and occupation should not be determined by factors over which one has no choice, one's gender, the social status of one's parents, or the part of the country in which one happens to live.

Some ministerial statements indicated that ability or aptitude (the latter being the preferred term) was a consideration in determining equality of opportunity.[21] The most explicit of these statements came from Dr Hillery in a Dáil debate. In March 1960, he stated that it would be an uplift to the morale of the country

> if it were generally understood that the child of even the poorer, if he is of sufficient ability, would have the opportunity of . . . climbing right to the top of the educational ladder (Randles, 1975, p. 45).

In the following year, Dr Hillery noted a 'serious defect in our social system . . . that the boy or girl who is poor but clever had often no adequate opportunity of receiving the entire course of education available'. He intended to remedy that defect by establishing 'the pattern of free education the whole way up for the poor but clever child' (Randles, 1975, p. 65).

There are other less explicit statements which seem to indicate that the promotion of equality of opportunity in the 1960s was based on a meritocratic principle. For example, there are references to an education suited to needs, talents, aptitudes, and abilities of children (Randles, 1975). Further, Dr Hillery in a statement in May 1963 envisaged that among students leaving at the end of a comprehensive three-year junior course would be those who 'had failed to benefit adequately from the opportunity they had been given' (OECD, 1969, p. 124). Opportunity for some would obviously end earlier than for others.

In our study, as well as considering participation and achievement rates of different groups of students, we shall carry out analyses which examine a model of opportunity based on a meritocratic assumption. We feel justified in doing this, not only because such analyses will provide data which will be similar, if not directly comparable, to those obtained in other countries, but also because some government policy statements on equality of opportunity, as we have seen, seemed to assume the operation of meritocratic principles.

To coincide with government statements on equality of opportunity, a series of reforms was proposed to promote equality. Most of these related to second-level education. However, there were also reforms at primary level, such as amalgamation of small schools. At third level, apart from a general expansion in the number of places available, a Higher Education Authority was established (1968), attempts were made to rationalize university resources, and colleges to promote technical and technological education were established. The reforms at second level included the raising of the minimum school-leaving age from fourteen to fifteen years (1972), the provision of government funds for capital expenditure on secondary schools (1964), the provision of free education and free transport to schools (1967), and the comprehensivization of second-level schools (1963) (cf. Coolahan, 1981; Mulcahy, 1981; Randles, 1975; Sheehan, 1975).

Perhaps the most obvious change in the system during the 1960s and 1970s was the large increase in the number of students attending second-

and third-level educational institutions. For example, in 1963, when Dr Hillery made his policy statement on post-primary education (OECD, 1969, pp. 119–126), there were 113,048 students in second-level schools (Ireland: Department of Education, 1964); by 1970, the figure had risen to 205,690 (Ireland: Department of Education, 1974), and by 1980, it was 281,608 (Ireland: Department of Education, 1981). Thus, attendance figures increased by 150% within twenty years. Though the numbers involved in third-level education are not as great, the proportionate increase at this level was even greater. Before attributing these increases entirely to the policies of the 1960s, it should be pointed out that numbers in second-level education had more than doubled in the twenty years preceding 1963.[22] As we have already seen, commentators on educational change have pointed out that the mechanisms which produce growth and change in educational systems are complex. Controls on the system, exemplified in policy statements or manipulations, may have relatively little impact when faced with the autonomy of the system itself as well as the role of other social interactions and structural factors inside and outside the system (cf. Archer, 1982; Meyer & Hannan, 1979). We do not propose to consider the relative influences of the many controls operating in the system here; however, neither should we ignore the fact that much of the increase in participation over the past twenty years can probably be attributed to factors other than policy proposals, including an increase in the general population. While reforms, such as the raising of the school-leaving age and the provision of free transport, may have facilitated increased participation, all such increased participation cannot be attributed to them.[23]

It does not follow that the over-all increase in numbers, which was matched by an improvement in participation rates for the general population (cf. National Economic & Social Council, 1983, Table 3.17), was also matched by a decrease in differences in participation rates for members of different social classes, for genders, or individuals living in different parts of the country. While comprehensive and systematic statistical data which would throw light on trends over time are not available, we saw that the available evidence indicates that there are still disparities in participation related to social class, gender, and geographical location.

The Present Investigation

In the study reported in this book, we set out to assess the extent to which one particular government policy objective, the attainment of equality of educational opportunity, was realized for a cohort of students, whose educational careers we followed from the time they were eleven years of age.

Our study focuses on participation and achievement, which are examined for a sample of 500 children, who had been identified towards the end of their primary-school careers in 1967, as they progressed through the system. Thus, the children were attending school during the period in which a number of reforms to promote equality of opportunity were implemented. The children were selected to be broadly representative of eleven-year-old Irish school children at the time. Base-line data were obtained on the children in the following areas: verbal reasoning ability, scholastic performance, personality characteristics, characteristics of the school they were attending, and background characteristics relating to family and location. Since 1967, information was collected annually on the whereabouts and school progress of the children. Information was obtained for each child on choice of post-primary school, age of leaving school, post-school destination and, where appropriate, performance on public examinations and performance in third-level education.

In our analyses we were able to examine the representation of groups (by gender, social class, and location) at varying levels in the educational system. We were also able to examine the achievement of the same groups at different levels in the system. When the student left school, we were able to compare the status of his or her first occupation with that of his or her parents' occupation. We were also in a position to examine the factors affecting participation and achievement. Since our study was longitudinal, we could go beyond cross-sectional data to examine the dynamics of equality of opportunity as it pertains to individuals.

Our analyses were not confined, as so many earlier analyses of equality of opportunity have been, to a consideration of scholastic attainment and achievement in terms of class membership. Variance within classes is known to be considerable on a wide range of variables (cf. Great Britain: Department of Education & Science, 1967; Wiseman, 1964) and we considered it important to allow such variance to show in our analyses. A basic concern was to establish to what extent individual students' achievements (in school and in occupation) seemed to be 'achieved' rather than 'ascribed'.

The variables in our study may be categorized into three groups. Firstly, there is a set of variables which are completely or largely outside the control of the child. These are the child's gender; the socio-economic status of his or her family; whether the child lives in an urban or rural area; the child's measured ability; and personality characteristics of '

child. Secondly, there are intervening variables which relate to the child's school experience. These include the type of school attended at both primary and post-primary level and variables representing the child's educational history in the primary school (the child's overall place in class, a measure of his/her general scholastic progress, and measures of his/her scholastic progress in specific areas of the curriculum). Finally, we have a series of dependent variables which are used as indices of equality of opportunity. They are based on measures of both participation and achievement: whether or not an individual stays in the formal educational system, his or her level of achievement on public examinations and, finally, his or her occupational status on leaving school.

It is assumed that any of the variables in the first two categories may affect the variables in the third. As we have seen, there is already considerable evidence from a variety of countries including Ireland, that there are large differences in the educational attainments and achievements of the socio-economic groups, whatever measure (father's occupation, income, or educational level) of socio-economic status is used or whatever measure of output is used: the type of secondary school one goes to, the length of time one spends at school, achievement on public examinations, or participation in third-level education.

Further, it has been shown that the educational attainments of students of the same level of measured ability vary according to the social origins of the students. For example, one finds that for individuals of equivalent ability in Britain, there are fewer from lower socio-economic backgrounds in third-level education than there are from higher social-status backgrounds. We do not have evidence on the relative contributions of ability and socio-economic class to achievement in Irish society. Analysis of the school progress of our longitudinal sample should throw light on this issue; in our analyses, we shall be particularly interested in the relative role of ability, on the one hand, and social class, gender, and location, on the other, in determining scholastic progress.

A final point should be made about our study before we proceed to a detailed description of it. As already indicated, the study was a longitudinal one in which the school and early occupational careers of a group of students was monitored over approximately ten years. Such a procedure has advantages in tracing the kind of relationships in which we are interested. However, it has the disadvantage that by the time the study is complete, changes that may have taken place in the system render it impossible to say with any confidence that one's findings reflect what is happening in the system today. In this particular study, the problem is exacerbated by the fact that the study was carried out at a time when facilities were being expanded and numbers were increasing in the system. Despite these problems, we feel it is unlikely that conditions have changed to such an extent that the findings do not have relevance today. While there has been a general increase in participation rates, it is likely that many of the relationships between the variables described in this study still hold.

FOOTNOTES

1 Not all commentators agree that educational expansion and reform were carried out solely in the interest of promoting equality. While the class-maintaining function of schooling has been recognized by both liberal and revisionist interpreters of the function of schooling, for the former, reforms were attempts to modify and improve existing structures of educational equality and class relations in society; the effect of the reforms should be a fairer and more effective re-distribution of educational opportunities. For some revisionist commentators, such talk is perceived merely as a cloak for manpower policies. While acknowledging that certain reforms such as programmes to discover talented youth and ones for the disadvantaged did result in greater equality of opportunity, particularly for women and members of minority ethnic groups, they claim the primary aim of the programmes was to ensure that manpower resources would not be lost rather than that the rights of individuals would be satisfied (Spring, 1976). More radical interpretations of the function of schooling, particularly those put forward by neo-marxist commentators, regard the primary function of schools as the production and reproduction of labour power in a way that will ensure the stability of productive relations in society (Matthews, 1980). In these interpretations, which vary in detail, the basic function of the educational system is perceived to be the legitimization and reproduction of the existing system of privilege, power, and resources in society and educational expansion has as its objective the production of a docile labour force rather than the removal of inequalities or the provision of the learning needed to preserve freedom or even the skills necessary for employment (cf. Bourdieu, 1977; Bourdieu & Passeron, 1977; Bowles, 1972; Bowles & Gintis, 1976; Gintis, 1972; Katz, 1971).

2 In Hopper's (1977) typology of educational systems, a system is centralized if it has a specialized department within a national civil service or its equivalent, which is concerned exclusively with problems of education, if an entire population is included within a nationally organized programme, and if there are not regional and local variations in the application of this programme.

3 Descriptions of the system and aspects of its development are to be found in Akenson (1970; 1975), Auchmuty (1937), Coolahan (1981), Ireland: Department of Education (1954), Kellaghan (in press b), MacGleannáin (1979), McDonagh (1977), McElligott (1966; 1981), Mulcahy (1981), Murphy (1980), Ó Súilleabháin (1971), and Tussing (1978).

4 For example, 80% of a sample of the Irish adult population in 1974 thought that young people needed a standard of education of at least the level of the Leaving Certificate if they were to make 'a decent living' (Madaus, Fontes, Kellaghan, &

Airasian, 1979). The examination was seen as affecting one's choice of further education and the kind of job one gets (Fontes, Kellaghan, Madaus, & Airasian, 1980).

5 The distinction between attainment and achievement is made by Green (1980). He defines educational attainment as the last level of the system reached while educational achievement is defined as the level of mastery of knowledge, skill, or the acquisition of taste. The two are only roughly related. At any grade level (level of attainment), one would expect a variety of levels of achievement. One cannot infer level of achievement from level of attainment or level of attainment from level of achievement.

6 Ten years later, this percentage had been halved.

7 In 1979–80, the number had fallen to 0.15% of second-level students (Ireland: Department of Education, 1981).

8 A number of analyses on sections of the data collected for the study reported in this book were carried out as the data became available and the findings were published. These include Greaney (1973) and Kellaghan & Greaney (1970).

9 The Primary-school Certificate Examination was held on the completion of sixth standard in the primary school from 1929 to 1967. It was optional up to 1942. A student had to pass this examination or an equivalent examination before he or she could be recognized as a student in a secondary school. During its operation, it evoked much opposition among primary-school teachers who claimed that it led to an undue emphasis in the primary school on the subjects which were tested in the examination — Irish, English, and Mathematics (Madaus & Greaney, 1982). The examination was abolished in 1967. There is now no public examination which can be used to select students for second-level schools. Some schools, particularly in urban areas, are faced with the fact that they have more applicants for places in their schools than they can accommodate. A variety of criteria, including an examination, may be used by a school to allocate places (McCluskey, 1977). While a student may not gain admission to the first school of his or her choice, he or she usually succeeds in gaining admission to the type of school desired.

10 It was unlikely that many of the students in the present study would have enrolled in a comprehensive or community school. Fewer than 1% of students enrolled in comprehensive schools in 1969 and community schools were not established until 1972. By 1980, 8% of post-primary students were attending 15 comprehensive and 30 community schools (Ireland: Department of Education, 1981).

11 The over-representation of girls in grammar-type secondary schools has also been noted in other countries, such as the United Kingdom and France. For example, almost 60% of students in long second-cycle courses in France are girls (Byrne, 1979). In Ireland, the figure is just under 57% (Ireland: Department of Education, 1981).

12 There are difficulties in making comparisons over time. There have been shifts in social class distributions as well as changes in the allocation of occupations to social groupings in the Census. Further, occupational classifications in different studies do not correspond exactly and categories have been aggregated in different ways. Some of these problems may be overcome to allow at least approximate comparisons by combining categories into broader groups. A less tractable problem arises in the case of errors in data gathering and classification procedures. An example of one aspect of this problem can be seen in the assignment of 471 students (6.74% of the total) to the 'unknown' category of socio-economic background in the *Accounts 1980 and student statistics 1980/81* of the Higher Education Authority (Ireland: Higher Education Authority, 1982a).

13 In one university, an increase in participation of students from lower socio-economic backgrounds was recorded in the late 1960s. This, however, was followed by a decrease in the late 1970s. The increase was attributed to the introduction of a student-grant scheme, the decrease to a decline in the real value of the grants which had not kept pace with inflation (MacHale, 1979). If these interpretations are correct, then financial barriers are creating inequality in access.

14 Since information on the socio-economic status of 13.2% of entrants to the technological sector was not available in 1980, the precise socio-economic constitution of different types of educational institution cannot be assessed with the data available at present.

15 Further analyses of Hutchinson's data on occupational mobility were carried out by Geary and Ó Muircheartaigh (1974) and Rottman *et al.* (1982). A study of educational mobility in Dublin in the early 1970s showed that upward mobility was greater than downward mobility (MacGréil, 1974).

16 The point at which differentiation occurs has obvious implications for students, particularly ones who may be borderline on the selection criteria. With early differentiation and a high degree of specialization, there is a greater probability that a 'suitable' student will be rejected because selection procedures, whether formal or informal, are too stringent. In the absence of early selection, there is a greater probability that an 'unsuitable' student will be accepted (Hopper, 1977).

17 It is always difficult to ascertain to what extent innovation in education is the result of factors within a society or factors outside it. In the former case, change is explained in terms of modernization theory as an indigenous norm-oriented movement in response to cultural and historical forces operating in a society (cf. Turner, 1975). In the latter case, change is seen to be the result of diffusion from other countries by which innovations elsewhere are selectively adopted (cf. Frank, 1969).

18 Mr George Colley, while Minister for Education, in a statement to the authorities of secondary and vocational schools in January 1966 expressed the view that 'our national survival demands the full use of all the talents of our citizens' (OECD, 1969, p. 128).

19 A realization of the meritocratic ideal would mean, according to one commentator, that by the beginning of the 21st century, English society would be transformed by the victory of the principle of achievement over ascription (Young, 1961).

20 The effort to identify 'talented' children and provide what were thought to be appropriate educational facilities was intensified following the 1944 Education Act in Britain. Concepts of talent and ability became more overt. What was meant by these terms has, however, been a matter of controversy. Operationally, ability may be defined as 'whatever it is on the basis of which the (educational) system distributes its benefits' (Green, 1980, p. 51). Intelligence, as measured by standardized tests, is frequently regarded as an important component of this kind of ability. A measure of intelligence was included in selection procedures for grammar school in Britain and the objective was to treat all children *of the same measured ability* in the same way; thus, access to different types of second-level education should depend on ability or aptitude and parental preference, not on the accidents of social origin or financial capacity (Westergaard & Little, 1967). Though the United States at the time had a less overtly selective educational system than Britain, it was not denied that the school played a role as a selective agency. The thinking of Warner, Havighurst & Loeb (1946) regarding the consideration that should be given to ability in the context of equality of opportunity was very similar to that which was prevalent in

Britain. They argued that we might speak of a realistic kind of equality of educational opportunity 'if all children and young people exceeding a given level of intellectual ability were enabled to attend schools and colleges up to some specified level'. While recognizing that selection based on intelligence test performance implied a selection based on social class, they accepted that equality of educational opportunity would exist to a considerable degree 'if all boys and girls with IQs over 100 were able to attend high school up to the age of eighteen, and if all young people with IQs over 110 were able to attend college for four years' (Warner *et al.*, 1946).

The provision of educational facilities for the more able children in society was not based solely on egalitarian principles. Perhaps of greater importance was the assumption that 'a pool of talent' existed in the population. This pool was usually defined in terms of children above a certain level of intelligence and was estimated in Britain to constitute something between 11% and 16% of the population (McIntosh, 1959). As one would expect to find these children distributed among all the social classes, it was important, in the interests of efficiency, if nothing else, that children likely to belong to that pool should be identified and their educational progress facilitated, whatever their socio-economic background, to help meet the demands of the economy for educated manpower.

21 The use of intelligence on which to base a policy of equality of opportunity raises a number of problems. One set of problems revolves around the nature of intelligence and its determinants (cf. Butcher, 1968; Herrnstein, 1973; Jensen, 1969, 1980; Resnick, 1976), and in particular the relationships between intelligence and socio-economic status (Carnoy, 1974; Coleman *et al.*, 1966) and achievement (Brody, & Brody, 1976). While intelligence might be a less conspicuous attribute, shifting the basis of selection from it to social class membership and gender meant that the selection was still based on a factor over which the child had little control. A further problem is that this form of meritocratic approach would maintain a social stratification, even if the basis of the allocation of individuals shifted. If successful, it could produce a stratification of society of the type envisaged by Michael Young (1961), one which was more rigid and less amenable to change than the one which it superseded. As things seem to be turning out, however, no mass mobility has occurred. Despite the efforts in this century to increase equality, many of them based on meritocratic principles, it has been claimed that mobility rates were as high in the United States in the 19th as in the 20th century (Thernstrom, 1964). A realization of this position has led to a definition of equality of opportunity that shuns the idea of equal treatment for children of similar levels of ability and demands instead as a criterion of equality a level of achievement that is similar for all groups. It is another matter how realistic this goal is.

22 There were 52,999 full-time students in second-level schools in the country in 1942–43 (Ireland: Department of Education, 1944).

23 Unguided change seems to predominate in societal development (Etzioni, 1968). Contemporary educational systems, like other social systems, take on 'a life of their own', which, though produced by human interaction, seems to escape its control. As such systems mature, they become increasingly independent as social institutions and decreasingly regulated by other parts of society (cf. Archer, 1982; Meyer & Hannan, 1979; Seidman, 1982). Further, since the ideologies on which educational systems are based are buttressed by cultural folk norms, they tend to change very slowly (cf. Hopper, 1977).

2 *The Design of the Study*

To monitor the scholastic progress of a cohort of students through the educational system and their early occupational choices, a sample of 500 eleven-year-old students was chosen in 1967. An attempt was made to select these students so that they would be representative of the population of eleven-year-old children in Ireland at the time.

Information was obtained on the students while they were still in primary school on a range of personal, educational, and background factors, as well as on the type of school they were attending. This information was then related to subsequent information that was collected annually about the students: their choice of post-primary school, their performance on public examinations, their age on leaving school, and their subsequent employment.

In this chapter, a description is provided of the sample which formed the basis of this longitudinal study, the variables for which information was collected, and the general procedures used in the investigation.

Sample

A sample of 500 eleven-year-old students was selected for the longitudinal study from a larger sample of 2,164 students who had taken part in the standardization of a verbal reasoning test in 1967 (Gorman, 1968). The students in the standardization sample were attending a representative sample of Irish primary schools (excluding special schools for the mentally and physically handicapped). In selecting the sample of schools for the standardization, the population of schools in the country had been divided into Catholic national schools (which were stratified by location, type of management, and size), Protestant national schools, and private schools. A number of schools were randomly selected from each sample stratum of Catholic national schools, the number being roughly proportional to the number of schools in the category in the population. Protestant and private schools, which were small in number, were not chosen randomly. Altogether 124 schools were selected. All children in each selected school who were aged between eleven and twelve years and were present on the day of testing were tested.

The longitudinal sample selected for the present study employed five categories of the standardization sample: children attending Catholic city national schools (i.e., located in one of five boroughs, Dublin, Cork, Limerick, Waterford or Dun Laoghaire), children attending Catholic town national schools (i.e., in towns with a population of 1,500 or more), children attending Catholic rural national schools (i.e., in areas with a population of less than 1,500), children attending Protestant schools, and children attending private schools. Children were selected randomly from each of these categories and the numbers selected were proportional to the numbers of children in each category in the population rather than to the numbers in the standardization sample which showed several biases (Table 2.1). An equal number of boys and girls was selected from each category.[1]

TABLE 2.1
Percentages of Students in Population, in Standardization Sample, and in Longitudinal Sample (with Numbers for the Two Samples by Sampling Strata)

Category of school	*Population* %	*Standardization sample* N	%	*Longitudinal sample* N	%
Catholic city	28.34	1,073	49.58	142	28.40
Catholic town	18.18	451	20.84	90	18.00
Catholic rural	46.93	464	21.44	236	47.20
Protestant	2.35	62	2.87	12	2.40
Private	4.20	114	5.27	20	4.00
Total	100.00	2,164	100.00	500	100.00

Variables Investigated

Information on student while in primary school

Information was obtained on 49 separate variables measured while the student was still attending primary school. The variables are categorized under four headings: home background (5 variables), educational history (12 variables), type of primary school attended (10 variables), and personal characteristics (22 variables).

Home background. (i) Socio-economic status (SES), assessed on the basis of the occupation of the student's father or guardian. Occupations were categorized according to the classification of the British Census (Great Britain: Registrar General, 1956) with certain modifications.[2] The following five categories were used: (a) higher professional, administrative, and managerial, and farmers with over 150 acres; (b) intermediate professional, administrative and managerial, and farmers with over 30 but less than 150 acres; (c) skilled occupations; (d) partly-skilled occupations and farmers with 30 acres or less; and (e) unskilled occupations. A code of 5 indicated high socio-economic status, a code of 1 low status. (ii) Number of children in family, i.e., the total number of children in the student's family. (iii) Modified ordinal position. This index was created by dividing each student's ordinal position by the number of children in the family and multiplying by 100 (cf. Kellaghan & Macnamara, 1972). For example, a student who was second in a family of five was allotted a modified ordinal position of 40. (iv.) Father living, i.e., whether or not the student's father was alive. (v) Mother living, i.e., whether or not the student's mother was alive.

Educational history. (i) Class place, i.e., student's rank position in class over all subjects as rated by the teacher. On the basis of a student's rank position and the total number of students in the class, each student was assigned to one of five categories: top ten percent; next twenty percent; middle forty percent; next lowest twenty percent; bottom ten percent. A code of five indicated high class place, a code of one low class place. (ii) General scholastic progress, rated by the teacher as being either satisfactory or unsatisfactory. In coding, one indicated satisfactory progress, while zero indicated unsatisfactory progress. (iii) Scholastic progress in eight specific areas of the curriculum: Irish Reading, Oral Irish, Written Irish, English Reading, Oral English, Written English, Mechanical Arithmetic, and Problem Arithmetic. Teachers were asked to indicate if a student had difficulties in any of the areas (yes or no); in coding, -1 indicated difficulty and +1 absence of difficulty. (iv) School attendance: the number of days the student had been absent during the school year (1967–1968). (v) School grade attained by students at the age of twelve years (in the school year 1967–1968). In June 1968, students were enrolled in Standard 4 (coded 0), Standard 5 (coded 1),

Standard 6 or 7 (coded 2), in first year post primary (coded 3), or in second year post primary (coded 4).[3]

Type of primary school attended. In describing the type of primary school attended by students, each school was categorized in terms of administration, size, gender composition of students, and location. The size of the student's class in the school was also included. Administration: (i) Catholic lay administration, i.e., a school in which the principal teacher was a lay Catholic. (ii) Catholic religious administration, i.e., a school in which the principal teacher was a member of a religious order or congregation. (iii) Protestant administration. (iv) Private administration, i.e., a school which was not in receipt of state funds. On each of these four variables, students who attended the type of school described above were coded +1 and all remaining students were coded -1. (v) Size of school, based on the number of teachers in the school, categorized as one, two, three, four to six, and seven or more teachers. (vi) All-male, i.e., schools in which all the students were boys. (vii) All-female, i.e., schools in which all the students were girls. (viii) Mixed gender, i.e., both boys and girls attended. For variables (vi) to (viii), students enrolled in a particular category were coded +1, while all others received a -1. (ix) Location of school: urban, if situated in one of the five boroughs; town, if in a town with a population of 1,500 or more; rural, if in a centre of population of less than 1,500 people. (x) Size of class: the number of children enrolled in the student's class.

Personal characteristics. (i) Verbal reasoning ability assessed on the Drumcondra Verbal Reasoning Test, a test designed to measure general verbal ability (cf. Gorman, 1968). The test was standardized in 1967 on an Irish population with a mean of 100 and a standard deviation of 15. (ii) Gender: girls were coded +1 and boys -1. (iii) Ratings on personality characteristics were obtained from teachers for each student on a Student Construct Scale. A five-point scale was provided for each of twenty personality characteristics: (1) keenness to get on, (2) enquiring mind, (3) achievement tendencies, (4) leadership, (5) concentration on own activities, (6) self-confidence, (7) dominance, (8) creativity, (9) dependence, (10) deference, (11) gregariousness, (12) common sense, (13) originality, (14) sense of humour, (15) popularity, (16) sensitivity, (17) appreciation of beauty, (18) intelligence, (19) health, (20) physical energy.[4] For each trait, five phrases were placed at approximately equal intervals on a line, which allowed the teacher to indicate the degree to which he/she considered the trait to be possessed by a student. The initial and final phrases represented both poles of the trait. The following example illustrates the format of the items.

Self-Confidence (assured, self-reliant)

Completely self-assured	Rarely seeks outside help	Average belief in own capacities	Usually looks for help when problems arise	Lacks self-confidence entirely

In an effort to ensure comparability of rating, teachers were asked to consider the traits only in light of the descriptions given. They were advised not to consider a trait as desirable or undesirable but simply to indicate whether the student was high or low in the possession of it. In making their judgments, they were requested to compare the student being rated with the average of all the children of the same age they had known. Teachers indicated their judgments by placing an X at any point on the line under the phrases describing the trait. Scoring of the completed personality ratings was carried out by dividing the line into five equal segments and by assigning values ranging from one to five to each trait. A score of five indicated that the student was considered to possess the trait to a high degree.[5]

Descriptive statistics on each of the 49 variables are presented in Table 2.2. Two types of descriptive statistic, the mean and the standard deviation, are given. The mean or average was obtained simply by summing the values of each of the variables and dividing by the number of students (i.e., 500). For example, the mean for Problem Arithmetic was obtained by summing the values for the 268 students who were not considered to have had difficulty and the values for the 232 who were considered to have had difficulty and dividing by 500, i.e., $(268 \times 1) + (232 \times -1) \div 500 = .07$. It is interesting to note that among the listed subject areas, more students were considered to have experienced difficulty in Problem Arithmetic than in any of the remaining seven subject areas (Greaney & Kellaghan, 1972; Kellaghan, Macnamara, & Neuman, 1969). Standard deviation values are also provided in Table 2.2 to give some indication of the amount of variation in scores. It can be seen from the table, for example, that teachers varied more in rating students in Written Irish (.98) than in Oral English (.59).

TABLE 2.2
Means and Standard Deviations on Variables Investigated while Students were at Primary School (N: 500)

Variables	M	SD
Home background		
1. Socio-economic status	2.80	1.13
2. Number of children	5.65	2.74
3. Modified ordinal position	62.79	26.53
4. Father living	.95	.23
5. Mother living	.98	.15
Educational history		
1. Class place	3.06	1.05
2. School progress	.75	.43
3. Irish Reading	.42	.91
4. Oral Irish	.34	.94
5. Written Irish	.21	.98
6. English Reading	.80	.60
7. Oral English	.81	.59
8. Written English	.60	.80
9. Mechanical Arithmetic	.60	.80
10. Problem Arithmetic	.07	1.00
11. Absenteeism	14.54	14.61
12. School grade at age twelve	1.95	.71
Type of school attended		
1. Catholic lay admin.	-.06	1.00
2. Catholic religious admin.	-.07	1.00
3. Protestant admin.	-.95	.31
4. Private admin.	-.92	.39
5. Number of teachers	3.69	1.10
6. All male	-.29	.96
7. All female	-.30	.98
8. Mixed gender	-.42	.91
9. School location	2.14	.90
10. Class size	2.46	1.56

TABLE 2.2 (contd.)

Variables	M	SD
Personal characteristics		
1. Verbal reasoning ability	100.15	15.46
2. Gender	.00	1.00
3. Keenness to get on	3.76	1.01
4. Enquiring mind	3.28	.89
5. Achievement tendencies	3.06	.95
6. Leadership	2.74	.91
7. Concentration on own activities	3.14	.98
8. Self-confidence	2.93	.96
9. Dominance	2.72	.88
10. Creativity	2.80	.93
11. Dependence	2.84	.82
12. Deference	3.21	.98
13. Gregariousness	3.48	1.02
14. Common sense	3.36	.76
15. Originality	3.10	.78
16. Sense of humour	3.31	.72
17. Popularity	3.40	.77
18. Sensitivity	3.34	.80
19. Appreciation of beauty	3.08	.72
20. Intelligence	3.21	.84
21. Health	3.52	.85
22. Physical energy	3.29	.77

Information on student while in post-primary school
Information was obtained on six variables while the student was attending post-primary school. The variables are categorized under two headings: educational history (4 variables) and characteristics of the school attended by the student (2 variables).

Educational history. (i) Level of post-primary education. On the basis of the stage at which a student ceased formal full-time post-primary schooling, he/she was assigned to one of four categories: finished during junior cycle, finished upon completing junior cycle, finished during senior cycle, or finished upon completing senior cycle. (ii) Public examinations taken. Students were categorized as having taken the Day Group

TABLE 2.3
List of Public Examination Subjects

Day Group Certificate (DGCE)	*Intermediate Certificate (ICE)*	*Leaving Certificate* (LCE)*
Irish	Irish (Higher Course)	Irish
English	Irish (Lower Course)	English
Mathematics	English (Higher Course)	Latin
History and Geography	English (Lower Course)	Greek
German	Latin	Hebrew
Spanish	Greek	French
French	Hebrew	German
Italian	French	Italian
Art	German	Spanish
Science A	Spanish	History
Rural Science	Italian	Geography
Magnetism and Electricity	History and Geography	Mathematics
Mechanical Drawing	Mathematics (Higher Course)	Applied Mathematics
Woodwork	Mathematics (Lower Course)	Physics
Metalwork	Science — Syllabus A	Chemistry
Commerce	Science — Syllabus B	Physics and Chemistry
Book-keeping	Home Economics	Agricultural Economics
Business Methods	Music	Engineering Workshop Theory and Practice
Shorthand (General)	General and Practical Musicianship	Technical Drawing
Shorthand (Secretarial)	General Musicianship	Building Construction
Typewriting (General)	Art	Mechanics
Typewriting (Secretarial)	Manual Training Woodwork	Applied Physics
Retail Practice	Manual Training Metalwork	Home Economics (Scientific and Social)
Commercial Arithmetic	Mechanical Drawing	Home Economics (General)
Domestic Science (Written)	Commerce	Accounting
Laundrywork and Home Management		Business Organisation
Cookery		Economics
Needlework		Economic History
		Art
		Music
		General and Practical Musicianship
		General Musicianship

*Separate ordinary and higher level papers were set in all subjects except Building Construction, Technical Drawing, and Engineering Workshop Theory and Practice. Common-level papers were set in these subjects.

Certificate Examination (DGCE), the Intermediate Certificate Examination (ICE), or the Leaving Certificate Examination (LCE). (iii) Performance on public examinations. The grade obtained on each public examination paper by each student was obtained from school records. A total of 25 subjects was offered at the ICE level, 28 at the DGCE level, and 32 at the LCE level. A list of these subjects is presented in Table 2.3. (iv) Repeat LCE. Students who repeated the LCE were identified.

Characteristics of post-primary school attended. (i) School type: secondary, vocational, and comprehensive. (ii) Boarding school attendance: students were categorized as boarders or non-boarders.

Information on students' third-level education. Information was obtained on variables relating to students' third-level education. The variables concerned the type of third-level institution attended by the student (one variable) and the student's educational history while at a third-level institution (four variables).

Type of third-level institution. Three categories were created. Category one consisted of universities, major seminaries, and colleges of education, art, and pharmacy. Category two consisted of technological and domestic colleges. Students in other third-level institutions were assigned to category three.

Educational history. (i) Persistence: students were categorized as either having completed the course of studies, as being still enrolled, or as having dropped out. (ii) Three indices of undergraduate attainment were created: (1) rate of progress, i.e., the number of years taken above the minimum normally required to complete a course; (2) number of times an examination was repeated; (3) level of final degree award (first-class honours; second-class honours, division one; second-class honours, division two; and general or pass).

Employment

The student's *first* job upon leaving school was categorized according to the classification system of the British Census (Great Britain: Registrar General, 1956) with some modifications. The system was the same as the one used to classify the occupations of students' parents.

Reduction of data on student personality characteristics

Rather than report teacher ratings on each of the 20 personality characteristics on which information was obtained, the data were factor analyzed at the outset to reduce the number of variables. This data reduction technique tells us which of the personality measures belong together and so can be interpreted as measuring underlying traits.

Personality ratings for each of the 500 students were returned by a total of 165 teachers. For each teacher, the rating of one student was selected at random. Separate factor analyses of the ratings of boys and girls revealed that the factors or terms of reference underlying both sets of ratings were comparable (Greaney, 1974). A single factor analysis of the 165 ratings was then computed, the results of which are presented in Table 2.4. The first four columns of numbers in the table represent loadings on four summary variables or factors which emerged from the analysis.[6] The figures in each of the columns indicate the extent to which each of the variables measures each factor. For example, the most important variables relating to Factor I are keenness to get on, enquiring mind, and concentration, while, at the other extreme, the variable gregariousness contributes nothing to this factor. Relatively high loadings (absolute values greater than .5) have been italicized in the table.

TABLE 2.4
Teacher-rated Student Personality Ratings: Varimax Factor Loadings

Variables	*Factor Loadings* I	II	III	IV	h^2
Keenness to get on	*.83*	.06	.01	.13	.71
Enquiring mind	*.81*	.20	.05	.06	.71
Concentration	*.81*	.16	.08	-.06	.68
Achievement tendencies	*.77*	.17	.23	.15	.70
Intelligence	*.67*	.18	.28	.24	.62
Common sense	*.61*	.16	.33	.17	.53
Originality	*.59*	.22	.28	.21	.52
Dependence	*-.55*	-.40	-.11	.07	.48
Self-confidence	*.52*	*.56*	.00	-.08	.59
Dominance	.14	*.70*	.20	.16	.57
Leadership	.32	*.68*	.31	.05	.66
Health	.13	.04	*.77*	-.13	.63
Physical energy	.13	.29	*.66*	.05	.54
Appreciation of beauty	.48	.14	.02	*.57*	.58
Sense of humour	.12	.46	.39	.46	.59
Popularity	.14	.24	.48	.32	.41
Creativity	.49	.35	.20	.29	.49
Sensitivity	.40	-.01	-.13	.23	.23
Gregariousness	.00	.31	.45	.12	.32
Deference	-.08	-.38	-.25	.11	.23

Factor I, clearly the most important one, describes what may be termed good student behaviour, since it emphasizes the characteristics normally associated with satisfactory classroom behaviour. Personality-motivational variables rather than purely cognitive ones have the highest loadings. A student rated highly on this factor generally is keen to get on, has an enquiring mind, works intently, and strives to excel. The factor has a minor cognitive component as evidenced by the moderate loadings on intelligence, common sense, and originality. The additional minor loadings for dependence (negative) and self-confidence, along with the loadings of the previously noted variables, suggest that a student with a high score on this factor is likely to require little teacher supervision. Factor I was labelled a 'satisfactory classroom behaviour' factor.

Factor II is a social one with moderate positive loadings on dominance, leadership, and self-confidence. The relatively low loading on popularity (.24) indicates that popularity with other students is not a consideration in the identification of apparently domineering, confident, and perhaps tough-minded students who attain a prominent position in their social group. This factor was termed a 'group leadership' one.[7]

Factor III refers mainly to health and physical energy and to a lesser extent to popularity and gregariousness. Physically active extroverted students would receive high scores on it. The factor was identified as a 'health-extroversion' one.

Factor IV is relatively poorly defined and may be described as a minor aesthetic factor. Only one variable, appreciation of beauty, loads above .5 on the factor.

The results of this analysis were used to compute four factor scores for each student in the sample. In this manner four new variables were created for use in subsequent analyses in place of the original 20 personality ratings.

Procedure

The verbal reasoning ability test was administered to all students in May 1967. In June 1968, teachers in the students' primary schools provided information in postal questionnaires on the home background of the students and on their educational history; they also rated each student on the 20 personality traits.

At a later stage, teachers were asked to provide information on the post-primary destination of all students.

Once the student had entered a post-primary school, the principal of that school became the main source of information about the student's scholastic progress. Information was sought each year about the student. The information included results of public examinations and, if the student had left school completely, details of the date of departure and type and place of employment. Where information on employment was not provided by the school, it was obtained through direct contact with the former student either by mail or by telephone. If the student had transferred to another post-primary school, this latter school was contacted and the relevant information was obtained.

Information on the academic performance of third-level university students was obtained from the National University of Ireland and from Trinity College, Dublin. In the case of students in colleges of education and in technical colleges, the information was provided by the college registrars and principals respectively.

A student's information file was considered complete when details of academic performance and length of schooling had been recorded and when a description of his or her first full-time type of employment had been ascertained.

Definition of Terms

The following definitions were used in describing the educational history of students.

Choice of school is used in a strictly operational sense; it is inferred from the school which a student is actually attending.

Junior cycle refers to the period between the time a student enrols in a post-primary school and the time he or she sits for either the Day Group Certificate Examination (DGCE) or the Intermediate Certificate Examination (ICE). For DGCE candidates, the junior cycle normally covers a period of two years of post-primary schooling, while for most ICE candidates, it covers a period of three years.

Senior cycle refers to the period between the time a student commences a two-year Leaving Certificate Examination (LCE) course and the time he or she takes the LCE.

Early leaver is the term applied to a student who leaves school before completing a senior-cycle course in a post-primary school. Students who terminate their full-time education at the end of primary school are termed primary-school terminal leavers. Students who attend a post-primary school and leave before sitting for the DGCE or the ICE are termed junior-cycle early leavers. Students who complete a junior-cycle course by sitting for the DGCE or ICE are termed junior-cycle terminal leavers. Students who attend senior-cycle classes and leave before taking the LCE are described as senior-cycle early leavers.

Topics Investigated

Following primary school, the majority of students in our sample enrolled in a post-primary school, while a small number left school altogether. The first topic we shall examine will be differences between students who went to secondary schools, those who went to vocational schools, and primary school terminal leavers (Chapter 3).

We shall then focus on those students who went to secondary school and describe their educational progress, paying particular attention to the selection procedures within the system that resulted in some students dropping out of school, while others persisted (Chapter 4). This will be followed by a similar description of students who enrolled in vocational schools (Chapter 5).

A series of analyses examines the characteristics of students in relation to the time they left school: at the end of primary school and at various stages in the post-primary school (during the junior cycle, at the end of the junior cycle, or during the senior cycle) (Chapter 6).

Either in their second or third year of post-primary school, students sit for one of two public examinations, the Day Group Certificate Examination or the Intermediate Certificate Examination. Two years after the Intermediate Certificate, they take the all-important Leaving Certificate Examination. The relationship between students' performance on these examinations and such factors as their verbal ability and social background are examined (Chapter 7).

A relatively small proportion of our sample advanced to third-level education. After taking the Leaving Certificate Examination, these students enrolled in universities, colleges of education, technological institutes, and other third-level institutions. The characteristics of students (ability, achievement, and social background) who entered third-level institutions are examined and compared with those of students who did not go on to third-level education. Among other issues that are addressed are the differences in the participation rates of male and female students, the criteria used to admit students to third-level institutions, and the extent to which differences in students' achievements at the time of entry to university are related to subsequent performance (Chapter 8).

Since a student's level of ability is taken into account in some meritocratic definitions of equality of opportunity, the results of a series of analyses are presented in which the scholastic progress of students with different levels of ability were examined (Chapter 9).

Finally, we look at the early post-school careers of students, exploring in the process the relationship between amount of education and the type of job secured (Chapter 10).

FOOTNOTES

1 Due to a clerical error four students too many were selected from the city group while four students too few were selected from the rural group. An error of this magnitude is unlikely to have any significant bearing on the results of the study.

2 The classification of occupations used in the British Census was considered more hierarchical than the classification in the Irish Census and thus more appropriate for the analyses we contemplated carrying out in this study. Unfortunately, the two systems are not directly comparable, even where the same headings are given to individual categories. For instance, a messenger is considered 'unskilled' under the British system whereas he is rated 'semi-skilled' under the Irish system. Similar inconsistencies occur at other levels. While it was not possible to identify five categories which were common to both systems, it was possible to identify three broad categories: (i) farmers, (ii) professionals, and (iii) others (skilled, semi-skilled, and unskilled). To get an estimate of the representativeness of our sample in terms of SES, our data were compared to the data obtained in the Irish national census of 1971. Each occupation listed in the *Census of Ireland, 1971* (Ireland: Central Statistics Office, 1975) was assigned to one of the three broad categories. To avoid inconsistencies between the two classification systems, non-farmers were classified as 'professional' or 'other' according to occupational status under the British classification system. A summary of the SES comparison of our sample with the 1971 national statistics for married males, aged 25 and over (exclusive of those who were not gainfully employed) is presented in Table 2.5. While the two sets of data are not strictly comparable, these figures suggest that our sample is very similar to the national sample in terms of the three broad social groupings.

TABLE 2.5
Percentages of Students' Parents and of the General Population of Married Males (1971 Census) in Occupation Categories

	Occupational category			
Group	*Farmer* %	*Professional* %	*Other* %	N
Students' Parents	22.4	18.2	59.4	500
Married Males (aged 25), 1971	22.8	17.4	59.9	444,716

3 A small number of students (N:7) were enrolled in post-primary schools when the standardization of the verbal reasoning test was carried out. By June 1968, these pupils were in second year post-primary.

4 Ten of the traits (2 to 11) were taken from Lightfoot's (1951) study of bright and gifted children. Traits 12 through 20 were used in Terman *et al.*'s (1926) and Parkyn's (1948) studies of children of high intelligence. Trait 1 was added for the present study.

5 A reliability study of the twenty personality ratings used in the present study was carried out as part of a separate investigation (Neuman, 1970). Sixty children of high verbal ability from the original larger sample were selected randomly nine months after the initial investigation and their teachers were asked to rate them again using an identical questionnaire. Separate Pearson product-moment correlations were computed for each of the twenty traits. The correlations varied from .34 to .76, the median value being .58. Highest correlations were obtained for achievement tendencies, intelligence, health, and concentration, while the lowest were for dependence and popularity. The re-administration of the questionnaire was complicated by the fact that in some cases the teacher had to rely on memory for the second rating, since during the nine-month interval the student had moved to the next class or had even left the school.

6 Slightly over half of the variation of the teachers' ratings of the 20 personality traits was attributable to four independent factors. Of the total of 54% of item variance accounted for by the rotated solution, 25.8% was attributable to the first factor, and 11.8%, 11.0% and 5.2% to the second, third, and fourth factors respectively.

7 The number and nature of dimensions which best describe teachers' perceptions of their students will naturally vary with the characteristics which teachers are asked to rate in the first place, as well as with the method of analysis employed in data reduction. Nevertheless, a variety of studies have provided evidence that, as in this study, teachers perceive students along a dimension representing classroom behaviour and along one representing social behaviour (cf. Airasian, Kellaghan, & Madaus, 1977).

3 The Post-Primary Destination of Students

At the end of primary school, students transferred to one of three types of post-primary school (secondary, vocational, comprehensive) or left school altogether. In the case of our sample, the majority of students (66.7%) enrolled in either a secondary or comprehensive school, about one quarter (25.6%) transferred to a vocational school, and the remaining students (7.4%) did not enrol in any second-level school (Table 3.1). In our analyses, we assigned the small number of comprehensive-school students (7) to the secondary category. In terms of verbal reasoning ability, socio-economic status, and primary-school achievement, the secondary and comprehensive students were quite similar. Furthermore, in terms of post-primary school state examinations, most of the small sample of comprehensive school students sat for the Intermediate Certificate Examination (rather than the Day Group Certificate Examination), an examination traditionally associated with the secondary school.

TABLE 3.1
Numbers (and Percentages) of Students Proceeding to Varying Post-Primary Destinations

	Destination				
	Secondary	*Comprehensive*	*Vocational*	*Terminal leaver*	*Emigrant**
N	326	7	128	37	2
%	*65.2*	*1.4*	*25.6*	*7.4*	*0.4*

*The two pupils who emigrated are not included in further analyses.

The primary purpose of this chapter is to compare the secondary-school entrants with the vocational-school entrants and the primary-school terminal leavers in terms of home background, educational history or records while at primary school, type of primary school attended, and personal characteristics. We shall be examining differences between the groups in their mean scores on the range of variables (33 in all) for which we obtained information when the students were still at primary school. The means and standard deviations on each variable for each group are set out in Table 3.2.[1]

Analysis of variance is used throughout to test the significance of the differences between means.[2] The procedure yields an F-ratio. The value of F which is required to justify a statement of the existence of a significant difference varies depending on the number of groups being compared and the number of individuals in the groups. In the present comparisons, an F value of approximately 3.00 is required at the .05 probability level, 4.60 at the .01 level, and 7.00 at the .001 level.

The results of a series of analyses of variance are summarized in Table 3.2. The largest F value (63.01) was recorded for verbal reasoning ability. The value was statistically significant beyond the .001 level. Thus, we may state that the probability that the differences in the mean verbal ability scores of secondary entrants, vocational entrants, and primary terminal leavers which we found were due to chance was less than 1 in a 1,000. Significant differences between the three groups were recorded on all of the educational history variables, on most of the type of primary school and personal-characteristic variables, and on two of the home-background variables. We will now look more closely at these differences.

Home-Background Variables

Socio-economic status

The mean socio-economic level of the secondary-school entrants was considerably higher than that of the vocational-school entrants which in turn was somewhat higher than that of the terminal leavers. While the children of professional and intermediate professional parents form 31.3% of our sample, they occupy 40.8% of entry places in secondary school, but only 13.3% of places in vocational school. The children of skilled and partly-skilled workers form approximately 50% of our overall sample. Their representation in secondary schools is also approximately 50%; in vocational schools, it is 55.5%, and among terminal leavers it is almost 38%. While children of unskilled workers constitute 18.3% of our sample, they make up only 9.3% of secondary-school entrants, 31.3% of vocational-school entrants, and 54.1% of terminal leavers (Table 3.3).

TABLE 3.2
Univariate Comparisons of Secondary Entrants, Vocational Entrants, and Primary-School Terminal Leavers

Variables	*Secondary (N:333)* M	SD	*Vocational (N:128)* M	SD	*Terminal leavers (N:37)* M	SD	F
Home background							
1. Socio-economic status	3.12	1.02	2.26	1.06	1.81	1.02	50.44***
2. Number of children	5.18	2.45	6.45	2.93	6.92	3.37	15.21***
3. Modified ordinal position	61.10	27.65	67.17	24.12	63.27	23.57	2.43
4. Father living	.95	.22	.93	.26	.97	.16	.62
5. Mother living	.97	.15	.97	.17	1.00	.00	.59
Educational history							
1. Class place	3.26	1.03	2.73	.96	2.38	.98	22.39***
2. School progress	.85	.36	.62	.49	.30	.46	40.48***
3. Irish Reading	.58	.82	.19	.99	-.24	.98	20.66***
4. Oral Irish	.49	.87	.16	.99	-.35	.95	18.20***
5. Written Irish	.40	.92	-.08	1.00	-.51	.87	23.90***
6. English Reading	.87	.49	.73	.68	.35	.95	14.28***
7. Oral English	.89	.45	.72	.70	.35	.95	16.88***
8. Written English	.72	.69	.45	.89	.03	1.01	16.65***
9. Mechanical Arithmetic	.71	.71	.52	.86	-.03	1.01	15.92***
10. Problem Arithmetic	.21	.98	-.08	1.00	-.67	.75	16.07***
11. Absenteeism	11.01	10.63	20.01	16.95	27.35	22.58	37.67***
12. School grade at age twelve	2.11	.68	1.73	.62	1.32	.63	33.07***

TABLE 3.2 (contd.)

Variables	*Secondary (N:333)*		*Vocational (N:128)*		*Terminal leavers (N:37)*		
	M	SD	M	SD	M	SD	F
Type of school attended							
1. Catholic lay admin.	-.21	.98	.25	.97	.24	.98	12.32***
2. Catholic religious admin.	.04	1.00	-.30	.96	-.24	.98	5.96**
3. Protestant admin.	-.94	.32	-.95	.30	-1.00	.00	.52
4. Private admin.	-.88	.47	-.00	.00	-1.00	.00	5.24**
5. Number of teachers	3.74	1.13	3.59	1.06	3.62	1.01	.91
6. All male	-.28	.96	-.28	.96	-.35	.95	.08
7. All female	-.22	.97	-.51	.86	-.19	.99	4.59*
8. Mixed gender	-.49	.87	-.20	.98	-.46	.90	4.68**
9. School location	2.13	.90	2.18	.89	2.03	.90	.42
10. Class size	2.46	1.53	2.44	1.67	2.46	1.46	.01
Personal characteristics							
1. Verbal reasoning ability	104.65	14.23	93.66	13.31	82.16	11.71	63.01***
2. Gender	.09	1.00	-.19	.99	-.08	1.01	3.66*
3. Satisfactory class. behav.	.34	.83	-.29	.88	-.72	.75	45.12***
4. Group leadership	.03	.86	-.02	.92	-.03	1.00	.20
5. Health/extroversion	.18	.82	.11	.81	-.46	.82	10.26***
6. Aesthetic behaviour	.12	.71	-.02	.68	-.29	.81	6.44**

*p <.05 **p <.01 ***p <.001

TABLE 3.3
Numbers (and Percentages) of Students Proceeding to each Post-Primary Destination, by Socio-Economic Class

	Socio-economic status					
Post-primary destination	*Profes-sional*	*Inter. Profes-sional-*	*Skilled*	*Partly-skilled*	*Un-skilled*	*Total*
Secondary school						
N	14	122	117	49	31	333
% of entrants	*4.2*	*36.6*	*35.1*	*14.7*	*9.3*	*66.9*
% of SES	*93.3*	*86.5*	*72.2*	*55.1*	*34.1*	
Vocational school						
N	1	16	38	33	40	128
% of entrants	*0.8*	*12.5*	*29.7*	*25.8*	*31.3*	*25.7*
% of SES	*6.7*	*11.3*	*23.5*	*37.1*	*44.0*	
No post-primary school						
N	0	3	7	7	20	37
% of leavers	*0.0*	*8.1*	*18.9*	*18.9*	*54.1*	*7.4*
% of SES	*0.0*	*2.1*	*4.3*	*7.9*	*22.0*	
Total	15	141	162	89	91	498
% of SES	*3.0*	*28.3*	*32.5*	*17.9*	*18.3*	

Looking at our data in another way, we can estimate that 87.2% of the children of professional and intermediate professional parents find their way to a secondary school while only 10.9% enrol in a vocational school. Among the children of skilled and partly-skilled parents, 66.1% go to a secondary school and 28.3% go to a vocational school. The preference for secondary school does not extend to the children of the unskilled SES group; only 34% of their children enrolled in secondary school, while 44% opted for vocational school.

The contrast between the post-primary school destinations of the children of unskilled parents and those in the other groups is most pronounced in the case of terminal school-leavers. While the percentage figure in the unskilled group which leaves school at the end of primary schooling is 22, the figures for the professional/intermediate professional and skilled/partly-skilled groups are 1.9% and 5.6% respectively.

Family size

While the correlation (.10) between number of children in family and SES was significant, it was quite small.[3] Mean family size was large in all SES groups (5.64 children). It ranged from 5.21 children for the intermediate professional, administrative, and managerial group to 6.12 children for the unskilled group.

Secondary-school entrants tended to come from families with fewer children (M = 5.18) than either vocational-school entrants (M = 6.45) or primary-school terminal leavers (M = 6.92). A closer look at the data (cf. Table 3.4) reveals that whereas approximately one-quarter of the secondary entrants came from families with seven or more children, a total of 46% of the vocational entrants and an even greater proportion (54%) of the primary-school terminal leavers came from families of this size.

TABLE 3.4
Numbers of Students from Families of Varying Sizes, by Post-Primary Destination

Post-primary destination		*Number of children in family*				
		1–3	4–6	7–9	10+	Total
Secondary school	N	80	169	67	17	333
	%	*24.0*	*50.8*	*20.1*	*5.1*	
Vocational school	N	20	49	38	21	128
	%	*15.6*	*38.3*	*29.7*	*16.4*	
No post-primary school	N	7	10	12	8	37
	%	*18.9*	*27.0*	*32.4*	*21.6*	
Total	N	107	228	117	46	498
	%	*21.5*	*45.8*	*23.5*	*9.2*	

Position in family

Significant differences related to the student's modified ordinal position in the family were not found between secondary-school entrants, vocational-school entrants, and terminal leavers.

Father/mother living

Whether or not the student's father or mother was alive was not related to the student's post-primary destination.

EDUCATIONAL HISTORY

The findings of the comparisons of secondary entrants, vocational entrants, and primary-school terminal leavers on the 12 educational history variables are strikingly consistent. In each instance the mean differences among the three samples are significant beyond the .001 level. Furthermore, in each instance, secondary entrants had received the most positive scores or ratings and were followed in turn by vocational entrants and then by terminal leavers.

Class place

The secondary entrants' comparatively higher mean score for class place (M = 3.26) indicates that students in this group tended to have been ranked higher in their primary-school classes than students in the other two groups. In fact, 39% of the secondary entrants had been ranked by their teachers in the top 30% of their primary classes, as opposed to 16.4% of the vocational entrants and 8.1% of the terminal leavers. At the other extreme, 51.3% of terminal leavers had been ranked in the bottom 30%, compared to 33.6% of vocational entrants and 18.6% of secondary entrants.

Unsatisfactory progress

While most students were rated satisfactory in their school progress, it is apparent that the progress of the secondary-school entrant group was considered more satisfactory than that of the vocational group, while the progress of the terminal-leaver group was rated lowest and, in general, was considered unsatisfactory (Table 3.5).

TABLE 3.5
Numbers of Students Judged as Making Satisfactory and Unsatisfactory Scholastic Progress, by Post-Primary Destination

Post-primary destination		*School-progress*	
		Satisfactory	*Unsatisfactory*
Secondary school	N	283	50
	%	*85.0*	*15.0*
Vocational school	N	79	49
	%	*61.7*	*38.3*
No post-primary school	N	11	26
	%	*29.7*	*70.3*
Total	N	373	125
	%	*74.9*	*25.1*

Difficulty in eight subject areas

As in the previous analyses, secondary entrants received the most favourable ratings and were followed at some distance by the vocational entrants, with the terminal leavers an even greater distance behind in last place. The majority of terminal leavers had, according to their teachers, experienced difficulty in Irish and Mathematics. Teachers do not seem to have been as demanding in evaluating English progress as in evaluating progress in either Irish or Mathematics. Among the vocational students, a slight majority appears to have experienced difficulty in both Written Irish and Problem Arithmetic.

Absenteeism

During the 1967–68 school year, the school attendance record of the secondary-school group was superior to that of the other two groups. Whereas secondary entrants had missed an average of 11 days from school in the year, vocational entrants had missed 20 days, and primary terminal leavers 27 days, that is, one out of every six school days. Fewer than 15% of the secondary entrants were absent for 20 or more days; the comparable figures for the vocational and terminal-leaver groups were 34.4% and 51.3% respectively (Table 3.6).

TABLE 3.6
Number of Students with Varying Numbers of Days Absent from School in 1967-68 School Year, by Post-Primary Destination

Post-primary destination		*Number of days absent from school*		
		0-19	20-39	40+
Secondary school	N	284	41	8
	%	*85.3*	*12.3*	*2.4*
Vocational school	N	84	28	16
	%	*65.6*	*21.9*	*12.5*
No post-primary school	N	18	13	6
	%	*48.6*	*35.1*	*16.2*
Total	N	386	82	30
	%	*77.5*	*16.5*	*6.0*

A separate analysis revealed that lower-SES children were less regular attenders than children from middle and upper-SES backgrounds. Furthermore, irregular school attenders also tended to receive poorer achievement ratings than students who attended more frequently.

School grade at age twelve
The final educational history variable describes the grade placement of the student at the age of twelve years. A comparison of the means indicates that secondary entrants as a group had completed more grades than either of the other two groups. The difference in the number of grades completed could be attributed to different rates of promotion from one grade to the next among the students in the three groups or to the fact that students did not commence school at the same age. At the time the data were gathered, all but 15.3% of the secondary entrants had completed fifth standard. Approximately one-quarter (26.6%) of the vocational entrants had not completed this grade, while 59.4% of the terminal leavers had not done so.

Type of Primary School Attended

Significant differences between the means of the three samples were recorded on five of the ten variables in this category. The significant variables referred either to the type of primary-school administration or to the gender composition of the school.

Type of administration

Students had attended either Catholic lay (47%), Catholic religious (46.6%), Protestant (2.4%), or privately administered (4%) primary schools. With the exception of those who had attended Protestant schools, significant differences were recorded in the post-primary school destinations of students from different administrative types of primary school. Among the secondary-entrant sample, students from Catholic lay primary schools were under-represented, while those from the Catholic religious and private schools were over-represented; although 53% of the total sample attended non-lay primary schools, 60.7% of the secondary entrants came from this sector (Table 3.7). (The Catholic religious schools in fact accounted for slightly over half of the total number of secondary entrants.) Turning to the vocational entrant and primary-school terminal-leaver groups, we find that whereas 47% of the sample had attended Catholic lay primary schools, the percentage of students from this sector in each of the vocational and terminal-leaver groups was approximately 62 percent.

TABLE 3.7
Number of Students from Primary Schools of Varying Types of Administration, by Post-Primary Destination

		Primary-school administration			
Post-primary destination		*Catholic lay*	*Catholic religious*	*Protestant*	*Private*
Secondary school	N	131	173	9	20
	%	*39.3*	*52.0*	*2.7*	*6.0*
Vocational school	N	80	45	3	0
	%	*62.5*	*35.2*	*2.3*	*0.0*
No post-primary school	N	23	14	0	0
	%	*62.2*	*37.8*	*0.0*	*0.0*
Total	N	234	232	12	20
	%	*47.0*	*46.6*	*2.4*	*4.0*

It seems obvious, therefore, that students from Catholic lay-administered primary schools are under-represented among secondary-school entrants and over-represented among the vocational-school entrant and primary-school terminal-leaver groups. One final point is worth making even though the numbers involved were very small: none of the primary-school terminal leavers had attended either Protestant or private primary schools.

Size of school

The size of the primary school (determined by the number of teachers in the school) which the student attended was not related to the student's post-primary destination.

Gender composition of the school

Students were categorized as having attended an all-male, all-female, or mixed-gender primary school. Comparisons of the means of the three groups indicate that significant differences in post-primary school destination were recorded on two (all-female, and mixed) of these three variables (Table 3.2). The data suggest that comparatively few students from all-female primary schools enrolled in vocational school. An examination of the frequency distribution (cf. Table 3.8) indicates that whereas the all-female group accounted for more than one-third (35.1%) of the overall sample, fewer than one in four (24.2%) of the vocational entrants came from this group. On the other hand, students who had attended mixed primary schools were over-represented among vocational entrants; they amounted to 39.8% of such entrants, though they constituted only 29.3% of the overall sample.

School location

Students from primary schools in urban, town, and rural locations were not differentially represented in either type of post-primary school or in the terminal-leaver category.

Class size

The size of the student's class (i.e., the number of students in the class) in primary school was not related to the student's post-primary destination.

TABLE 3.8
Numbers of Students from Primary Schools of Varying Types of Gender Composition, by Post-Primary Destination

Post-primary destination		*Gender composition of primary school*		
		All Male	*All Female*	*Mixed*
Secondary school	N	119	129	85
	%	*35.7*	*38.7*	*25.5*
Vocational school	N	46	31	51
	%	*35.9*	*24.2*	*39.8*
No post-primary school	N	12	15	10
	%	*32.4*	*40.5*	*27.0*
Total	N	177	175	146
	%	*35.5*	*35.1*	*29.3*

PERSONAL CHARACTERISTICS

Significant differences were recorded on five of the six personal characteristic variables (Table 3.2). Three of these variables are factors which were derived from the teachers' ratings of students' personality traits.

Verbal reasoning ability
The mean verbal reasoning score of the secondary group was 104.64, while the mean for the vocational entrants was more than 10 points lower at 93.66. The lowest mean score (82.16) was recorded by the primary-school terminal leavers. Thus, in terms of verbal reasoning ability, the most able students enrol in secondary school, those somewhat less than average go to vocational school, while the least able tend to drop out altogether.

Against this background of clear-cut mean differences, it should be emphasized that there is considerable overlap in scores, especially between the secondary and vocational groups. An examination of the original data reveals that in the vocational group, the spread of scores was from 70 to 130, while in the secondary group the range was 70 to 140. Almost 9% of the vocational group had verbal reasoning scores in excess of 110 (Table 3.9). At the other extreme, 13.2% of the secondary

TABLE 3.9
Number of Students with Varying Verbal Reasoning Scores by Post-Primary Destination

Post-primary destination		*Verbal reasoning score*				
		70-89	90-99	100-109	110-129	130-140
Secondary school	N	44	67	99	113	10
	%	*13.2*	*20.1*	*29.7*	*33.9*	*3.0*
Vocational school	N	45	39	33	10	1
	%	*35.2*	*30.5*	*25.8*	*7.8*	*0.8*
No post-primary school	N	27	5	5	0	0
	%	*73.0*	*13.5*	*13.5*	*0.0*	*0.0*
Total	N	116	111	137	123	11
	%	*23.3*	*22.3*	*27.5*	*24.7*	*2.2*

entrants scored lower than 89; indeed, one-third of them recorded verbal reasoning scores of 99 or lower.

The verbal reasoning scores of the terminal leavers were more homogeneous than those of the other two groups. The vast majority (86.5%) fell in the lower half of the distribution of scores. In fact, almost threequarters (73%) scored less than 90 points and 40.5% had scores of less than 79; in a national sample, we would expect only about one-quarter of pupils to score below 90.

Gender

Girls were in the majority among the secondary entrants and in the minority among the vocational entrants and primary-school terminal leavers (Table 3.10). A frequency distribution for the variable gender indicates that girls accounted for 54.4% of the secondary entrants, while boys accounted for 58.2% of the vocational and terminal-leaver samples (Table 3.10). When secondary and vocational entrants are considered together, we find that 50.5% of the total number of post-primary school entrants were female. Turning to the terminal leavers, it is interesting to note that a slight majority (59.5%) had attended urban primary schools. Most (60%) of the urban leavers were girls; in contrast, 80% of the rural leavers were boys.

TABLE 3.10
Number of Boys and Girls by Post-Primary Destination

Post-primary destination		*Gender of student*	
		Male	*Female*
Secondary school	N	152	181
	%	*45.6*	*54.4*
Vocational school	N	76	52
	%	*59.4*	*40.6*
No post-primary school	N	20	17
	%	*54.1*	*45.9*
Total	N	248	250
	%	*49.8*	*50.2*

Personality characteristics
As in the case of verbal reasoning scores, the teacher-rated personality traits of students were normally distributed. This means that for the overall sample, values of these variables tended to be concentrated around the mean and decreased in frequency the further one departed from the mean in either direction. Significant differences between groups were recorded for three personality factors: satisfactory classroom behaviour, health-extroversion, and aesthetic behaviour. In each instance, the secondary-school entrants recorded the highest mean score; vocational-school entrants had the next highest score, and terminal leavers the lowest. On the satisfactory classroom behaviour factor, for example, 68.4% of the secondary entrants had scores greater than zero (the mean score was approximately zero) as compared to 39% of the vocational entrants and 16.2% of the terminal leavers. Thus, of the three groups, students who went to secondary school were most likely to have manifested personality-motivational characteristics associated with success in the primary-school classroom. On the second of the significant factors, health-extroversion, the major difference was between the terminal leavers and each of the other two groups. On this variable, a total of 73% of the terminal leavers had scored below zero (as opposed to 52.4% of vocational entrants and 49.6% of secondary entrants). Finally, on the rather poorly-defined aesthetic measure,

almost three-quarters (73%) of terminal leavers scored below zero compared to somewhat more than half (52.3%) of the vocational entrants and somewhat less than half (45.9%) of the secondary entrants.

Overall Differences Between Groups

The findings which we have been considering relating to the comparisons of secondary-school entrants, vocational-school entrants, and primary-school terminal leavers present some difficulties in interpretation. Many of the variables on which the comparisons were made correlate highly among themselves. It should not surprise us, for example, to find out that groups which differed significantly from one another in Written Irish would also differ in Written English. (The correlation between these two ratings was .54.) Due to the overlap between variables, it is difficult from an examination of correlations and means for individual variables to identify the dimensions or variables that are most important in differentiating between the three groups. Clearly, no single variable can capture the essence of the differences among the groups. However, by identifying several variables and combining them in some manner we would hope to find one, or at most two, dimensions which might clarify the nature of the differences.

At the outset, through the use of multivariate analysis of variance, it was established, not surprisingly in view of the results of our earlier univariate analyses, that secondary entrants, vocational entrants, and primary-school terminal leavers differ *overall* from one another. Further, the variable which maximally separates the three groups is verbal reasoning ability; again this should not surprise us since it was the variable for which the largest mean differences were found among the three groups. The next variable which, taken *in conjunction with* verbal reasoning ability, leads to the greatest degree of separating among the groups is socio-economic status. Verbal reasoning ability and socio-economic status prove to be the best combination of two variables for discriminating between secondary-school entrants, vocational-school entrants, and primary-school terminal leavers. A stepwise procedure[4] was continued until a subset of 18 variables was identified which helped to discriminate among the three groups almost as well as the total set of variables.[5] Through the use of a further statistical procedure, known as discriminant analysis, two new variables[6] which maximized the difference between the three groups were created from the 18 variables. The primary-school variables and their relationship to the two new variables or functions are presented in Table 3.11. The first of these two new

TABLE 3.11
Discriminant Function Coefficients: Secondary School Entrants, Vocational School Entrants, and Primary-School Terminal Leavers

Variables	*Standardized coefficients*
Function 1	
1. Socio-economic status	.43
2. Verbal reasoning ability	.31
3. Gender	.27
4. School progress	.27
5. School grade at age twelve	.14
6. School location	.14
7. English Reading	.12
8. Oral English	.11
9. Mechanical Arithmetic	.10
10. Health/extroversion	.09
11. Satisfactory classroom behaviour	.04
12. Class place	-.05
13. Group leadership	-.11
14. Modified ordinal position	-.11
15. Number of teachers in school	-.15
16. Number of children in family	-.28
17. Catholic lay administration	-.28
18. Absenteeism	-.35
Function 2	
1. Health/extroversion	.48
2. School progress	.45
3. Catholic lay administration	.42
4. Mechanical Arithmetic	.38
5. Modified ordinal position	.37
6. Number of teachers in school	.35
7. English Reading	.34
8. School grade at age twelve	.22
9. School location	.17
10. Number of children in family	.16
11. Verbal reasoning ability	.15
12. Oral English	.14
13. Absenteeism	.09
14. Gender	-.18
15. Group leadership	-.21
16. Socio-economic status	-.29
17. Class place	-.36
18. Satisfactory classroom behaviour	-.43

variables proved to be considerably more important than the second. On this variable, secondary-school entrants had secured the highest mean score and were followed in turn by vocational-school entrants and primary-school terminal leavers (cf. Table 3.12). An examination of the data on this new composite variable shows that students with high scores (i.e., secondary-school students) tend to be of relatively high socio-economic level, had seldom been absent from primary school, have high verbal reasoning ability, had attended a non-lay administered primary school, are likely to come from a comparatively small family, tend to be female, and had been judged by teachers as having made satisfactory progress while in primary school. Students with low scores on the variable (i.e., primary-school terminal leavers) tend, on the other hand, to be of relatively low socio-economic level, had been frequently absent from primary school, have relatively low verbal reasoning ability scores, had attended Catholic lay-administered primary schools, tend to be male, and had generally been judged by teachers as having made unsatisfactory progress at primary school. A fuller description of these analyses is presented at the end of this chapter.[7]

TABLE 3.12
Centroids of Groups on Discriminant Functions

Destination	*First function* M	*Second function* M
Secondary entrants	.59	-.06
Vocational entrants	-.90	.37
Primary-school terminal leavers	-2.14	-.70

To determine the effectiveness of the two new variables in predicting the destination of students on leaving primary school, the profile of each of the 498 students was compared with the profiles of the typical secondary-school entrant, the typical vocational-school entrant, and the typical primary-school terminal leaver. These typical profiles were derived from the two new variables. Each student's *predicted* category was determined from his or her scores on the two new variables. The probability of the student being classified in each of the three destination categories (secondary, vocational, or terminal leaver) was determined. For instance, a student's scores might indicate that he or she had a probability of .68 (i.e., 68 chances out of 100) of being classified as a secondary entrant, a probability of .24 of being classified as a vocational entrant, and a probability of .08 of being classified as a primary-school terminal leaver. If in fact this student entered a secondary school this predication would be recorded as a 'hit'. If, on the other hand, the student entered a vocational school or dropped out of school after leaving primary school, the prediction would be recorded as a 'miss'.

Clearly, if a large percentage of our sample is classified correctly, the selected variables could be considered effective in discriminating among the three groups. The criterion for determining whether or not the variables were effective discriminators was arbitrarily set at a 'hit' rate of 66.7%, or twice the 'hit' rate one would expect on the basis of random assignment to each of the groups.

How accurate were the two discriminant functions in classifying students according to their destinations after leaving primary school? The classification table is reproduced in Table 3.13. 'Hits' for each group are represented in the diagonal of the table and are italicized. The row totals equal the actual group totals while the column totals equal the predicted totals. The overall 'hit' rate is 73.3%, which is greater than the arbitrary significance level of 66.7%.

An interesting aspect of the data in Table 3.13 is the distribution of 'misses'. Most of the misclassified secondary-school entrants (79.7%) fall into the vocational-entrants group. This, in effect, means that in terms of the 18 variables used in the analysis, the misclassified secondary-school entrants were more like the vocational-school entrants than the correctly classified secondary-school entrants. A total of 15 secondary-school entrants were misclassified as primary-school terminal leavers.

TABLE 3.13
Numbers of Students by Actual and Predicted (on the Basis of Discriminant Functions) Post-Primary Destination

	Predicted group		
Actual group	*Secondary*	*Vocational*	*No post-primary school*
Secondary school	*259*	59	15
Vocational school	25	*79*	24
No post-primary school	0	10	*27*

When the magnitude of the difference between secondary-school entrants and primary-school terminal leavers is taken into account, this latter finding strongly suggests that these 15 students were atypical of the secondary-school entrants. Among the vocational entrants, 61.7% were correctly classified. In terms of the 18 variables, 27% of the terminal leavers possessed attributes similar to those of the vocational-school entrants, while none of the leavers would have been 'more at home' with the secondary-school group than with the other groups.[8]

Conclusion

The first thing that strikes one about the findings of our analyses in this chapter is the large proportion (almost two-thirds) of students who went to secondary school. It is unusual in European countries to have such a large proportion proceed to an academic type post-primary school. The reason is no doubt partly historical; the early growth in post-primary education in this country was marked by a strong emphasis on classical academic studies and the number of secondary schools today is still considerably larger than the number of other types of school. As we have already noted, the preference for an academic type of secondary education may also reflect people's perception of this type of education as the best means of advancing to higher social and economic positions (O'Leary, 1962).

Perhaps even more striking than the numbers going to secondary schools is the clear pattern that emerges of a selective post-primary system. The 'type' of student who goes to a secondary school can be clearly distinguished from the one who goes to a vocational school, who in turn can be distinguished from one who does not proceed to any type of post-primary education. Secondary-school students tend to be of relatively high verbal ability and social class while terminal school-leavers tend to be low on these measures. Vocational-school students occupy an intermediate position. Students in the three groups could also be differentiated in terms of their attendance record at primary school (terminal leavers had the poorest attendance) and their general scholastic progress while still at primary school. It was also possible to distinguish students in the three groups in terms of personality-motivational variables (satisfactory classroom behaviour, health/extroversion), but these were less conspicuous in our analyses than the more obviously cognitive variable, verbal ability.

While evidence for three 'types' of student emerges from our analyses, it does not follow that the type of student one would expect to go to a particular type of post-primary school always does. There was, in fact, considerable over-lap in scores between students with varying post-primary destinations. For example, the spread of students' scores on the verbal ability test was quite large for both secondary and vocational-school entrants. The scores of terminal school-leavers were more homogeneous than those of the others groups: more than four out of five of these students fell in the lower half of the distribution of scores.

It is perhaps surprising that a considerable number (a third) of secondary-school entrants also scored in the lower half of the distribution of scores. This finding must at least raise a question about the ability of many students entering secondary schools to follow a classical academic curriculum.

Apart from socio-economic status, other non-personal variables did not, with one exception, figure prominently in distinguishing between students of varying post-primary destinations. That exception was the type of administration of the primary school which the student attended. Students who attended a Catholic lay-administered primary school were less likely to go to secondary school and more likely to go to a vocational school or not to go to any post-primary school than students attending Catholic religious-administered, or private schools. It is of interest to note that other characteristics of the primary school which the student attended such as location (whether in a city, a town, or a rural area), size of school, or size of class, were not related to the student's post-primary destination.

FOOTNOTES

1 To facilitate the interpretation of the data in Table 3.2 and in later tables the reader may have to refer from time to time to the section in Chapter 2 on the description and coding of the variables. The findings should be interpreted in light of the values assigned to the variables. For example, on the first variable in Table 3.2, SES, high scores denote high socio-economic status. Thus, the sample of secondary entrants (M = 3.12) is likely to have proportionately more students from middle and upper-SES families than either the vocational or terminal-leaver samples, both of which have lower mean SES values (2.26 and 1.81 respectively). Again, on the variable lay administration, it should be remembered that students who had attended a Catholic lay-administered primary school were coded 1 and those who had attended non-lay schools (i.e., Catholic-religious, Protestant, or private) were coded -1. Thus, the

minus sign before the mean for secondary entrants (-.21) indicates that the majority of these students had attended non-lay primary schools while the values .25 for vocational entrants and .24 for terminal leavers show that the majority in both of these groups had attended lay primary schools. Similarly for gender (girls = 1; boys = -1), the mean for the secondary entrants (.09) indicates that girls were in the majority in this group while boys were in the majority among vocational entrants and terminal-leaver samples.

2 Very often the key question in educational research is whether or not differences in mean scores from different samples are due to chance. If, for instance, it is found that two samples of students who had been exposed to two different reading methods differed by four points on a reading test, it is necessary to determine if the difference is due to chance or to the fact that one method is superior to another. The results of comparisons of this nature are reported as either statistically significant or not statistically significant. If a difference is found to be statistically significant, it is normal to infer that it was not due to chance. There are conventional procedures for deciding whether or not a difference is statistically significant. A common practice is to accept the .05 level of significance, which means that the probability of an observed difference occurring as a result of chance is only 5 out of 100. More stringent levels of significance are ones at the .01 and .001 levels. The notations p (probability) $<.05$, $p<.01$, and $p<.001$ are used to indicate levels of significance. To return to the reading sample, if a difference of four points in reading scores was significant beyond the .05 level ($p<.05$), one would conclude that the difference would occur by chance less than 5 times in a 100. Obviously, the smaller the value of p, the greater one's confidence will be that an observed difference is a 'real' one.

3 Correlation coefficients indicate the degree of relationship between two measures or variables (e.g., between intelligence test scores and performance on an arithmetic test). The correlation coefficient ranges in size from +1.00 to -1.00. Coefficients close to 1.00 or -1.00 indicate that there is a strong relationship, either positive or negative, between the variables, while coefficients close to 0 suggest that there is little or no relationship. Positive correlations indicate that high values of one variable are associated with high values of the other (e.g., marks in examinations in arithmetic and algebra, intelligence of parents and their off-spring). Negative correlations indicate that low values of one variable are associated with high values of the other (e.g., number of days absent from school and scores on an Irish test, weight of adults and running speed).

4 The order of entry of the 18 variables was as follows: (1) verbal reasoning ability; (2) socio-economic status; (3) unsatisfactory school progress; (4) absenteeism; (5) gender; (6) number of children in family; (7) health/extroversion; (8) difficulty in Oral English; (9) grade at age twelve; (10) Catholic lay administration; (11) number of teachers in school; (12) modified ordinal position; (13) group leadership; (14) satisfactory classroom behaviour; (15) difficulty in English Reading; (16) difficulty in Mechanical Arithmetic; (17) class place; and (18) school location.

5 The discriminatory power based on 31 variables was .4929 and on 18 variables .4736. Students who had attended Catholic religious or mixed-gender schools served as reference groups and were not included in the analysis.

6 Two functions proved to be statistically significant ($\chi^2 = 317.15$; $df = 36$; $p<.001$ and $\chi^2 = 35.03$; $df = 17$; $p<.01$). The first function accounted for 91.3% of the total discriminatory power and the second for 8.7 percent.

7 The objective of discriminant analysis is to weight and linearly combine variables in

such a fashion that the groups are forced to be as statistically distinct as possible (Tatsuoka, 1970). Each linear combination creates a new transformed variable which can then be used as a basis for describing the nature of differences among the groups. Since there were only three groups (secondary entrant, vocational entrant, primary-school terminal leaver) in our analysis, discriminant analysis permits a comparison of the groups in terms of one or at most two new transformed variables or functions. The problem of deciding the number of significant *transformed* variables (i.e., discriminant functions) was solved by means of Bartlett's V statistic. The weights or coefficients, arranged in order of magnitude, for the two significant functions which were identified are presented in Table 3.11.

The weights indicate the relative importance to the function of the variables with which they are associated. Each of the functions will be interpreted separately in the light of the variables which weigh on it and of the centroids of each of the three groups. The group centroids arranged in order of magnitude are presented in Table 3.12.

The total discriminatory power (Tatsuoka, 1970) of the two functions was estimated to be .4763. Thus almost 48% of the total variability of the two discriminant functions is attributable to group differences.

The purpose of these analyses was to reduce the dimensionality of the data and to identify the variables that contribute most to differentiating among the groups. When the mean scores (centroids) on the first and obviously most important function are compared, it is apparent (Table 3.12) that secondary-school entrants receive the highest score (.59) and are followed in turn by the vocational entrants and primary-school terminal leavers. An examination of this function reveals that the four largest positive weights (.43 for socio-economic status, .31 for verbal reasoning ability, .27 for gender and for school progress) are considerably larger than the remaining positive weights. Similarly, the negative weight with largest absolute value (–.35 for absenteeism) is considerably larger than the remainder of the weights. The next highest negative weights recorded are for Catholic lay administration (–.28) and number of children in family (–.28). Due to the relatively large absolute values of weights attaching to these seven variables, it is reasonable to focus on them in interpreting the meaning of this first function. While it is difficult to subsume even these seven characteristics under one label, several of them seem to reflect scholastic aptitude and home-background factors.

The second function is more difficult to interpret. In considering it, it is important to remember that it is uncorrelated with the first and represents the dimension along which the largest group differences, which have not been accounted for by the first dimension, may be found. The highest score on this function is recorded by the vocational entrants (.37). Secondary-school entrants received a somewhat lower score, while the primary-school terminal leavers are rated the lowest of the three groups. The weights suggest that students with high scores tended to be physically active extroverted types, who had recorded satisfactory general scholastic progress but unsatisfactory classroom behaviour. In addition, these students are likely to have attended Catholic lay-administered primary schools.

8 Ideally, it would have been more appropriate to have computed the discriminant-function coefficients from half of the sample and to have cross-validated the functions on the rest of the sample. However, the size of the overall sample was considered too small to justify this type of cross-validation. Had the discriminant-function coefficients been applied to a different sample of students, clearly fewer 'hits' would have been recorded.

4 Secondary School

After completing their primary schooling, two out of every three students in our sample transferred to a secondary school, i.e., to a classical, academic type post-primary school. Most of these students subsequently completed a five-year course of studies and sat for the Leaving Certificate Examination. A considerable number, however, ceased full-time formal education at some time during the five years. Some students dropped out during the junior-cycle period, i.e., without having taken either the Group or Intermediate Certificate Examination. The Intermediate Certificate (and in two instances the Group Certificate) Examination signified the termination of formal full-time education for some others. Finally, some students dropped out during the final two years after having embarked on a senior-cycle course.

The purpose of this chapter is to describe the progress of the secondary-school students through the system and to compare them with the original national sample, of which they were a sizeable subsample. We were primarily concerned with trying to determine some of the selection or sorting procedures that operated within the system. For instance, we wished to find out if there was a tendency at each stage or time period for the more able students (determined by performance on a verbal reasoning test while at primary school) to advance while the less able dropped out. Or were home factors (such as social status and size of family) related to a student's perseverance in or termination of his or her school career?

In addressing these questions, we compared the characteristics of a diminishing secondary-school sample (as students dropped out at various stages) with the characteristics of the original sample at a number of points in time. Four such points were selected: (1) the time of entry into secondary school, (2) the completion of the junior-cycle course (normally three years), (3) the commencement of the senior-cycle course, and (4) the completion of the senior-cycle course by sitting for the Leaving Certificate Examination (normally two years). In our analyses, the mean score of the secondary-school students on each of the home-background, educational-history, school and personal characteristics was calculated for the sample of students in secondary school at each of the four time points and compared with the corresponding mean score for the original sample. If, for instance, the mean verbal reasoning ability score was higher at a later point in time than at an earlier one, it would indicate that, on average, the students in the system at the later point were more able in terms of verbal ability than those at the earlier point, in effect suggesting a degree of selectivity in terms of verbal ability. Similarly, on SES, a higher score at a later point than at an earlier one would indicate selectivity in terms of SES; no change in mean score over time would lead to the conclusion that socio-economic status was not a factor in determining persistence in secondary school. The school-subject variables had been coded 1 to denote that the student had not experienced difficulty in the subject and -1 to denote difficulty. An increase in score in a particular subject (e.g., .21 to .40 for Written Irish in Table 4.1) would provide evidence that students in the system at the later point had, on average, a better primary-school record in that subject than students at the earlier point; the increase would suggest that weaker pupils in that subject area had dropped out between the two time points.

Variable values differed due to differences in coding. For example, the values for many of the variables (e.g., subject areas, lay administration, all male) ranged from -1 to 1, while school grade at age twelve ranged from 0 to 4, number of children in family from 1 to 16, and verbal reasoning ability from 70 to 140. To compare the extent to which mean scores changed over time, it would have been inappropriate to compare variables in terms of their original numerical values. To facilitate variable comparisons, it was necessary to transform differences between means into a common metric or scale. To do this, each mean difference was expressed in terms of a standard score. Two examples should clarify the procedure. The mean socio-economic status score for the original sample (2.80) in Table 4.1 was subtracted from the corresponding mean for the secondary-school entrant sample (3.12). The raw score difference (.32) was then divided by the standard deviation for the original sample (1.13) to express the difference in terms of standard deviation units away from the original mean. The resulting .28 indicated that the mean for secondary entrants had moved .28 standard units towards the higher values (i.e., the higher SES levels). Similarly, the standard score for English reading was obtained by subtracting .80 (i.e., the mean for the original sample) from .87 (the mean for secondary entrants) and dividing by .60 (the standard deviation for the original sample). The resulting standard score of .12

indicates the extent to which the secondary-school entrants' sample differed from the original sample in terms of the mean and standard deviation of the original sample. When the standard scores for both socio-economic status and English Reading are compared, it would appear that the secondary-school entrants differed from the original sample more in terms of the former than of the latter. Stated another way, the difference between the means for the secondary entrants and the original sample, expressed in standard scores, was greater for SES than for English Reading.[1] Thus, selection is greater for socio-economic status than for English-Reading ability.

SECONDARY-SCHOOL ENTRANTS

Descriptive statistics for the sample of students who enrolled in secondary school (N:333) are presented in Table 4.1. These may be compared with the means (and standard deviations) of the total sample on the same variables.

Table 4.2 presents the mean scores of the secondary-school entrants in terms of standard scores and it is to these scores that we will pay most attention. The values in the first column of the table indicate the extent to which the mean scores for the subset of secondary-school entrants differ from the corresponding mean scores of the original larger sample.

Within the home-background set of variables, the scores for SES (.28) and number of children in family (−.17) were much larger than those for any other variables. This indicates that there was a tendency for children from the lower social-class groupings to be under-represented in the secondary-school entrant sample. Furthermore, students who entered secondary school were more likely to come from slightly smaller families than students in the total sample.

A clear pattern emerges when we examine the data on the educational-history variables. The achievements of secondary-school entrants in a variety of school subject areas had been consistently perceived by teachers as being superior to the achievements of the total sample. By comparison with the overall sample in each subject area, a lower proportion of the secondary-school entrants had experienced difficulty. Furthermore, secondary-school entrants were more likely to have had better primary-school attendance records, to have completed more primary-school grades by the age of twelve, to have received more positive general progress ratings, and to have had higher class rankings than students in the original sample.

TABLE 4.1
Means (and Standard Deviations) on all Variables of Students Attending Secondary School at Varying Points in the Secondary School Course

	Total Sample (N:500)		*Secondary entrants (N:333)*		*Completed junior cycle (N:287)*		*Commenced senior cycle (N:221)*		*Completed senior cycle (N:212)*	
Variables	M	SD	M	SD	M	SD	M	SD	M	SD
Home background										
1. Socio-economic status	2.80	1.13	3.12	1.02	3.18	.99	3.26	1.01	3.25	1.02
2. Number of children	5.65	2.74	5.18	2.45	5.08	2.38	5.05	2.44	5.08	2.45
3. Modified ordinal position	62.79	26.53	61.10	27.65	60.86	27.80	60.81	28.07	60.77	28.13
4. Father living	.95	.23	.95	.22	.94	.23	.95	.22	.95	.22
5. Mother living	.98	.15	.97	.15	.98	.15	.97	.16	.97	.17
Educational history										
1. Class place	3.06	1.05	3.26	1.03	3.30	1.04	3.40	1.00	3.41	1.01
2. School progress	.75	.43	.85	.36	.87	.34	.90	.30	.90	.31
3. Irish Reading	.42	.91	.58	.82	.60	.80	.67	.74	.68	.74
4. Oral Irish	.34	.94	.49	.87	.50	.87	.54	.84	.54	.85
5. Written Irish	.21	.98	.40	.92	.45	.90	.55	.84	.55	.84
6. English Reading	.80	.60	.87	.49	.89	.46	.90	.44	.91	.43
7. Oral English	.81	.59	.89	.45	.90	.43	.91	.42	.91	.43
8. Written English	.60	.80	.72	.69	.76	.66	.77	.63	.76	.65
9. Mechanical Arithmetic	.60	.80	.71	.71	.71	.70	.75	.67	.76	.66
10. Problem Arithmetic	.07	1.00	.21	.98	.23	.97	.31	.95	.32	.95
11. Absenteeism	14.54	14.61	11.01	10.63	10.81	10.89	9.92	10.50	9.93	10.64
12. School grade at age twelve	1.95	.71	2.11	.68	2.13	.68	2.20	.68	2.21	.68

TABLE 4.1 (contd.)

Variables	Total Sample (N:500)		Secondary entrants (N:333)		Completed junior cycle (N:287)		Commenced senior cycle (N:221)		Completed senior cycle (N:212)	
	M	SD	M	SD	M	SD	M	SD	M	SD
Type of school attended										
1. Catholic lay admin.	-.06	1.00	-.21	.98	-.22	.98	-.20	.98	-.23	.98
2. Catholic religious admin.	-.07	1.00	.04	1.00	.04	1.00	-.01	1.00	.01	1.00
3. Protestant administration	-.95	.31	-.94	.32	-.94	.33	-.94	.35	-.93	.36
4. Private admin.	-.92	.39	-.88	.47	-.88	.49	-.86	.52	-.85	.53
5. Number of teachers	3.69	1.10	3.74	1.13	3.75	1.12	3.70	1.10	3.71	1.10
6. All male	-.29	.96	-.28	.96	-.32	.95	-.27	.97	-.25	.97
7. All female	-.30	.98	-.22	.97	-.18	.99	-.28	.96	-.26	.97
8. Mixed gender	-.42	.91	-.49	.87	-.50	.87	-.46	.87	-.48	.88
9. School location	2.14	.90	2.13	.90	2.15	.89	2.24	.86	2.24	.86
10. Class size	2.46	1.56	2.46	1.53	2.44	1.49	2.33	1.46	2.36	1.46
Personal characteristics										
1. Verbal reasoning ability	100.15	15.46	104.65	14.23	105.30	14.18	107.44	14.09	107.81	13.82
2. Gender	.00	1.00	.09	1.00	.14	.99	.06	1.00	.05	1.00
3. Satisfactory class. behav.	.10	.91	.34	.83	.42	.80	.51	.77	.52	.78
4. Group leadership	.01	.89	.03	.86	.04	.85	.08	.84	.07	.83
5. Health/extroversion	.12	.83	.18	.82	.20	.81	.20	.79	.21	.79
6. Aesthetic behaviour	.05	.72	.12	.71	.13	.72	.13	.73	.13	.72

TABLE 4.2
Deviations of Means from Total Sample Means of Students Attending School at Varying Points in the Secondary-School Course

Variables	*Secondary entrants (N:333)*	*Completed junior cycle (N:287)*	*Commenced senior cycle (N:221)*	*Completed senior cycle (N:212)*
Home background				
1. Socio-economic status	.28	.34	.41	.40
2. Number of children	-.17	-.21	-.22	-.21
3. Modified ordinal position	-.06	-.07	-.07	-.08
4. Father living	.00	-.04	.00	.00
5. Mother living	-.07	.00	-.07	-.07
Educational history				
1. Class place	.19	.23	.32	.33
2. School progress	.23	.28	.35	.35
3. Irish Reading	.18	.20	.27	.29
4. Oral Irish	.16	.17	.21	.21
5. Written Irish	.19	.24	.35	.35
6. English Reading	.12	.15	.17	.18
7. Oral English	.14	.15	.17	.17
8. Written English	.15	.20	.21	.20
9. Mechanical Arithmetic	.14	.14	.19	.20
10. Problem Arithmetic	.14	.16	.24	.25
11. Absenteeism	-.24	-.26	-.32	-.32
12. School grade at age twelve	.23	.25	.35	.37
Type of school attended				
1. Catholic lay admin.	-.15	-.16	-.14	-.17
2. Catholic religious admin.	.11	.11	.06	.08
3. Protestant admin.	.03	.03	.03	.06
4. Private admin.	.10	.10	.15	.18
5. Number of teachers	.05	.05	.01	.02
6. All male	.01	-.03	.02	.04
7. All female	.08	.12	.02	.04
8. Mixed gender	-.08	-.09	-.04	-.07
9. School location	-.01	.01	.11	.11
10. Class size	.00	-.01	-.08	-.06
Personal characteristics				
1. Verbal reasoning ability	.29	.33	.47	.50
2. Gender	.09	.14	.06	.05
3. Satisfactory class. behav..	.26	.35	.45	.46
4. Group leadership	.02	.03	.08	.07
5. Health/extroversion	.07	.10	.10	.11
6. Aesthetic behaviour	.10	.11	.11	.11

As far as the type of primary school attended by the student was concerned, in general, the statistics for the total sample and for the subsample of secondary entrants are similar. There was, however, as indicated by the negative sign before .15, a tendency for students from Catholic lay-administered primary schools to be slightly under-represented and for students from primary schools run by Catholic religious and from private schools to be over-represented among the secondary-school entrants.

Among the personal characteristic variables, it is evident that the secondary entrants tended to have higher verbal ability scores and to have received higher ratings from their teachers on the characteristics normally associated with satisfactory classroom behaviour than the overall sample of students. On the verbal ability test, the difference in favour of the secondary-school entrants was 4.5 points.

Finally, it should be noted that the major differences in order of magnitude were recorded for verbal ability, socio-economic status, satisfactory classroom behaviour, absenteeism, satisfactory scholastic progress, and school grade at age twelve. Clearly many of these variables are intercorrelated and, in general, they seem to suggest the pervasive influence of scholastic ability and home-background factors, as did the analyses in the previous chapter.[2]

Secondary-School Students Who Completed Junior Cycle

Of the 333 students who embarked on a junior-cycle course in a secondary school, 30 dropped out at some stage during the junior-cycle period. Two others died and one emigrated. A further 13 students transferred to vocational schools.[3] Thus, at the end of the junior-cycle period, the total number in secondary schools had been reduced by 13.8% (from 333 to 287). Considerably more than half (57.4%) of the national sample completed junior-cycle education in secondary school. (Other students, as we shall see in the next chapter, completed junior cycle in vocational schools.)

A summary of comparisons of students who completed junior cycle in secondary school with the total sample is presented in Table 4.1. Table 4.2 presents similar comparisons in terms of deviation scores. In the latter table, it is also possible to make comparisons between the degree of 'selectivity' at the time of entry to secondary school and at the completion of the junior cycle. For example, in the first row of Table 4.2, the first figure (.28) tells us that the mean for the socio-economic status of the secondary entrant group was .28 standard deviation units above the mean for the national sample, indicating that students from middle and higher socio-economic groups are over-represented among secondary-school entrants. The first figure in the second column (.34) indicates that middle and higher socio-economic groups are over-represented in the sample of students who completed junior cycle at secondary school; further, when compared with the value of secondary-school entrants (.28), it is clear that there has been a shift towards further selectivity in terms of socio-economic status between the commencement and the completion of the junior cycle. Another family factor that was related to perseverance throughout the junior cycle was family size. Students who completed junior cycle tended to have, on average, fewer brothers and sisters (5.08) than students in the total sample (5.65) (Table 4.1). The change in the deviation values was from -.17 to -.21 (Table 4.2).

Students who had completed junior cycle had as a group received more positive ratings from their teachers on each of the educational history variables than students in the overall sample. Further, students who completed junior cycle had received higher ratings on most of these variables than the sample of students who had entered secondary school. The differences between the means for the two time periods were most pronounced in the case of unsatisfactory progress while in primary school in Written Irish and Written English.

The type of primary school the student had attended did not appear to be strongly related to staying on in secondary school to complete the junior cycle. The tendency for students from Catholic lay-administered primary schools to be slightly under-represented and for students from Catholic religious-administered schools to be over-represented which we found among secondary-school entrants was again in evidence in the group of students that completed junior cycle. By comparison with the secondary-entrant group, there was an increase in the proportion of students from all-female primary schools in the persisting group indicating that fewer girls than boys dropped out of secondary school during the junior-cycle years. Girls had been in a slight majority among secondary-school entrants; differential attrition during the junior-cycle years had the effect of further increasing the proportion of girls relative to boys in secondary school.

Finally, data on personal characteristics indicate that in terms of satisfactory classroom behaviour and verbal reasoning ability, the ratings or scores for the sample of students who completed the junior cycle were superior to those for the overall sample. Further, the sample that persisted in school to the end of junior cycle was superior to the secondary-entrant group in verbal reasoning ability and, more obviously, in satisfactory classroom behaviour.

So far we have described the progress of students through the secondary school system in terms of information obtained when the students were still attending primary school. Information on the scholastic performance of students while attending post-primary school was also available. This information took the form of students' performance on public examinations. It included for each student in the case of the Intermediate Certificate Examination letter grades for each examination subject taken by the student, as well as an overall pass-fail rating. Similar data were obtained for the small number (N:14) of students who took the Day Group Certificate Examination, an examination which is normally associated with the vocational system. Of the total number of secondary students for whom ICE results were available (N:280),[4] 244 or 87.1% passed. The overall pass rate, based on ICE results for 335 secondary and vocational-school students, was 84.78%.

Not surprisingly, given the vocational nature of the examination, very few secondary students sat for the DGCE. A total of 11 of the 14 students (i.e. 78.6%) who took the examination passed. Here again, the pass rate of the secondary-school candidates was superior to the overall pass rate (69.41%) of the 85 secondary and vocational students in the sample that took this examination. Of the total of 14 DGCE secondary-school candidates, 12 sat for the ICE the following year. Each one of the 12 who took both examinations obtained a junior-cycle certificate by passing either the ICE or the DGCE; none failed both examinations. In the case of each examination, ten passed and two failed.

Altogether, 87.2% of the secondary students who completed the junior-cycle course obtained a junior-cycle certificate.

Secondary-School Students Who Commenced Senior Cycle

Of the 287 students who completed junior cycle, all but four sat for the Intermediate Certificate Examination.[5] Traditionally, this examination has marked a major decision point for the student. Students who possessed the Intermediate Certificate could apply for certain positions, both in the public and private sectors. They could also apply for training or apprenticeship schemes. Alternatively, they could elect to remain in school for the two-year senior-cycle course, at the end of which time they would normally sit for the Leaving Certificate Examination.

At the end of junior cycle, of the cohort of 287 students who had completed the junior cycle, a total of 220 (i.e., 76.7%) commenced a senior-cycle course. Sixty-five students (22.6%) ceased formal full-time education at this stage. Two students transferred from a secondary to a vocational school and one further student from a vocational to a secondary school. Thus, 221 (i.e., 44.2% of the original national sample) embarked on a two-year senior-cycle course in a secondary school.

In this section we compare the sample of senior-cycle entrants (N:221) with the original sample (N:500) and also with the sample of students who completed junior cycle. Comparisons in terms of mean scores are presented in Table 4.1 and in terms of deviation scores in Table 4.2.

The pattern of findings for the home-background data is very similar to that found in the two preceding analyses. Senior-cycle entrants were found to differ markedly from the original sample on two variables, socio-economic status (.41) and number of children in the family (-.22). In effect, this means that, compared to the original sample, senior-cycle entrants tended to come from middle and higher socio-economic groups and from smaller families. Furthermore, the change in standardized mean difference from .34 to .41 indicates that of those students who completed junior cycle, ones from middle and higher SES levels were somewhat more likely to commence the senior-cycle course.

Two relatively clear-cut patterns emerge when we examine the educational-history variables. Firstly, the scholastic progress ratings awarded by primary-school teachers to students who subsequently entered senior-cycle courses in secondary schools were consistently superior on each of ten measures to the ratings awarded to students in the overall sample. Further the senior-cycle entrants had comparatively better primary-school attendance records and tended to have completed more grades.

A comparison of senior-cycle entrants with students who entered secondary school indicates that on all educational-history variables, the former received more positive ratings. The variables which were most sensitive to change between time of entry to secondary school and entry to senior cycle (as measured by the size of the standardized mean difference) were the grade the student had reached at age twelve and the teacher ratings of students' general progress and of students' progress in Written Irish. Thus, it would appear that achievement-related selection factors continued to operate up the commencement of senior cycle.

Although the extent of change in mean scores is smaller for the type of primary school attended than for other categories of variables, nevertheless there are a number of interesting findings. As in the previous analyses, students who had attended Catholic non-lay primary schools (especially the small number who had been in private primary schools) were more likely than their lay-primary peers to enter the senior-cycle programme. When the data for the senior-cycle entrants and those who completed junior cycle are compared, it is evident that there was a decrease in the proportion of students from all-female primary schools and an increase in the proportions both from all-male and mixed primary schools. (In the next paragraph we shall see that far more girls than boys left secondary school at the end of junior cycle.) The second notable change is related to school location. It would appear that during the short time interval between the end of junior cycle and the commencement of senior cycle there was a decrease in the proportion of secondary students who had attended urban primary schools. Taken together, these findings indicate that school leavers at the Intermediate Certificate stage tend to be girls, probably from urban backgrounds.

Among the personal characteristics, once again, verbal reasoning ability and teachers' ratings of students on characteristics normally associated with satisfactory classroom behaviour proved to be relatively good predictors of persistence in secondary school. The mean difference between the senior-cycle entrant group and the total sample in verbal reasoning ability was 7.29 points, which is almost one-half a standard deviation on the test. Similarly, the mean on the satisfactory classroom behaviour variable for the senior-cycle group was almost half a standard deviation above that of the original sample. On both these variables, the mean scores for the senior-cycle group were substantially greater than the mean for students who had completed junior cycle. The decrease in the standardized mean on the variable gender from .14 to .06 for the sample who entered senior cycle indicates that while girls were still in the majority within the secondary school, the extent of this majority had decreased. Actually at the end of the junior cycle, more than twice as many girls (N:46) as boys (N:20) left secondary school.

Earlier we saw that 87.1% of Intermediate Certificate Examination candidates passed the examination. The pass rate for students who entered senior cycle was 91.2%.[6] An additional measure of achievement was the letter grades which students obtained on the six subjects on which they performed best on the ICE. The mean performance of the senior-cycle entrants on a separate index of level of performance on the ICE, computed from letter grades (see Chapter 7) was 6.39, as opposed to 6.21 for the total number of students who took the ICE while at secondary school. Lastly, seven of the eight senior-cycle entrants who had taken the Day Group Certificate Examination passed, giving a pass rate of 87.5%, as against 78.6% for the total of 14 secondary students who had taken the examination.

So far the evidence suggests that there was a slight tendency for the students with the better examination records to advance to senior cycle while those with the somewhat weaker records tended to finish school at the end of junior cycle. In a direct comparison between persisters and early leavers on the ICE index, a significant difference in favour of the former was found.[7] In a separate (discriminant) analysis of differences between senior-cycle entrants and junior-cycle terminal leavers in which the ICE index and the primary-school measures were used, the ICE index was identified as the most powerful discriminator between the two groups of students.

Secondary-School Students Who Completed Senior Cycle

The two-year senior-cycle course culminates in the Leaving Certificate Examination. Of the 221 who commenced the course, 212 (95.9%) sat for the examination. Therefore, 42.4% of the original sample completed a Leaving Certificate course of studies in secondary school.

Given the high persistence rate of this senior-cycle sample, it is not surprising to find that the statistics derived from the school variables for the comparison of the sample with the original sample were very similar to those for students who commenced senior cycle described in the last section (Tables 4.1 and 4.2). On the ICE, the performance of all the senior-cycle students (with a 91.2% pass rate) was superior to that of the 9 students who failed to complete the cycle (55.6%). On the DGCE a pass rate of 87.5% was recorded.[8]

Finally, at the end of secondary school, 199 of the 212 candidates succeeded in passing the LCE, i.e., a pass rate of 93.9% was achieved.

The Most Selective Variables

It is clear that the standardized mean values for some variables were subject to a relatively sizeable change as the secondary-school cohort decreased in size, while the means for other variables varied little for successive samples of secondary students (cf. Table 4.2).

The changes in mean scores for the home-background, educational-history and personal characteristics variables are presented in visual format in Figure 4.1. The bar graphs extend above and below the base or overall mean line to denote positive and negative deviations from the mean of the original sample. For example, the standardized mean socio-economic status level of secondary entrants (.28) was *above* the mean for the original sample; by the end of the senior cycle, the mean value had increased still further (.40). On the other hand, the standardized mean number of children in the families of secondary entrants was *below* the mean for the original sample (-.17); at the end of senior cycle, it had decreased slightly further (-.21).

The three variables which showed the greatest change in standardized mean values for primary school until the end of secondary school were verbal reasoning ability, satisfactory classroom behaviour, and socio-economic status. Following these were a number of variables that referred almost exclusively to the primary-school educational history of the students (grade achieved at age twelve, general school progress, teacher ratings in a variety of school subjects, class place, and absenteeism). Variables relating to the type of primary school attended by the student evidenced little change and appeared to have had relatively little effect on secondary-school selection procedures from one stage to the next.

When we examine more closely the verbal reasoning ability scores of samples, at different time points, the nature and extent of the selection process becomes most apparent. We find that for students who scored at or below the mean (100) on the verbal ability test, both their entrance and persistence rates in secondary school are comparatively low. For each successive time point, the number of students at the mean or below it diminishes. By the end of senior cycle, the percentage of students of this level of ability has dropped from 49.0% (for secondary entrants) to 22.9%. On the other hand, when we examine the entrance and persistence rates of students of above-average ability, a quite different picture emerges. Of the total sample of students who scored above the mean on the verbal ability test, 83.5% entered secondary school and 61.2% completed senior cycle. The entrance and persistence rates (89.7% and 75.6%, respectively) were even more pronounced for secondary entrants who had a score of 116 or higher on the ability test (Table 4.3).

Viewed from a somewhat different perspective, the data in Table 4.3 indicate that the probability of a primary-school student who scored below 85 completing secondary school is 15/87 or .17 (i.e., 17 chances in 100) and that of a secondary entrant who had recorded a score in this category is 15/33 or .45. For students in the 86–100 verbal reasoning ability range, the comparable figures are .26 and .47, respectively. For

FIGURE 4.1

Deviations of Means from Total Sample Means of Students Attending School at Varying Points in the Secondary-School Course

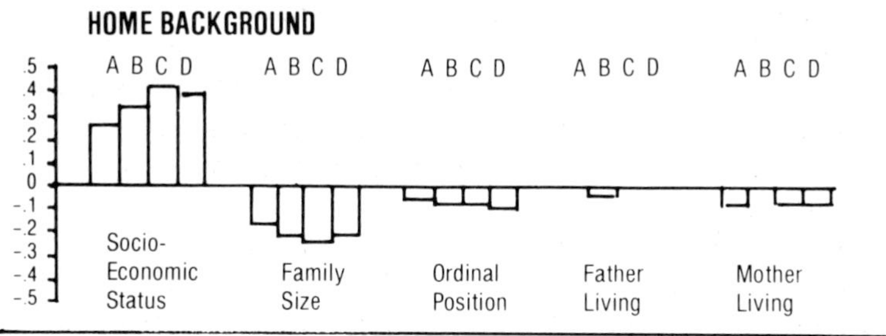

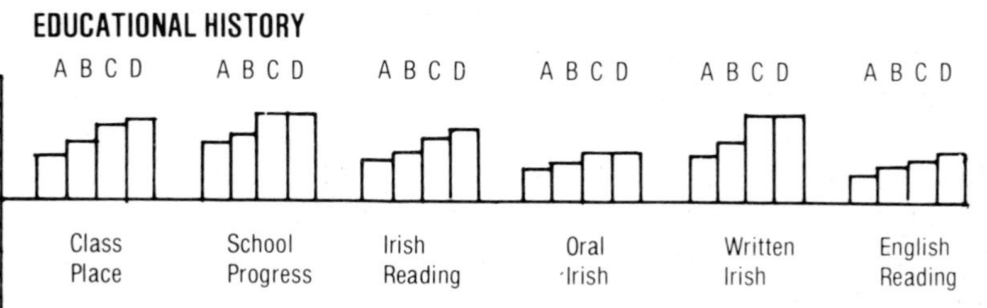

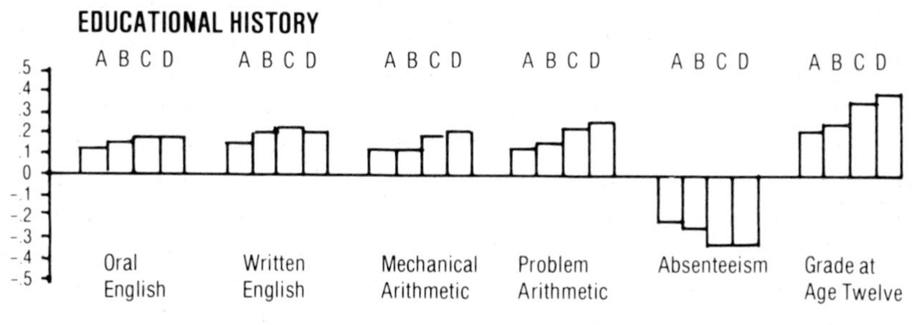

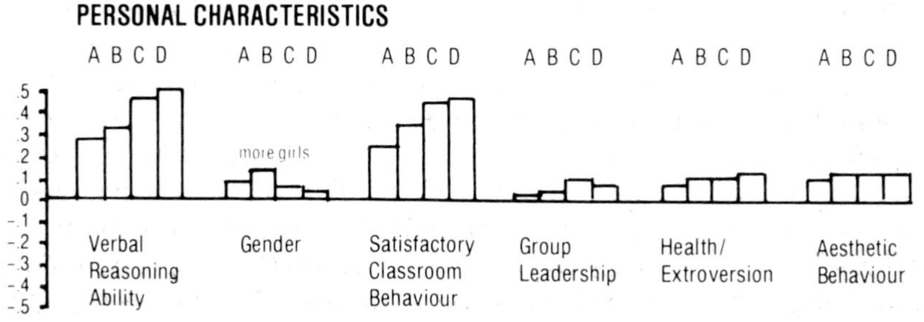

TABLE 4.3
Numbers (and Percentages) of Students with Varying Scores on the Verbal Reasoning Test at Varying Points in the Secondary-School Course

Sample		*Verbal reasoning scores* -85	86-100	101-115	116-130	131+	Total
Total sample	N	87	158	177	68	10	500
	%	*17.4*	*31.6*	*35.4*	*13.6*	*2.0*	
Secondary entrants	N	33	87	143	60	10	333
	%	*9.9*	*26.1*	*42.9*	*18.0*	*3.0*	
Completed junior cycle	N	28	69	125	55	10	287
	%	*9.8*	*26.0*	*43.6*	*19.2*	*3.5*	
Commenced senior cycle	N	18	42	100	51	10	221
	%	*8.1*	*19.0*	*45.2*	*23.1*	*4.5*	
Completed senior cycle	N	15	41	97	49	10	212
	%	*7.1*	*19.3*	*45.8*	*23.1*	*4.7*	

TABLE 4.4
Numbers (and Percentages) of Students with Varying Degrees of Satisfactory Classroom Behaviour at Varying Points in the Secondary-School Course

Sample		*Standard score on satisfactory classroom behaviour* -2.00	-1.99 *to* -1.00	-0.99 *to* 0.00	0.00 *to* *0.99*	1.00 *to* *1.99*	2.00 *to* *2.99*	Total
Total sample	N	6	54	155	202	76	7	500
	%	*1.2*	*10.8*	*31.0*	*40.4*	*15.2*	*1.4*	
Secondary entrants	N	3	14	88	155	66	7	333
	%	*0.9*	*4.2*	*26.4*	*46.5*	*19.8*	*2.1*	
Completed junior cycle	N	2	7	74	136	61	7	287
	%	*0.7*	*2.4*	*25.8*	*47.4*	*21.3*	*2.4*	
Commenced senior cycle	N	1	4	45	114	51	6	221
	%	*0.5*	*1.8*	*20.4*	*51.6*	*23.1*	*2.7*	
Completed senior cycle	N	1	4	42	109	50	6	212
	%	*0.5*	*1.9*	*19.8*	*51.4*	*23.6*	*2.8*	

those in the 100–115 score range, the figures are .55 and .68, while the probabilities for students in the 116–130 ability range are .72 and .82. Finally, since every student who had scored 130+ on the verbal ability test entered and completed secondary school, both probabilities in this instance were 1.00.

The second variable most sensitive to change was satisfactory classroom behaviour. Scores on this composite variable were derived from the primary teachers' ratings of students on such personality characteristics as keenness to get on, enquiring mind, concentration, and achievement tendencies. Details of scores on the variable for various time points are summarized in Table 4.4. An examination of these data indicates that students who had scored relatively poorly on this variable were much less likely to complete secondary school than were students who had scored highly. For example, of the 215 students who had scored below the mean (0.0) in the overall sample, a mere 21.9% (N:47) completed secondary school. On the other hand, 165, or 57.9% of the original sample, who had scored above the mean completed senior cycle. Fewer than 30% of students who had scored –1.00 or less enrolled in secondary school while at the other extreme, almost 90% of those who had satisfactory classroom behaviour scores of 1.00 or greater entered secondary school. In terms of probability, the data indicate that students with low scores on this variable (i.e., –1.00 or less) had a probability of .28 of enrolling in secondary school and of .08 of finishing senior cycle; for the small number (N:17) who enrolled in secondary school, the probability of completing (.29) was still relatively small. For the large group (N:357) who scored between –0.99 and +0.99, the probability of completing senior-cycle secondary education was .42, while for those who entered secondary school, the comparable probability was .62. Lastly, for students who received high satisfactory classroom behaviour ratings (i.e., 1.00 or greater), the probability of completing senior cycle was .67, while for those who had enrolled in secondary school, the probability of completing rose to .77.

Socio-economic status was the third among the three variables which showed most sensitivity to change in the secondary-school samples. Reading down the columns in Table 4.5 we note that the representation of the professional and intermediate professional categories tended to increase, as that of the partly-skilled and unskilled tended to decrease. At one extreme, 87% (i.e., 13 of 15 children) from the professional SES category completed senior cycle. In sharp contrast, a mere 15 of 92 children, or 16% from the unskilled category attained this level of education. Indeed approximately two out of three students in this latter category did not enrol in secondary school at all. Students in the

TABLE 4.5
Numbers (and Percentages) of Students of Varying Socio-Economic Levels at Varying Points in the Secondary-School Course

Sample		*Socio-economic status*					
		Profes-sional	*Inter. profes-sional*	*Skilled*	*Partly-skilled*	*Un-skilled*	*Total*
Total sample	N	15	141	163	89	92	500
	%	*3.0*	*28.2*	*32.6*	*17.8*	*18.4*	
Secondary entrants	N	14	122	117	49	31	333
	%	*4.2*	*36.6*	*35.1*	*14.7*	*9.3*	
Completed junior cycle	N	13	112	97	44	21	287
	%	*4.5*	*39.0*	*33.8*	*15.3*	*7.3*	
Commenced senior cycle	N	13	94	67	32	15	221
	%	*5.9*	*42.5*	*30.3*	*14.5*	*6.8*	
Completed senior cycle	N	13	88	65	31	15	212
	%	*6.1*	*41.5*	*30.7*	*14.6*	*7.1*	

unskilled and partly-skilled categories accounted for 36.2% of the overall sample but for only 21.7% of those who completed senior cycle. Students from the professional and intermediate professional categories on the other hand, amounted to 31.2% of the overall sample but as much as 47.6% of the sample which completed the senior cycle in secondary school. The probability that a student from the professional category would enter secondary school was .93, for students from the intermediate professional category it was .87, from the skilled category .72, from the partly-skilled category .55, and from the unskilled category .34. For those who enrolled in secondary school the probabilities of completing senior cycle in secondary school were as follows: .93 for the professional category, .72 for intermediate professional, .56 for skilled, .63 for the partly-skilled, and .48 for the unskilled category.

It might be argued that the three most selective variables, verbal reasoning ability, satisfactory classroom behaviour, and socio-economic status, are inter-correlated and measure aspects of the same basic trait. However, for those students who entered secondary school, correlations among these variables are not substantial. Both socio-economic status and satisfactory classroom behaviour are significantly correlated with verbal reasoning ability (.17 and .39, respectively), but the correlations are not very large. The correlation between socio-economic status and satisfactory classroom behaviour (.15) was not significant. Given the size of the correlations, we are forced to conclude that all three factors are important selection variables throughout the secondary school.

Boarding-School Students

Before concluding this chapter, we turn our attention briefly to a special sample of secondary-school students, those attending boarding school. In 1969–70, boarders amounted to 16.95% of all secondary-school students (Ireland: Department of Education, 1974), and in 1974–75, 12.29% (Ireland: Department of Education, 1977). In our sample, boarders accounted for 7.20% of secondary-school entrants and 10.85% of the students that completed senior cycle. Therefore, it would appear that boarders are under-represented somewhat in the sample.

In the earlier sections of this chapter we traced the progress of the decreasing sample of students through secondary school and attempted to explain this progress in terms of primary-school variables and examination performance. It is not possible to duplicate this procedure for the sample of boarders since only 1 of the 24 boarders (a boy) left school without taking the LCE. Instead we present a brief description of the boarding school sample.

Although 48.3% of boarders came from the professional and intermediate professional socio-economic categories, there are no significant differences between the distributions of boarders and non-boarders on socio-economic status. Similarly the differences between boarders and non-boarders on the remaining home-background variables, number of children in family, ordinal position in family, and whether or not the student's father and mother were living were not significant. On the educational-history variables, the ratings for boarders and non-boarders were similar. Turning to the type of primary school attended by the student, it was found that none of the private or Protestant primary school students attended boarding schools. Almost two out of three (62.5%) had attended all-female primary schools as compared to 38.1% of non-boarders. A total of 70.8% had attended a rural primary school (as opposed to 46.7% of non-boarders), while none had attended a city primary school (34.7% of non-boarders had attended city schools). Finally, in terms of personal characteristics, scores of boarders and non-boarders on the four personality variables were similar. The mean verbal reasoning ability score of the boarders (105.75) did not differ from that of the non-boarders (104.53) by a significant amount. Girls were over-represented among boarders; of the initial total of 24 boarders, 15 were girls.

Conclusion

In this chapter we examined the extent to which secondary-school students at different stages of the secondary-school programme, which normally lasts five years, differ from the larger overall sample of students, of which they were a sizeable component. We noted that students who remained in school differed from those who finished school on some characteristics much more than on others. A macro-view of the changing nature of the secondary-school cohort was presented in Table 4.2.

The biggest changes in deviations were recorded by the entrants sample (Table 4.2, column 1). In other words, in the first selection process, i.e., in the selection of the secondary-entrant sample from the overall sample, the changes in variable mean scores tended to be more pronounced than the changes between any other two time periods. The next most pronounced change in variable mean scores occurred between the end of junior cycle (column 2) and the beginning of senior cycle (column 3). The changes between the beginning and end of the senior cycle were small which is not surprising since the difference in sample size over this period amounts to a mere nine students.

It is evident that the mean socio-economic level of students still at school tended to increase as students left school at various stages,[9] thus indicating an increase in selectivity in terms of social class. Furthermore, the mean number of children in the student's family tended to get smaller, though in absolute terms, the difference between the mean size of family in the total sample (5.65) and of the sample of students who completed senior cycle (5.08) is not very large. None of the other home-background variables (the student's ordinal position in family and whether or not his or her father or mother were living) appears to be related to the length of time students spend in secondary school.

When we turn to the primary-school measures of attainment, it would appear that at each of the four decision points which we examined, the students with the more positive ratings tended to advance to the next higher level, while those who had received poorer ratings tended to drop out of school. A similar finding was observed in the case of absenteeism; students who entered secondary school had, on average, been absent from primary school on fewer occasions (11 days) than the overall sample (14.54 days), while within secondary school, students at each succeeding higher level tended to have had better attendance records at primary school than students at preceding levels.

In general, the mean standardized scores for type of school attended showed less change than scores for variables in the other three categories. From the outset, students who had attended Catholic lay-administered primary schools were under-represented among secondary-school entrants and continued to be so throughout the five years of secondary school. Students from the other three administrative types, Catholic religious, Protestant, and especially private, were over-represented. With one exception, there was little change in the means for the three school-gender variables (all-male, all-female, and mixed). The exception was the drop in the proportion of students from all-female primary schools at the end of junior cycle, a drop that was attributable in the main to the relatively high drop-out rate among girls at this point. As the proportion of students from all-female primary schools dropped, there was an increase in the proportion of students who had attended rural primary schools.

The most striking deviation changes over time were observed for the personal characteristics of students. At each time point, the mean verbal ability score for the sample was higher than that recorded at the preceding point, thus suggesting the existence of an ability selection factor. The relatively large deviation (.50) for the sample which finished senior cycle, however, should not blind us to the fact that the mean difference between entrants to secondary school and those who completed senior cycle was only 3.16 points on the ability test.

The trend for students at each succeeding secondary level to have higher mean scores than those at the preceding level was repeated in the case of the index of satisfactory classroom behaviour. Students who had been rated highly by their primary teachers on personality variables associated with satisfactory behaviour in the classroom tended to spend longer in secondary school than students who had received less satisfactory ratings. On the three remaining personality variables derived from factor scores, while the deviations tended to increase in a positive direction from one time point to the next, the trend was not so pronounced.

At each point in time there were more girls than boys in our secondary-school samples. Furthermore, between the time of entry

(54.5% girls; 46.6% boys) and the end of junior cycle, boys were more likely than girls to drop out of school. Of the 287 students who completed junior cycle, 163 (56.8%) were girls. After junior cycle, more girls than boys dropped out and the percentage of girls had dropped to 52.9% by the beginning of senior cycle. While the superiority in numbers of girls remained through the senior cycle, the percentage of girls in the sample had decreased very slightly (to 52.4%) by the end of the cycle.

Lastly, students who elected to commence senior cycle tended to have performed much better on public examinations than those who terminated school at the end of junior cycle. Indeed, a measure of performance on the Intermediate Certificate Examination was identified as the best discriminator between senior cycle entrants and junior cycle terminal leavers.

FOOTNOTES

1 Standard scores derived in this manner need to be interpreted with caution. A problem arises especially in the case of dichotomously-coded variables where the value of the mean score is close either to the minimum or maximum score value. Two such variables are student's mother living (M = .95; maximum value = 1.00) and Protestant school administration (M = -.98; minimum value = -1.00). If a small subsample had one or two deviant scores on one such variable, it would result in an unduly large standard deviation score.

2 For example, the correlation between verbal reasoning score and SES was .17 ($p < .001$) and between verbal reasoning score and satisfactory classroom behaviour .39 ($p < .001$).

3 The mean verbal reasoning ability and SES scores (101.77 and 2.85 respectively) of the students who transferred were close to those of the original sample (100.15 and 2.80). Ten of the students who transferred were boys.

4 Four students who completed junior cycle did not take the ICE and the results of one further student were lost by the school.

5 These four students attended a secondary school which did not present students for the ICE.

6 Four students who did not sit for the ICE have not been considered in the calculation of these figures.

7 $F = 41.46$; $df = 1{,}274$; $p < .001$. ICE indices were not computed for those students who had taken fewer than six examination subjects.

8 Eight LCE students had taken the DGCE. None of these dropped out of school during the senior cycle.

9 The statistic .40 in column 4 is an exception to this trend. The minor decrease from .41 to .40 is due to the fact that six of the nine pupils who dropped out during the final two years had been classified as intermediate professional.

5 *Vocational School*

Traditionally vocational schools have emphasized practical subjects and the preparation of students for trades, business, and agriculture (cf. O'Leary, 1962). Until the mid-1960s students in such schools were expected to sit for the Day Group Certificate Examination (DGCE) which was normally taken two years after entry. Since then, students may, after three years, sit for the Intermediate Certificate Examination (ICE) — an examination traditionally associated with secondary schools. A relatively small number of vocational school students complete the Leaving Certificate Examination (LCE) course each year.

In Chapter 3, we saw that students in our sample who had enrolled in vocational schools could be distinguished from secondary-school entrants and also from primary-school terminal leavers mainly in terms of general scholastic ability and home-background factors. In this chapter we will examine the educational progress of those students who transferred to vocational schools on completion of their primary education. Firstly, we compare the vocational entrants with the original national sample on measures of home background, educational history, school, and personal characteristics. Secondly, we describe the characteristics of students who completed the junior cycle by sitting for either the DGCE or the ICE. Thirdly, we examine the examination performances of students who completed the junior cycle. Fourthly, we focus our attention on students who elected to enrol in a senior-cycle course in a vocational school. Finally, we describe the characteristics of the small number of students who remained at school until the end of the senior cycle and actually sat for the LCE. As in the case of the previous chapter, we will be examining the characteristics of a diminishing sample as students drop out at various stages at four distinct points in time. These time points are (1) the time of entry into vocational school, (2) the completion of the junior-cycle course, (3) the commencement of the two-year senior-cycle course, and (4) the completion of the senior-cycle course.

In Chapter 1, we observed that approximately 25% of students in Irish schools normally transfer to vocational school after completing the primary-school course. In the present study, a total of 128 pupils (25.6%)

of the original sample enrolled in a vocational school.

As in Chapter 4, the mean score for each sample of students on each of the primary-school measures was calculated and compared with the corresponding mean score for the original sample (N:500). Differences in raw scores have been transformed into standard scores thus allowing us to express all differences in terms of a common metric and to identify those variables, the mean values of which were most subject to change.

Vocational-School Entrants

The data in Table 5.1 permit a comparison of the sample of vocational entrants (N:128) and the original sample (N:500) of which the vocational entrants were a part. The deviation values in Table 5.2 indicate the extent to which the mean for the vocational entrants on a particular variable differed from the mean for the original national sample on that variable in standard-score units.

When we look at the home-background variables, we see that vocational-school entrants tended to belong to families of relatively low socio-economic status. The mean socio-economic index for such entrants was almost one-half a standard deviation below that of the national sample. The difference was largely attributable to the fact that 57.1% of the entrants had been classified as children of semi-skilled or unskilled workers as opposed to 36.2% of the overall sample, while at the other extreme, as few as 13.3% of the entrants were in the professional and intermediate-professional classes, as opposed to 31.2% of the overall sample. On the second variable (number of children in family), vocational entrants tended to have more siblings (M = 6.45) than the overall average (M = 5.65). As many as 46.1% of them were members of families which had seven or more children; the comparable figure for the overall sample was 32.7 per cent. In fact, almost one in six (16.5%) of vocational-school entrants came from a family with ten or more children (as opposed to 9.2% of the overall sample). Lastly, vocational entrants, compared to children in the overall sample, tended to be the later-born children in families.

Taken together, the educational-history data clearly indicate that, in terms of primary-school attainment, vocational entrants were generally below average. In contrast to the overall sample, their class rank or place tended to be poorer; they were more likely to have completed fewer primary-school grades by the age of twelve and they were also more likely to have been judged by teachers to have made unsatisfactory

TABLE 5.1
Means (and Standard Deviations) on all Variables of Students Attending Vocational School at Varying Points in the Vocational-School Course

	Total sample (N:500)		*Vocational entrants (N:128)*		*Completed junior cycle (N:90)*		*Commenced senior cycle (N:23)*		*Completed senior cycle (N:10)*	
Variables	M	SD	M	SD	M	SD	M	SD	M	SD
Home background										
1. Socio-economic status	2.80	1.13	2.26	1.06	2.38	1.07	2.57	.99	2.30	1.16
2. Number of children	5.65	2.74	6.45	2.93	6.52	2.79	6.30	2.03	6.60	2.46
3. Modified ordinal position	62.79	26.53	67.17	24.12	65.07	23.65	58.91	23.41	66.60	27.02
4. Father living	.95	.23	.93	.26	.96	.21	.91	.29	.90	.32
5. Mother living	.98	.15	.97	.17	.98	.15	1.00	.00	1.00	.00
Educational history										
1. Class place	3.06	1.05	2.73	.96	2.89	.84	2.96	1.15	3.10	.99
2. School progress	.75	.43	.62	.49	.70	.46	.78	.42	.90	.32
3. Irish Reading	.42	.91	.19	.99	.31	.96	.39	.94	.80	.63
4. Oral Irish	.34	.94	.16	.99	.36	.94	.30	.97	.80	.63
5. Written Irish	.21	.98	-.08	1.00	.13	1.00	.22	1.00	.40	.97
6. English Reading	.80	.60	.73	.68	.71	.71	.65	.78	.80	.63
7. Oral English	.81	.59	.72	.70	.76	.66	.74	.69	1.00	.00
8. Written English	.60	.80	.45	.89	.53	.85	.57	.84	.60	.84
9. Mechanical Arithmetic	.60	.80	.52	.86	.62	.79	.65	.78	.80	.63

TABLE 5.1 (contd.)

Variables	*Total sample (N:500)*		*Vocational entrants (N:128)*		*Completed junior cycle (N:90)*		*Commenced senior cycle (N:23)*		*Completed senior cycle (N:10)*	
	M	SD	M	SD	M	SD	M	SD	M	SD
10. Problem Arithmetic	.07	1.00	-.08	1.00	.18	.99	.30	.97	.60	.84
11. Absenteeism	14.54	14.61	20.01	16.95	18.96	16.21	17.17	13.28	20.60	11.68
12. School grade at age twelve	1.95	.71	1.73	.62	1.88	.60	2.00	.74	2.00	.47
Type of school attended										
1. Catholic lay admin.	-.06	1.00	.25	.97	.20	.98	.30	.97	.40	.97
2. Catholic religious admin.	-.07	1.00	-.30	.96	-.24	.98	-.39	.94	-.40	.97
3. Protestant admin.	-.95	.31	-.95	.30	-.98	.21	-1.00	.00	-1.00	.00
4. Private admin.	-.92	.39	-1.00	.00	-.98	.21	-.91	.42	-1.00	.00
5. Number of teachers	3.69	1.10	3.59	1.06	3.58	1.03	3.43	1.04	3.30	.95
6. All male	-.29	.96	-.28	.96	-.27	.97	-.13	1.01	-.40	.97
7. All female	-.30	.98	-.51	.86	-.58	.82	-.74	.69	-.40	.97
8. Mixed gender	-.42	.91	-.20	.98	-.16	.99	-.13	1.01	-.20	1.03
9. School location	2.14	.90	2.18	.89	2.22	.90	2.26	.75	2.40	.52
10. Class size	2.46	1.56	2.44	1.67	2.54	1.63	2.70	1.55	2.60	1.65
Personal characteristics										
1. Verbal reasoning ability	100.15	15.46	93.66	13.31	95.98	14.42	98.83	15.33	96.30	11.00
2. Gender	.00	1.00	-.19	.99	-.27	.97	-.48	.90	.00	1.05
3. Satisfactory class. behav.	.10	.91	-.29	.88	-.06	.85	.10	.77	.34	.63
4. Group leadership	.01	.89	-.02	.92	-.07	.88	.00	.73	.15	.57
5. Health/extroversion	.12	.83	.11	.82	.21	.79	.01	.55	-.17	.49
6. Aesthetic behaviour	.05	.72	-.02	.68	-.02	.63	-.16	.40	-.09	.40

scholastic progress. While the majority of vocational-school entrants were not considered to have experienced difficulty in individual subjects (Problem Arithmetic and Written Irish being two exceptions), as a group the proportion that experienced difficulty was above average for each of eight subject areas. Lastly, the primary-school attendance record of the vocational entrants was, on average, approximately five and a half days poorer than that of the overall sample.

Students who had attended Catholic lay-administered primary schools were over-represented among the vocational entrants. In fact, students from such schools accounted for 62.5% of the vocational-entrant sample as opposed to 47% of the overall sample. Students from Catholic religious-administered primary schools, on the other hand, were under-represented among vocational entrants, accounting for 35.2% of them, compared to 46.6% of the overall sample. Even more pronounced is the finding that of students who had attended private primary schools (N:20), none transferred to a vocational school. Girls from all-female primary schools tended not to enrol in vocational school; out of a total of 175 girls from this type of school, 31, or 17.7%, transferred to a vocational school. Students who had attended mixed-gender primary schools were over-represented among vocational-school entrants; they accounted for 39.8% of the entrants as opposed to 29.2% of the overall sample.

Findings relating to the personal characteristics of the students are relatively clear. The mean verbal reasoning ability score for the vocational entrants was, on average, 6.5 points below that of the overall sample. In fact, over one-third (35.1%) had scored less than 90 on the verbal reasoning test; the comparable figure for the overall sample was 23.3%. In terms of satisfactory classroom behaviour, vocational entrants tended to have received poorer ratings than students in the overall sample. Finally, boys were over-represented among vocational entrants, making up 59.4% of the sample.

Vocational-School Students Who Completed Junior Cycle

Of the sample of 128 students who had enrolled in vocational school, one left school during the junior cycle and emigrated. However, the sample of vocational students was augmented by the transfer of 13 students from the secondary-school sector. The students who transferred had a mean score of 101.72 on the verbal reasoning test. Their transfer had the effect of raising the mean verbal reasoning score of the vocational sample. Of

TABLE 5.2
Deviations of Means from Total Sample Means of Students Attending School at Varying Points in the Vocational-School Course

Variables	*Vocational entrants (N:128)*	*Completed junior cycle (N:90)*	*Commenced senior cycle (N:23)*	*Completed senior cycle (N:10)*
Home background				
1. Socio-economic status	-.48	-.37	-.20	-.44
2. Number of children	.29	.32	.24	.35
3. Modified ordinal position	.17	.09	-.15	.14
4. Father living	-.09	.04	-.17	-.22
5. Mother living	-.07	.00	.13	.13
Educational history				
1. Class place	-.31	-.16	-.10	.04
2. School progress	-.30	-.12	.07	.35
3. Irish Reading	-.25	-.12	-.03	.42
4. Oral Irish	-.19	.02	-.04	.49
5. Written Irish	-.30	-.08	.01	.19
6. English Reading	-.12	-.15	-.25	.00
7. Oral English	-.15	-.08	-.12	.32
8. Written English	-.19	-.09	-.04	.00
9. Mechanical Arithmetic	-.10	.03	.06	.25
10. Problem Arithmetic	-.15	.11	.23	.53
11. Absenteeism	.37	.30	.18	.41
12. School grade at age twelve	-.31	-.10	.07	.07
Type of school attended				
1. Catholic lay admin.	.31	.26	.36	.46
2. Catholic religious admin.	-.23	-.17	-.32	-.33
3. Protestant admin.	.00	-.10	-.16	-.16
4. Private admin.	-.21	-.15	.03	-.21
5. Number of teachers	-.09	-.10	-.24	-.35
6. All male	.01	.02	.17	-.11
7. All female	-.21	-.29	-.45	-.10
8. Mixed gender	.24	.29	.32	.24
9. School location	.04	.09	.13	.29
10. Class size	-.01	.05	.15	.09
Personal characteristics				
1. Verbal reasoning ability	-.42	-.27	-.09	-.25
2. Gender	-.19	-.27	-.48	.00
3. Satisfactory class. behav.	-.43	-.18	.00	.26
4. Group leadership	-.03	-.09	-.01	.16
5. Health/extroversion	-.01	.11	-.13	-.35
6. Aesthetic behaviour	-.10	-.10	-.29	-.19

the new total of 140 students attending vocational school, 90 (or 64.3%) completed the junior cycle by taking either the DGCE or the ICE. Thus 18% of the overall sample completed a junior-cycle course in a vocational school.

Characteristics of the sample of vocational students who completed junior cycle (N:90) may be compared with the original sample in Table 5.1. Comparisons in terms of standard-score means are presented in Table 5.2. For most variables, values for the vocational entrants differed more from the values for the overall sample than did the values for students who completed the junior-cycle programme. Thus, the sample of students who completed junior cycle was less atypical of students in general than was the sample of students who had entered vocational school on leaving primary school.

The mean standard scores for socio-economic status (-.37) and number of children in family (.32) of students who completed junior cycle were substantially larger than those for the other variables in the home-background category. As in the case of vocational-school entrants, there was a tendency for relatively low SES families to be over-represented in the sample of students that completed junior cycle in a vocational school. In fact, slightly over half of this sample had been classified in the two lowest socio-economic status categories — partly-skilled (25.8%) and unskilled (31.3%). A change in standard score from -.48 to -.37 during the junior-cycle period, however, indicates that the mean socio-economic level of the vocational-school students had moved upwards slightly during this period. An examination of frequency data revealed that the change could be attributed for the most part to the disproportionate drop-out rate of students from the lowest SES categories.

The trend towards the mean of the overall sample did not apply in the case of the number of children in students' families. The mean for this variable in fact increased marginally during the junior-cycle period, suggesting that large family size on its own was not an important factor in a student's decision to remain in vocational school to complete the junior cycle.

On most of the educational-history variables, students who completed junior cycle in a vocational school received more negative ratings than students in the overall sample. In general, however, the differences in mean ratings for the two samples were not pronounced. The greatest difference was recorded for the variable absenteeism; those who completed junior cycle had, on average, been absent from primary school more frequently than students in the overall sample. When we compare vocational-school entrants with students who completed the junior cycle, we find that on eleven of the twelve educational history variables, the values of the standard scores decrease, indicating that the students with more positive achievement ratings tended to persist in school and complete the junior-cycle terminal examination, while those with poorer ratings tended to leave school early. For example, among vocational-school entrants classified in the bottom 30% in terms of class place, more than half (53.2%) dropped out of junior cycle, while of those classified in the top 70%, only 26.9% dropped out.

As in the case of vocational entrants, students from Catholic lay-administered and mixed-gender primary schools were over-represented while those from Catholic religious and, in particular, all-female primary schools were under-represented among the sample of vocational students who completed junior cycle. The proportion of students from all-female primary schools dropped during the junior-cycle period; during this time, 15 of the already small number of 34 students from all-female primary schools ceased to attend vocational school.

Students who completed junior cycle in vocational school had, compared to the overall sample, a lower than average mean score for verbal reasoning ability (M = 95.98) and a slightly below-average score for satisfactory classroom behaviour. On both variables, the changes in standard score indicate that students who completed junior cycle tended to be superior to the sample of vocational entrants. The former also scored higher on the health-extroversion rating. Boys were over-represented, making up 63.3% of the sample, among students who completed junior cycle. Their over-representation at this stage was even greater than it had been at the point of entry to vocational school. During the junior cycle period, 40% of girls, as opposed to 32.9% of boys, left school.

Students in vocational schools could present themselves for the Day Group Certificate Examination (DGCE) after two years or for the Intermediate Certificate Examination (ICE) after three years. They could also take both examinations in separate years. Unlike candidates in secondary schools, ICE candidates in vocational schools were required to take in addition to Irish, three other subjects — English, Mathematics, and one other (Mechanical Drawing or Art, if they were boys, and Home Economics or Commerce, if they were girls).

Details of the junior-cycle examination performance of the 90 vocational-school candidates are summarized in Table 5.3. The data reveal that 60% of the sample sat for either the DGCE or the ICE, while 40% took both examinations. The overall pass rate for the students who sat only for DGCE (N:35) was 62.9%. Most of these students were boys

TABLE 5.3
Numbers of Students in Vocational Schools Who Sat for Junior-Cycle Public Examinations, Together with Pass Rates

Examination	*Number of candidates*	*Pass*	*Fail*	*Awarded junior cycle certificate*
Day Group Certificate	35	22	13	62.9%
Intermediate Certificate	19	11	8	57.9%
Both Day Group and Intermediate Certificate	36	DGCE 26 ICE 29	10 7	88.9%
Total	90	DGCE or ICE 65	25	72.2%

(N:29). The mean verbal reasoning score for the group was low (88.49). Students who took only the ICE had a pass rate of 57.9 per cent. Boys and girls are fairly equally represented in this group, and scored more than 10 points better (98.79) on the verbal reasoning test than the 35 students who sat only for the DGCE. Students who sat for both the DGCE and ICE had the highest mean verbal reasoning score (101.78); again, boys and girls were approximately equally represented in the group. There were 36 examination candidates in this group; of these, 32 (88.9%) obtained a junior-cycle certificate by passing one or other of the examinations while four candidates failed both examinations. The pass rate of students who took both examinations was higher on both examinations than that of students who opted for only one; for the latter group, the pass rate on the DGCE was 67.6% while on the ICE, it was 72.7 per cent. Altogether, a total of 72.2% of the examination candidates obtained a junior-cycle certificate.

Vocational-School Students Who Commenced Senior Cycle

After completing junior cycle, approximately three-quarters (N:68) of vocational-school students ceased formal full-time schooling. A minority elected to enrol in a senior-cycle course. One student transferred to a senior-cycle course in a secondary school; the remaining 21 students commenced the senior-cycle course in a vocational school. This number was augmented by the transfer of two students from the secondary-school sector. Thus, a total of 23, or fewer than 5% of the original sample of 500, enrolled in a Leaving Certificate course in a vocational school. Over three-quarters (N:18) of these students had taken the ICE.

How did this small senior-cycle entrant group compare with the original sample in terms of primary-school measures? An examination of the standardized mean scores in Table 5.2 (column 3) indicates that in general the differences were small and amount to less than .20 of a standard score for approximately two-thirds of the variables.

Looking first at the home-background measures, it is evident that the mean socio-economic level of senior-cycle entrants in vocational schools was slightly below the average of the total sample. Furthermore, there was a slight upward shift in mean SES level from the group which completed junior cycle to the group which commenced senior cycle. This upward shift can be attributed to the relatively low transfer rate from junior to senior cycle of students from the lowest SES group (unskilled); in fact, only four of the 15 students from this group who had completed junior cycle transferred to senior cycle. As far as number of children in family is concerned, it is evident that the senior-cycle group is somewhat above the total mean but below the mean for the sample that completed junior cycle. The data on ordinal position in family indicate that the weighted ordinal position of senior-cycle students is slightly below the mean for the overall sample and somewhat more below the mean for the sample that completed junior cycle. It is of interest to note that whereas 13.0% of the senior-cycle entrant sample had family ordinal positions of six or greater, 24.4% of the group who completed junior cycle had such ordinal positions. The –.17 standard-score difference for 'father living' in Table 5.2 can be explained by the fact that the fathers of two of the 23 pupils in the sample had died.

On most of the educational-history measures, the mean achievement-related ratings for senior-cycle entrants were quite close to those of the original sample. On Problem Arithmetic, senior-cycle entrants had received more positive ratings than students in the original sample. On most of the measures, students who had transferred to senior cycle had more positive ratings, on average, than students who completed junior cycle. The data on absenteeism revealed a similar trend; while senior-cycle entrants had a below-average primary-school attendance record, they showed a slight improvement (M = 1.79 days) on the record of the larger sample of students who had completed junior cycle.

Following the transfer from junior to senior cycle, the proportion of vocational-school students who had attended Catholic lay primary schools increased to the extent that virtually two of every three (65.2%) senior-cycle vocational-school students had attended such a primary school. None of the small number who had attended a Protestant school (N:12) and only one student from a private primary school (N:10) in the original sample enrolled in a senior-cycle course in a vocational school.[1] Students from primary schools administered by religious were under-represented, accounting for 30.4% of the sample, compared to 46.6% of the overall sample.

The representation of students from all-female primary schools in vocational schools decreased still further after the junior cycle. Whereas, approximately one student out of every three in the original sample had attended an all-female primary school, as few as one out of eight (approximately) of these students enrolled in a senior-cycle vocational-school course. Students from mixed-gender primary schools continued to be over-represented at this level.

Turning to the personal characteristics of students, there was a pronounced bias in favour of boys among senior-cycle entrants; out of the total of 23 entrants, 17 were boys. A comparison with the sample of students who had completed junior cycle revealed that the over-representation of males increased (from 63.3% to 73.9%) following the junior cycle. Mean scores on both the verbal reasoning ability and the satisfactory classroom-behaviour variables increased. At the same time, means on the health/extroversion and aesthetic factors decreased.

The examination results for students who commenced the senior-cycle course were somewhat better than for students who completed junior cycle. Those staying on after junior cycle recorded a pass rate of 83.3% on the ICE and a pass rate of 75% on the DGCE. When both sets of results were combined, it was found that 78.3% of the senior-cycle entrants had qualified for a junior-cycle certificate.

Vocational-School Students Who Completed Senior Cycle

The relatively high drop-out rate of the early stages of the vocational-school course continued during the senior-cycle course. Over half (N:13) of the students who had embarked on the two-year course leading to the LCE (N:23) left school without taking the examination. Thus, only ten students completed the course. In describing the characteristics of this group, the small number of cases on which our data are based should be kept in mind. In this situation, one or two unusual or deviant values for a variable can have an unduly large effect on the mean value for that variable. This will be especially true for dichotomously-coded variables with small standard deviations.[2]

In each of the preceding sections, we observed that at each successive time period, the mean SES level of the vocational students who remained in school, though generally below the mean for the original sample, tended to move towards it. There was a reversal of this trend for a number of variables in the case of students who completed senior cycle. The fact that the mean SES level of students who completed senior cycle was lower than that of those who commenced the cycle indicates that persistence at this level was better among students from relatively low-SES backgrounds than it was among students from relatively high backgrounds. On both family variables (number of children in family and modified ordinal position), the mean values recorded were greater than those for students in the original sample and also greater than those for students in the somewhat larger sample (N:23) which had commenced senior cycle in vocational school.

An interesting and consistent pattern emerges from an analysis of the educational-history variables. On almost all of these variables, the means of students who completed senior cycle in vocational schools were greater than those of students in the overall sample, indicating that in terms of perceived achievements and general primary-school performance, students who persevered through senior cycle were above average. Furthermore, the mean ratings of those who completed senior cycle were superior to those of students who had commenced senior cycle. Students who completed senior cycle, however, were below average for the total sample in their primary-school attendance.

Students from Catholic lay-administered schools (N:7) were over-represented among students who sat for the LCE, while students from other types of primary school were either under-represented (Catholic religious, N:3) or not represented at all (Protestant, Private). None of the ten students who completed the senior cycle had attended a city primary school. Although most of the senior-cycle students left school during the final two years, none of those who had attended all-female primary schools did so. As a result, the proportion of students from all-female primary schools had increased by the end of the senior cycle.

For the first time in a vocational-school sample, boys and girls were equally represented at the end of the senior cycle. This was achieved through a high drop-out rate on the part of boys during the senior cycle: 12 of the 13 leavers during this period were boys. Students who completed the senior cycle scored approximately four points below the national mean on the verbal reasoning test and also scored somewhat lower (2.5 points) than the sample that had commenced senior cycle. On both the health/extroversion and aesthetic personality factors, the mean values for those who completed senior cycle were also below those of the original sample and, in the case of health/extroversion, below the mean for senior-cycle entrants. The opposite was true for the two remaining personality factors: students who completed senior cycle had been rated above average on satisfactory classroom behaviour and on group leadership and also above the average of the senior-cycle entrants.

On variables which measured aspects of primary-school achievement, students who completed senior cycle tended to have higher ratings than those who began it, indicating that those who left school during this period were lower achievers in the primary school than those who remained to the LCE. Yet on three other variables which one might reasonably expect to be associated with length of schooling a similar tendency was not revealed: a comparison of the mean scores of those who commenced senior cycle and those who completed it, on measures of socio-economic status, verbal reasoning ability and absenteeism, indicates that those who stayed in school had slightly lower scores than those who dropped out. The importance of achievement in school is further underlined by a tendency which we found for students with better examination records to stay on to the Leaving Certificate Examination. All students who persisted in school to the LCE had passed the ICE (compared to 83.3% of those who commenced senior cycle). Furthermore, six of the seven students who had taken the DGCE some years previously had also passed this examination (compared to 75% of those who commenced senior cycle). Finally, it should be noted that nine of the ten students who remained at school to the end of the senior cycle passed the Leaving Certificate Examination.

Conclusion

Clearly, the most striking findings in the present chapter relate to the changes in the numbers of students in vocational school over the period of post-primary schooling. More than one student out of three who enrolled in a vocational school left school without completing the junior-cycle course. This rate of attrition, however, is mild by comparison with the rate recorded at the end of junior cycle, when over three-quarters of the students that had taken either the DGCE or ICE elected to terminate their formal schooling. Of the relatively small sample of students who enrolled in the senior-cycle course, fewer than half stayed to sit for the Leaving Certificate Examination. Thus, for the vast majority of vocational-school students in our sample, formal full-time education in effect meant junior-cycle education only.

In terms of the primary-school measures, the entrants' sample differed from the larger original sample, of which it was a part, on many variables. The subset of students who completed the junior cycle had lower standardized mean deviations than the vocational entrants, indicating that the more atypical students (those with relatively low ratings on socio-economic status, educational history, verbal ability, etc.) tended to leave school during the junior-cycle years. A similar selection process appears to have operated between the end of junior cycle and the commencement of senior cycle. Given the small number of students who completed the senior-cycle course, it is not surprising to note that the fairly clear-cut trends observed during the junior-cycle years were not as evident at the senior cycle; nevertheless, on the student achievement ratings (educational history and satisfactory classroom behaviour), it is evident that among the senior-cycle students, those with the higher ratings tended to complete the course.

Vocational entrants had relatively high family ordinal positions. Subsequently the mean family ordinal position moved downwards (Figure 5.1) up to the commencement of senior cycle. The trend was reversed during the senior-cycle period. As in the case of secondary-school students, with the exception of the 10 students who completed senior cycle, the mean socio-economic status level of the sample moved upwards (though it was still below the national mean in the case of vocational students) as the persistence rate of students from the intermediate-professional and skilled classes proved superior to that of students from the partly-skilled and unskilled classes. For example, the percentage of vocational entrants from the intermediate-professional and professional categories who completed junior cycle was 81.5% as opposed to 63.0% for entrants from the partly-skilled and unskilled categories.

A fairly consistent selection pattern emerges when we examine the data for the set of twelve educational-history variables. At each time period, the students who had received the more positive primary-school ratings tended to progress to the next highest level, while those who had received relatively poor ratings tended to leave school. Out of eight

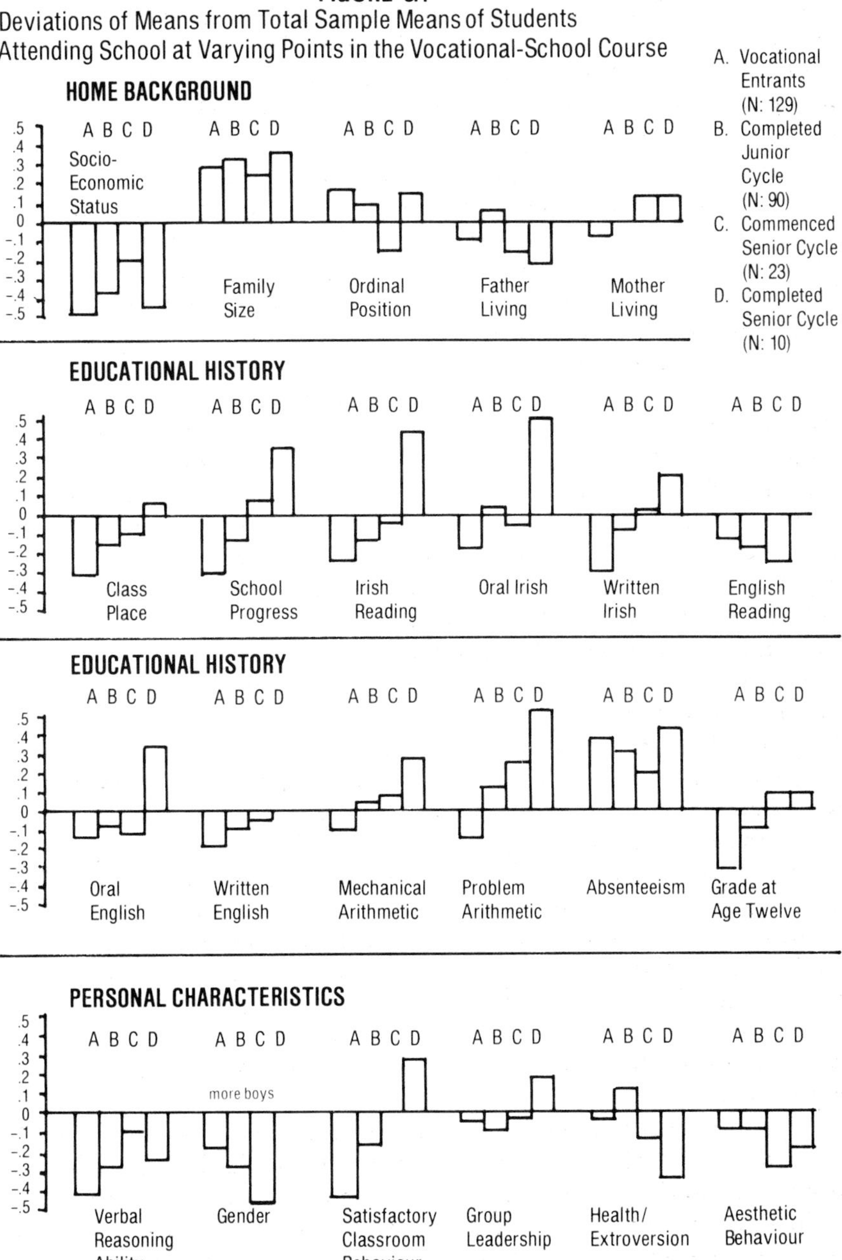
FIGURE 5.1
Deviations of Means from Total Sample Means of Students Attending School at Varying Points in the Vocational-School Course
A. Vocational Entrants (N: 129)
B. Completed Junior Cycle (N: 90)
C. Commenced Senior Cycle (N: 23)
D. Completed Senior Cycle (N: 10)
HOME BACKGROUND
A B C D
Socio-Economic Status
Family Size
Ordinal Position
Father Living
Mother Living
EDUCATIONAL HISTORY
Class Place
School Progress
Irish Reading
Oral Irish
Written Irish
English Reading
EDUCATIONAL HISTORY
Oral English
Written English
Mechanical Arithmetic
Problem Arithmetic
Absenteeism
Grade at Age Twelve
PERSONAL CHARACTERISTICS
more boys
Verbal Reasoning Ability
Gender
Satisfactory Classroom Behaviour
Group Leadership
Health/ Extroversion
Aesthetic Behaviour
.5
.4
.3
.2
.1
0
-.1
-.2
-.3
-.4
-.5

TABLE 5.4
Numbers (And Percentages) of Students of Varying Socio-Economic Levels at Varying Points in the Vocational-School Course

		Socio-economic status					
Sample		*Profes-sional*	*Inter. profes-sional*	*Skilled*	*Partly-skilled*	*Un-skilled*	*Total*
Total sample	N	15	141	163	89	92	500
	%	*3.0*	*28.2*	*32.6*	*17.8*	*18.4*	
Vocational entrants	N	1	16	38	33	40	128
	%	*0.8*	*12.5*	*29.7*	*25.8*	*31.3*	
Completed junior cycle	N	0	15	29	21	25	90
	%	*0.0*	*16.7*	*32.2*	*23.3*	*27.8*	
Commenced senior cycle	N	0	4	9	6	4	23
	%	*0.0*	*17.4*	*39.1*	*26.1*	*17.4*	
Completed senior cycle	N	0	2	2	3	3	10
	%	*0.0*	*20.0*	*20.0*	*30.0*	*30.0*	

subject areas, the English Reading rating was the only exception to this trend. While the tendency for students with better attendance records to remain in school persisted to the commencement of senior cycle, it was reversed during the senior-cycle years.

The pattern of results relating to the type of primary school attended by students presents a fairly consistent picture. Students who had attended Catholic lay primary schools were over-represented at each period in vocational schools while those who had attended Catholic religious schools tended to be under-represented. Students in the two smaller categories of primary school, Protestant and private, were under-represented at all stages. Proportionately few students from all-female primary schools were enrolled in a vocational school at any time. The reverse was true for students from mixed-gender schools, who were over-represented at each time period. Finally, the data on school location and school size (based on the number of teachers in the school) suggest that the initial slight tendency for vocational students to come from relatively small town and rural schools (as opposed to city schools) increased at each successive stage throughout the vocational-school programme.

Among the set of personal-characteristic measures, the pattern of ratings on the satisfactory classroom behaviour variable was similar to that on the educational-history variables. At each succeeding vocational-school level, students who remained in school had received higher satisfactory classroom behaviour ratings than those at the preceding level. Boys, who had been over-represented (59.4%) among the vocational-school entrants, increased in percentage to 65.3% of the sample that completed junior cycle and to 73.9% of the sample that commenced senior cycle. By the end of senior cycle, however, boys and girls were equally represented among the small number of students who were still at school at this stage. Finally, the decrease in the standardized means on the verbal ability measure between commencement of the junior and senior cycles suggests the operation of selection based on ability: students who commenced senior cycle had scored, on average, approximately 5 points higher on the verbal ability test than the larger sample of vocational entrants. It is of interest to note, however, that this trend did not persist to the end of senior cycle; those who left school during the senior cycle had scored slightly higher on the verbal ability test than those who completed the senior cycle.

The findings for the post-primary achievement measure, i.e., performance on public examinations, suggest the operation of selection based on achievement in the latter half of the vocational-school programme. Vocational students recorded a 72.7% pass rate on the ICE. Those who commenced the senior-cycle course had a pass rate of 83.3%, while the pass rate for the small number that completed the senior-cycle course was 100 percent. On the DGCE, the corresponding pass rates were 67.6%, 75%, and 85.7 percent. Lastly, while 72.2% of all ICE and DGCE candidates in vocational schools qualified for a junior-cycle certificate, the percentage of senior-cycle entrants that qualified was 78.3%, while for those that completed the senior-cycle programme, it was 100 percent.

Overall, while the mean values of most of the variables included in our investigation changed for vocational-school students during the course of second-level education, those for the achievement-related variables, i.e., those relating to educational history and satisfactory classroom behaviour, were subject to most change. At both junior and senior levels, students who remained in school had received more positive achievement ratings than those who left without completing the cycle.

FOOTNOTES

1 The change in the standard score value for the private-school variable from -.15 to .03 does not represent a change in the number of students in this category; it merely represents a change in the proportion of private-school students from 1 in 90 (the sample that completed junior cycle) to 1 in 23 for the senior-cycle entrants. It highlights the sensitivity of standard scores to *small* changes in dichotomous variables in small samples and emphasizes the need for caution in interpreting this type of data.

2 For example, in the case of father living, one of the 10 fathers of students who completed senior cycle had died. Although this number is small, it represents approximately twice the death rate of fathers in the overall sample. Had this one father lived, the standardized mean value for father living would have been +.22 (instead of -.22).

6 *Early Leavers*

Prior to its abolition in 1967, the Primary-school Certificate Examination, taken at the end of sixth class in primary school, acted as the terminal school-leaving examination for many pupils. With the introduction of free post-primary education and the raising of the school-leaving age from fourteen to fifteen years of age, the number of students who proceeded to some type of post-primary education increased markedly. Not all however, as we have seen, complete the junior cycle in a post-primary school. Students who drop out before the end of junior cycle effectively deny themselves admission to a range of recognized apprenticeship schemes and to many occupations which require a junior-cycle certificate as a minimum entry criterion[1]. On the other hand, students who complete junior cycle can enrol in apprenticeship schemes or training courses or seek employment directly. Other positions require the possession of the Leaving Certificate as a minimum entry requirement. Thus, for an individual student, early school leaving can result in a lowering of career goals.

The term 'early school leaver' is used in a variety of ways and does not in itself indicate the amount of schooling the student has received before dropping out. In this chapter, four categories of school leavers are identified. The term *Primary-school terminal leaver* (PSTL) refers to the small number of pupils who did not transfer to a vocational or secondary school after leaving primary school. *Junior-cycle early leaver* (JCEL) refers to students who attended junior-cycle courses in vocational or secondary schools and left school without taking either the Intermediate or Day Group Certificate Examinations. *Junior-cycle terminal leaver* (JCTL) describes vocational- or secondary-school students who left full-time formal education after taking the Intermediate or Day Group Certificate Examinations. The final term, *Senior-cycle early leavers* (SCEL) refers to students who, having completed the junior-cycle course, commenced the two-year senior-cycle course but left school without sitting for the Leaving Certificate Examinations.

Two types of analysis are used to examine the characteristics of school leavers at varying stages of the educational process. In the first type of analysis, school leavers in each of the four categories are compared with the total original sample of 500 students (of which they are a part) in terms of home background, educational history, school and personal characteristics to determine the extent to which they are representative subsamples of the original sample with respect to each of the original primary-school variables.

The second set of analyses is confined to leavers in three categories — junior-cycle early leavers, junior-cycle terminal leavers, and senior-cycle early leavers. The leavers in each of these categories, as well as being compared with the overall sample, are compared with students who elected to remain in school. Thus, for example, junior-cycle early leavers are compared with students who completed junior cycle.[1] Since we know that entrants to secondary school differ from entrants to vocational school in a variety of ways, separate analyses were carried out for students in the two types of school.

Primary-School Terminal Leavers

A total of 37 students, or 7.4% of the overall sample, did not transfer to a post-primary school. Did these students differ from students in the original sample? To answer this question we used two separate approaches in comparing the two groups on the set of primary-school variables. First, on each variable, the mean for the sample of primary-school terminal leavers (PSTLs) was compared with the corresponding mean for the overall sample and the difference between the two was expressed in standard scores. Secondly, the distribution for the PSTLs on each variable was compared with the corresponding distribution for the overall sample to determine the degree of similarity or 'goodness of fit'.

A summary of the comparisons of the PSTL and original samples is presented in Table 6.1. Among the set of five home-background measures, the most pronounced differences between the groups were found for socio-economic status and size of family. While slightly over one-third (36.2%) of students in the original sample had been classified in the two lowest categories (partly-skilled and unskilled), the percentage of students in these categories among PSTLs amounted to 73.0%, i.e., approximately double that of the overall sample. At the other extreme, students from the two highest SES categories were under-represented among PSTLs, accounting for 8.1% of this sample, as against 31.2% of the overall sample. The mean number of children in the

TABLE 6.1
Statistics on Primary-School Variables for Primary-School Terminal Leavers and Overall Sample

Variables	*Terminal leavers (N:37)*		*Overall sample (N:500)*		*Standard score difference*	*Goodness of fit (p)*
	M	SD	M	SD		
Home background						
1. Socio-economic status	1.81	1.02	2.80	1.13	-.88	Sig.***
2. Number of children	6.92	3.37	5.65	2.74	.46	Sig.*
3. Modified ordinal position	63.27	23.57	62.79	26.53	.02	N.S.
4. Father living	.97	.16	.95	.23	.09	N.S.
5. Mother living	1.00	.00	.98	.15	.13	N.S.
Educational history						
1. Class place	2.38	.98	3.06	1.05	-.65	Sig.***
2. School progress	.30	.46	.75	.43	-1.05	Sig.***
3. Irish Reading	-.24	.98	.42	.91	-.73	Sig.***
4. Oral Irish	-.35	.95	.34	.94	-.73	Sig.***
5. Written Irish	-.51	.87	.21	.98	-.73	Sig.***
6. English Reading	.35	.95	.80	.60	-.75	Sig.***
7. Oral English	.35	.95	.81	.59	-.78	Sig.***
8. Written English	.03	1.01	.60	.80	-.71	Sig.***
9. Mechanical Arithmetic	-.03	1.01	.60	.80	-.79	Sig.***
10. Problem Arithmetic	-.67	.75	.07	1.00	-.74	Sig.***
11. Absenteeism	27.35	22.58	14.54	14.61	.88	Sig.***
12. School grade at age twelve	1.32	.63	1.95	.71	-.89	Sig.***

TABLE 6.1 (contd.)

Variables	*Terminal leavers (N:37)*		*Overall sample (N:500)*		*Standard score difference*	*Goodness of fit (p)*
	M	SD	M	SD		
Type of school attended						
1. Catholic lay admin.	.24	.98	-.06	1.00	.30	N.S.
2. Catholic religious admin.	-.24	.98	-.07	1.00	-.17	N.S.
3. Protestant admin.	-1.00	.00	-.95	.31	-.16	N.S.
4. Private admin.	-1.00	.00	-.92	.39	-.21	N.S.
5. Number of teachers	3.62	1.01	3.69	1.10	-.06	N.S.
6. All male	-.35	.95	-.29	.96	-.06	N.S.
7. All female	-.19	.99	-.30	.98	.11	N.S.
8. Mixed gender	-.46	.90	-.42	.91	-.04	N.S.
9. School location	2.03	.90	2.14	.90	-.12	N.S.
10. Class size	2.46	1.46	2.46	1.56	.00	N.S.
Personal characteristics						
1. Verbal reasoning ability	82.16	11.71	100.15	15.46	-1.16	Sig.***
2. Gender	-.08	1.01	.00	1.00	-.08	N.S.
3. Satisfactory class. behav.	-.72	.75	.10	.91	-.90	Sig.***
4. Group leadership	-.03	1.00	.01	.89	-.04	N.S.
5. Health/extroversion	-.46	.82	.12	.83	-.70	Sig.*
6. Aesthetic behaviour	-.29	.81	.05	.72	-.47	Sig.**

*$p < .05$ **$p < .01$ ***$p < .001$

families of PSTLs was 6.92, or 1.27 above that for the overall sample. The number of children in the families of the PSTL group ranged from one to 15; 35.1% of the group were members of families of nine or more children.

The difference between the PSTL and overall samples was sizeable on the educational-history variables — more than one-half a standard deviation on each variable. Furthermore, the distribution for each of the variables for the PSTL group differed from that for the overall sample. Students in the PSTL group had a consistent pattern of relatively poor achievement, school progress, and school attendance. For example, the school progress of 70.3% of these students was considered unsatisfactory, as compared to 25% in the overall sample. Compared to students in the overall sample, a greater percentage of PSTLs had experienced difficulty in each of eight listed subject areas. For most subject areas, most PSTLs were considered to have experienced difficulties; in the overall sample, however, the majority of students was not perceived by teachers to have experienced learning difficulties. Problem Arithmetic and Written Irish were judged by teachers to be the most difficult subjects for PSTLs; over three-quarters of the group were rated as having experienced difficulties with these subjects. On average, PSTLs had been absent from school almost twice as many days during the school year as students in the overall sample. Lastly, the educational progress of the PSTLs, as indicated by class place (or rank) and number of grades completed at age twelve, was substantially inferior to that of the overall sample.

A comparison of the types of primary school attended by students in the PSTL and overall samples indicates no significant bias. Thus, we may conclude that attendance at a particular type of primary school was not related to dropping out at the end of primary school.

The mean verbal reasoning ability score for the PSTL group (82.16) was more than one standard deviation below that of the overall sample; it corresponded to the twelfth percentile rank on the original distribution of scores on this test. Of the 37 PSTLs, 27 (73.0%) scored below 90 and 15 of these (40.5%) scored below 80 on the verbal ability measure. The PSTL students could not be considered representative of the original sample with respect to satisfactory classroom behaviour, health/extroversion, or aesthetic behaviour either. On each of these variables, their scores were considerably lower than those of the overall sample. For both satisfactory classroom behaviour and health/extroversion, 86.5% had been rated below the overall average, while 73% had been rated below average on the aesthetic measure.

Junior-Cycle Early Leavers

Secondary School

Of the 333 students who enrolled in a secondary school, 13 transferred to vocational school, two died, and one emigrated during the course of the three-year junior cycle. Of the remaining 317, a total of 30 (9.5%) dropped out of school during junior cycle. This group of 30 leavers (JCEL) is the focus of this section.

Comparison with the total sample
A comparison between junior-cycle early leavers and the original total sample of students showed that differences between these groups were quite small (Table 6.2). In almost all instances, the differences were less than .3 of a standard score. While junior-cycle early leavers had somewhat poorer ratings than the overall sample on many of the variables related to school achievement, a series of 'goodness of fit' tests revealed that the early leavers could not be considered atypical of the original sample on any of the variables.

Comparison of leavers and persisters
The group of secondary entrants who persisted and completed the junior cycle was more than nine times (N:287) the size of the group that left during junior cycle (N:30). The groups were compared with each other to determine if there were overall differences between them. The comparison revealed that the groups did in fact differ from each other in terms of the primary-school measures.[2]

The two groups were then compared on each of the original variables (Table 6.3). Statistically significant differences between them were recorded for socio-economic status and number of children in family. Within the two highest SES categories (professional and intermediate-professional), students in the JCEL group were under-represented; the percentage of JCELs in these two categories was 23.3%, as against 44.5% for the persisters. At the other extreme, 43.4% of the JCEL group belonged to the two lowest categories (partly-skilled and unskilled), as opposed to 22.6% of the persisters. Students in the JCEL sample had, on average, one sibling more than students in the sample of persisters; JCEL students were under-represented among small families of three or fewer children (3.3% vs 25.8% for persisters) and over-represented among large families of seven or more children (36.6% vs 23% for persisters).

Statistically significant differences between the two groups were also recorded on four of the educational-history variables. By comparison with persisters, a significantly greater proportion of the early leavers had been rated as having difficulty in Written Irish and in Written English and as having made unsatisfactory school progress. Further, the mean number of school grades which the early leavers had completed at age twelve was less than the number completed by the persisters.

None of the mean differences relating to the type of primary school attended was statistically significant. Significant differences, however, were recorded on two of the personal variables — verbal reasoning ability and satisfactory classroom behaviour. Half of the JCEL group had scored below 100 on the verbal ability measure as compared to 31.3% of the persisters, while only one of the 30 early leavers scored above 120 as against 15.9% of the persisters. Similarly, on the satisfactory classroom behaviour variable, JCEL students were over-represented among the lower scorers and under-represented among the higher scorers.

Not surprisingly, a number of the significant variables which we have examined are highly inter-related. To help identify a general dimension which would maximally differentiate between the early leavers and persisters, a separate (discriminant function) analysis was carried out. This analysis showed that an early leaver was more likely than a persister to have come from a low socio-economic background, to have experienced difficulty in Written Irish, not to have attended an all-female primary school (i.e., had attended an all-male or mixed-gender school), and to have received a low rating for satisfactory classroom behaviour.[3]

Vocational School

In Chapter 3, we saw that 128 students enrolled in a vocational school after completing their primary education. Subsequently, the size of the sample in junior-cycle courses in vocational schools increased to 140 due to the transfer of students from secondary school. (One further student emigrated from vocational school.)

A vocational student could have completed a junior-cycle course either by taking the Day Group Certificate Examination after two years or the Intermediate Certificate Examination after three years. While the majority of students completed a junior-cycle course, a total of 50 left school without doing so. This drop-out rate of approximately one in three (35.7%) is substantially greater than that recorded by the much larger secondary junior-cycle group (9.5%).

TABLE 6.2

Statistics on Primary-School Variables for Secondary Junior-Cycle Early Leavers and Overall Sample

	Early leavers (N:30)		*Overall sample* (N:500)		*Standard score difference*	*Goodness of fit (p)*
Variables	M	SD	M	SD		
Home background						
1. Socio-economic status	2.53	1.14	2.80	1.13	-.24	N.S.
2. Number of children	6.06	1.86	5.65	2.74	.15	N.S.
3. Modified ordinal position	61.17	28.08	62.79	26.53	-.06	N.S.
4. Father living	.97	.18	.95	.23	.09	N.S.
5. Mother living	.97	.18	.98	.15	-.07	N.S.
Educational history						
1. Class place	2.97	.85	3.06	1.05	-.09	N.S.
2. School progress	.70	.47	.75	.43	-.12	N.S.
3. Irish Reading	.33	.96	.42	.91	-.10	N.S.
4. Oral Irish	.40	.93	.34	.94	.06	N.S.
5. Written Irish	-.13	1.01	.21	.98	-.35	N.S.
6. English Reading	.87	.51	.80	.60	.12	N.S.
7. Oral English	.80	.61	.81	.59	-.02	N.S.
8. Written English	.47	.90	.60	.80	-.16	N.S.
9. Mechanical Arithmetic	.47	.90	.60	.80	-.16	N.S.
10. Problem Arithmetic	-.13	1.01	.07	1.00	-.20	N.S.
11. Absenteeism	11.83	8.24	14.54	14.61	-.19	N.S.
12. School grade at age twelve	1.83	.53	1.95	.71	-.17	N.S.

TABLE 6.2 (contd.)

Variables	*Early leavers* (N:30)		*Overall sample* (N:500)		*Standard score difference*	*Goodness of fit (p)*
	M	SD	M	SD		
Type of school attended						
1. Catholic lay admin.	-.27	.98	-.06	1.00	-.21	N.S.
2. Catholic religious admin.	.20	1.00	-.07	1.00	.27	N.S.
3. Protestant admin.	-.93	.37	-.95	.31	.06	N.S.
4. Private admin.	-1.00	.00	-.92	.39	-.21	N.S.
5. Number of teachers	3.83	1.23	3.69	1.10	.13	N.S.
6. All male	-.13	1.01	-.29	.96	.17	N.S.
7. All female	-.47	.90	-.30	.98	-.17	N.S.
8. Mixed gender	-.40	.93	-.42	.91	.02	N.S.
9. School location	2.00	.98	2.14	.90	-.16	N.S.
10. Class size	2.63	1.87	2.46	1.56	.11	N.S.
Personal characteristics						
1. Verbal reasoning ability	98.60	11.32	100.15	15.46	-.10	N.S.
2. Gender	.00	1.02	.00	1.00	.00	N.S.
3. Satisfactory class. behav.	-.20	.89	.10	.91	-.33	N.S.
4. Group leadership	-.10	.84	.01	.89	-.12	N.S.
5. Health/extroversion	-.03	.81	.12	.83	-.18	N.S.
6. Aesthetic behaviour	.16	.70	.05	.72	.15	N.S.

TABLE 6.3
Means and Standard Deviations on Primary-School Variables for Secondary Junior-Cycle Early Leavers and Persisters

Variables	*Early leavers (N:30)*		*Persisters (N:287)*		
	M	SD	M	SD	F
Home background					
1. Socio-economic status	2.53	1.14	3.18	.99	11.22***
2. Number of children	6.06	1.86	5.08	2.38	4.80*
3. Modified ordinal position	61.17	28.08	60.86	27.80	.00
4. Father living	.97	.18	.94	.23	.27
5. Mother living	.97	.18	.98	.15	.09
Educational history					
1. Class place	2.97	.85	3.30	1.04	2.81
2. School progress	.70	.47	.87	.34	6.50*
3. Irish Reading	.33	.96	.60	.80	2.97
4. Oral Irish	.40	.93	.50	.87	.34
5. Written Irish	-.13	1.01	.45	.89	11.24***
6. English Reading	.87	.51	.89	.46	.06
7. Oral English	.80	.61	.90	.43	1.40
8. Written English	.47	.90	.76	.66	4.90*
9. Mechanical Arithmetic	.47	.90	.71	.70	3.20
10. Problem Arithmetic	-.13	1.01	.23	.97	3.83
11. Absenteeism	11.83	8.24	10.81	10.89	.25
12. School grade at age twelve	1.83	.53	2.13	.68	5.23*

TABLE 6.3 (contd.)

Variables	*Early leavers (N:30)*		*Persisters (N:287)*		
	M	SD	M	SD	F
Type of school attended					
1. Catholic lay admin.	-.27	.98	-.22	.98	.06
2. Catholic religious admin.	.20	1.00	.04	1.00	.71
3. Protestant admin.	-.93	.37	-.94	.33	.03
4. Private admin.	-1.00	.00	-.87	.49	2.00
5. Number of teachers	3.83	1.23	3.75	1.12	.15
6. All male	-.13	1.01	-.32	.95	1.09
7. All female	-.47	.90	-.18	.99	2.37
8. Mixed gender	-.40	.93	-.50	.87	.34
9. School location	2.00	.98	2.15	.89	.75
10. Class size	2.63	1.87	2.44	1.49	.46
Personal characteristics					
1. Verbal reasoning ability	98.60	11.32	105.30	14.18	6.28*
2. Gender	.00	1.02	.14	.99	.51
3. Satisfactory class. behav.	-.20	.89	.42	.80	15.85**
4. Group leadership	-.10	.84	.04	.85	.68
5. Health/extroversion	-.03	.81	.20	.81	2.16
6. Aesthetic behaviour	.16	.70	.12	.72	.07

$^*p < .05$ $^{**}p < .01$ $^{***}p < .001$

Comparison with the total sample

A comparison of vocational junior-cycle leavers with the total original sample of 500 students on each of the 33 variables indicated that on 13 variables the distributions for the JCEL group did not conform to the distribution for the overall sample (Table 6.4).

Compared to the overall sample, early leavers were more likely to belong to skilled, partly-skilled, and unskilled families; 92% of leavers were in these three categories as opposed to 68.8% of the overall sample. None of the remaining comparisons among the home-background variables produced evidence of a significant difference.

The results of the comparisons of the two samples on the educational-history variables are quite clear. Students who dropped out of vocational school during the junior cycle tended to have had poorer primary-school achievement records, poorer scholastic progress, and poorer school attendance than students in the overall sample. For example, the school progress of 52% of the JCEL group was considered unsatisfactory, as against 25% for the overall sample. Problem Arithmetic, Written Irish, and Oral Irish were the subjects which seem to have caused most difficulty for the early leavers; they were also the subjects on which their ratings differed markedly from those of the students in the overall sample. For example, in Problem Arithmetic, 72% of early leavers had been rated as having difficulty, as against 46.4% of the overall sample. Lastly, students who left school during the junior cycle had been absent from primary school an average of 6.10 school days more than students in the overall sample.

Students who had attended Catholic lay primary schools were over-represented (62%) among the JCEL sample. While this percentage differs considerably from that for the overall sample (47.0%), it is not surprising since it merely reflects the percentage of students enrolled in vocational school who had attended lay primary schools (60.7%).

Finally, significant differences were recorded for two of the personal characteristics of the students. On the first, verbal reasoning ability, the mean score of the JCEL group (91.34) corresponded to approximately half a standard deviation below the mean for the overall sample. A total of 18% of the sample scored below 80 on the verbal measure. To avoid the danger of typecasting all JCELs as having low verbal reasoning ability, however, it should be pointed out that 22% of these students obtained above-average scores on this measure. On the second measure, satisfactory classroom behaviour, approximately three out of every four early leavers had been rated below the overall average by their former primary-school teachers.

Comparisons of leavers and persisters
Junior-cycle early leavers (N:50) and persisters (N:90) were compared to ascertain if there was an overall difference between the two groups in terms of the original primary-school measures. The comparison indicated that the overall difference between the groups was not statistically significant.[4]

Significant univariate differences were found between the groups in their educational history (Table 6.5). Compared to persisters, more of the JCELs tended to have had difficulty in Problem Arithmetic (72% vs 41.1%), in Written Irish (66% vs 43.3%), and in Oral Irish (54% vs 32.2%); more of them also tended to have made unsatisfactory progress at school (52% vs 30%). Furthermore, their level of attainment as measured by the number of grades they had completed by age twelve and their achievements as indicated by their place or rank in class tended to be poorer. On the set of personal characteristics, early leavers received lower ratings than persisters for both satisfactory classroom behaviour and health/extroversion.

Junior-Cycle Terminal Leavers

Secondary School

At the end of the junior-cycle course, approximately one-fifth (N:65) of the secondary entrants left school. Virtually all (N:63) of these students had spent three years in a secondary school before taking the Intermediate Certificate Examination. The remaining two left school some time after taking the Day Group Certificate Examination.

Comparison with the total sample
An examination of the standardized mean scores for secondary junior-cycle terminal leavers (JCTLs) and the overall sample indicates that, in general, the means for both samples are relatively similar (Table 6.6). Significant differences on the goodness of fit test were found for three variables relating to the type of primary school which students had attended. A fourth variable which evidenced a significant difference was the gender of the student.

Students who had attended all-male primary schools were not proportionately represented among the sample of JCTLs; they accounted for 21.5% of the sample, compared to 35.6% of the overall sample. Students who had attended all-female primary schools, on the

TABLE 6.4

Statistics on Primary-School Variables for Vocational Junior-Cycle Early Leavers and Overall Sample

Variables	*Early leavers (N:50)*		*Overall sample (N:500)*		*Standard score difference*	*Goodness of fit (p)*
	M	SD	M	SD		
Home background						
1. Socio-economic status	2.18	1.04	2.80	1.13	-.55	Sig.***
2. Number of children	6.02	3.58	5.65	2.74	.14	N.S.
3. Modified ordinal position	70.28	24.79	62.79	26.53	.28	N.S.
4. Father living	.90	.30	.95	.23	-.22	N.S.
5. Mother living	.96	.20	.98	.15	-.13	N.S.
Educational history						
1. Class place	2.52	1.13	3.06	1.05	-.51	Sig.**
2. School progress	.48	.50	.75	.43	-.63	Sig.***
3. Irish Reading	.08	1.01	.42	.91	-.37	Sig.**
4. Oral Irish	-.08	1.01	.34	.94	-.45	Sig.**
5. Written Irish	-.32	.96	.21	.98	-.54	Sig.***
6. English Reading	.72	.70	.80	.60	-.13	N.S.
7. Oral English	.68	.74	.81	.59	-.22	N.S.
8. Written English	.32	.96	.60	.80	-.35	Sig.*
9. Mechanical Arithmetic	.44	.91	.60	.80	-.20	N.S.
10. Problem Arithmetic	-.44	.91	.07	1.00	-.51	Sig.***
11. Absenteeism	20.64	17.24	14.54	14.61	.42	Sig.**
12. School grade at age twelve	1.62	.70	1.95	.71	-.46	Sig.**

TABLE 6.4 (contd.)

Variables	*Early leavers (N:50)*		*Overall sample (N:500)*		*Standard score difference*	*Goodness of fit (p)*
	M	SD	M	SD		
Type of school attended						
1. Catholic lay admin.	.24	.98	-.06	1.00	.30	Sig.*
2. Catholic religious admin.	-.32	.96	-.07	1.00	-.25	N.S.
3. Protestant admin.	-.92	.40	-.95	.31	.10	N.S.
4. Private admin.	-1.00	.00	-.92	.39	-.21	N.S.
5. Number of teachers	3.52	1.16	3.69	1.10	.15	N.S.
6. All male	-.28	.97	-.29	.96	.01	N.S.
7. All female	-.40	.93	-.30	.98	-.10	N.S.
8. Mixed gender	-.32	.96	-.42	.91	.11	N.S.
9. School location	2.14	.86	2.14	.90	.00	N.S.
10. Class size	2.32	1.77	2.46	1.56	.09	N.S.
Personal characteristics						
1. Verbal reasoning ability	91.34	12.92	100.15	15.46	-.57	Sig.***
2. Gender	-.12	1.00	.00	1.00	-.12	N.S.
3. Satisfactory class. behav.	-.66	.80	.10	.91	-.84	Sig.***
4. Group leadership	.04	.97	.01	.89	.03	N.S.
5. Health/extroversion	-.08	.87	.12	.83	-.24	N.S.
6. Aesthetic behaviour	-.04	.76	.05	.72	-.13	N.S.

*$p < .05$ **$p < .01$ ***$p < .001$

TABLE 6.5
Means and Standard Deviations on Primary-School Variables for Vocational Junior-Cycle Early Leavers and Persisters

Variables	*Early leavers (N:50)*		*Persisters (N:90)*		
	M	SD	M	SD	F
Home background					
1. Socio-economic status	2.18	1.04	2.38	1.07	1.12
2. Number of children	6.02	3.58	6.52	2.79	.85
3. Modified ordinal position	70.28	24.79	65.07	23.65	1.51
4. Father living	.90	.30	.96	.21	1.65
5. Mother living	.96	.20	.98	.15	.36
Educational history					
1. Class place	2.52	1.13	2.89	.84	4.82*
2. School progress	.48	.50	.70	.46	6.84**
3. Irish Reading	.08	1.01	.31	.96	1.81
4. Oral Irish	-.08	1.01	.36	.94	6.56*
5. Written Irish	-.32	.96	.13	1.00	6.84**
6. English Reading	.72	.70	.71	.71	.01
7. Oral English	.68	.74	.76	.66	.39
8. Written English	.32	.96	.53	.85	1.85
9. Mechanical Arithmetic	.44	.91	.62	.79	1.54
10. Problem Arithmetic	-.44	.91	.18	.99	13.28**
11. Absenteeism	20.64	17.24	18.96	16.21	.33
12. School grade at age twelve	1.62	.70	1.88	.60	5.32*

TABLE 6.5 (contd.)

Variables	*Early leavers (N:50)* M	SD	*Persisters (N:90)* M	SD	F
Primary school attended					
1. Catholic lay admin.	.24	.98	.20	.99	.05
2. Catholic religious admin.	-.32	.96	-.24	.98	.20
3. Protestant admin.	-.92	.40	-.98	.21	1.27
4. Private admin.	-1.00	.00	-.98	.21	.55
5. Number of teachers	3.52	1.16	3.58	1.03	.09
6. All male	-.28	.97	-.27	.97	.01
7. All female	-.40	.93	-.57	.82	1.38
8. Mixed gender	-.32	.96	-.16	.99	.90
9. School location	2.14	.86	2.22	.90	.28
10. Class size	2.32	1.77	2.54	1.63	.57
Personal characteristics					
1. Verbal reasoning ability	91.34	12.92	95.98	14.42	3.57
2. Gender	-.12	1.00	-.27	.97	.72
3. Satisfactory class. behav.	-.66	.80	-.06	.85	16.82***
4. Group leadership	.04	.97	-.07	.88	.50
5. Health/extroversion	-.08	.87	.21	.79	4.04*
6. Aesthetic behaviour	-.04	.76	-.02	.63	.02

*$p < .05$ **$p < .01$ ***$p < .001$

TABLE 6.6

Statistics on Primary-School Variables for Secondary Junior-Cycle Terminal Leavers and Overall Sample

Variables	*Terminal leavers (N:65)*		*Overall sample (N:500)*		*Standard score difference*	*Goodness of fit (p)*
	M	SD	M	SD		
Home background						
1. Socio-economic status	2.86	.93	2.80	1.13	.05	N.S.
2. Number of children	5.18	2.23	5.65	2.74	-.17	N.S.
3. Modified ordinal position	61.14	27.32	62.79	26.53	-.06	N.S.
4. Father living	.92	.27	.95	.23	-.13	N.S.
5. Mother living	.98	.12	.98	.15	.00	N.S.
Educational history						
2. Class place	2.97	1.07	3.06	1.05	-.09	N.S.
2. School progress	.78	.41	.75	.43	.07	N.S.
3. Irish Reading	.38	.93	.42	.91	-.04	N.S.
4. Oral Irish	.38	.93	.34	.94	.04	N.S.
5. Written Irish	.14	1.00	.21	.98	-.07	N.S.
6. English Reading	.85	.54	.80	.60	.08	N.S.
7. Oral English	.88	.48	.81	.59	.12	N.S.
8. Written English	.69	.73	.60	.80	.11	N.S.
9. Mechanical Arithmetic	.63	.78	.60	.80	.04	N.S.
10. Problem Arithmetic	.02	1.01	.07	1.00	-.05	N.S.
11. Absenteeism	14.00	11.70	14.54	14.61	-.04	N.S.
12. School grade at age twelve	1.83	.57	1.95	.71	-.17	N.S.

TABLE 6.6 (contd.)

Variables	*Terminal leavers (N:65)*		*Overall sample (N:500)*		*Standard score difference*	*Goodness of fit (p)*
	M	SD	M	SD		
Type of school attended						
1. Catholic lay admin.	-.23	.98	-.06	1.00	-.17	N.S.
2. Catholic religious admin.	.14	1.00	-.07	1.00	.21	N.S.
3. Protestant admin.	-.97	.25	-.95	.31	-.06	N.S.
4. Private admin.	-.94	.35	-.92	.39	-.05	N.S.
5. Number of teachers	3.88	1.17	3.69	1.10	.17	N.S.
6. All male	-.57	.83	-.29	.96	-.29	Sig.*
7. All female	.17	.99	-.30	.98	.48	Sig.***
8. Mixed gender	-.60	.81	-.42	.91	-.20	N.S.
9. School location	1.88	.94	2.14	.90	-.29	Sig.*
10. Class size	2.71	1.54	2.46	1.56	.16	N.S.
Personal characteristics						
1. Verbal reasoning ability	98.18	12.03	100.15	15.46	-.13	N.S.
2. Gender	.45	.90	.00	1.00	.45	Sig.***
3. Satisfactory class. behav.	.13	.80	.10	.91	.03	N.S.
4. Group leadership	-.09	.91	.01	.89	-.11	N.S.
5. Health/extroversion	.16	.86	.12	.83	.05	N.S.
6. Aesthetic behaviour	.08	.72	.05	.72	.04	N.S.

$*p < .05$ $***p < .001$.

other hand, were over-represented in the JCTL sample. These latter students accounted for 58.5% of the leavers, which is considerably more than their 35% representation in the original sample. It appears that students who had attended town or rural primary schools were less likely to leave school at this stage than were students who had attended city schools; town and rural primary-school students accounted for 49.2% of leavers as opposed to 66% of the overall sample. The finding for the fourth and final variable, gender, is consistent with the findings for the all-female and all-male school variables. Of the total of 65 leavers, 47 (72.3%) were girls. Thus, girls who accounted for 50% of the overall sample were over-represented among JCTLs. Despite this comparatively high drop-out rate, girls still maintained a slight numerical superiority in the sample of senior-cycle entrants (52.9% vs. 47.1%).

A total of 335 (67%) of the original sample took the Intermediate Certificate Examination. Of this total, 284 (84.8%) passed the examination. Among the 62 JCTLs for whom ICE examination results were available, 46 (74.2%) had been successful. A comparison of the ICE performance of the JCTLs with the performance of all ICE candidates indicated that the JCTLs, with their lower pass rate, could not be considered representative of the larger sample.[5] Seven of the JCTLs had taken the DGCE. In this instance, the pass rates for the JCTLs (71.4%) and for the total number (N:85) of DGCE candidates (69.4%) were similar.

Comparison of leavers and persisters

A comparison of junior-cycle terminal leavers (N:65) and persisters or senior-cycle entrants (N:221) revealed that the two groups were different from one another.[6] Statistically significant differences were found in each of the four categories of variables (Table 6.7).

Early leavers, by comparison with persisters, were likely to have been members of families of middle and lower socio-economic status. Almost three-quarters of the leavers (73.9%) were from these categories, while only approximately half of the persisters (51.6%) were. Although the percentage of leavers from the middle and lower socio-economic categories exceeded the corresponding percentage for the persisters, the actual number of students from these categories who remained in school greatly exceeded the number who left; 114 students remained, while 48 left.

Leavers also tended to have received poorer general primary-school progress and achievement ratings than persisters. Specifically,

TABLE 6.7
Means and Standard Deviations on Primary-School Variables for Secondary Junior-Cycle Terminal Leavers and Senior-Cycle Entrants

	Terminal leavers (N:65)		*Senior-Cycle entrants (N:221)*		
Variables	M	SD	M	SD	F
Home background					
1. Socio-economic status	2.86	.93	3.26	1.00	8.23**
2. Number of children	5.18	2.23	5.05	2.44	.17
3. Modified ordinal position	61.14	27.32	60.81	28.07	.01
4. Father living	.92	.27	.95	.22	.70
5. Mother living	.98	.12	.97	.16	.29
Educational history					
1. Class place	2.97	1.07	3.40	1.00	9.08**
2. School progress	.78	.41	.90	.30	6.22*
3. Irish Reading	.38	.93	.67	.74	6.80**
4. Oral Irish	.38	.93	.54	.84	1.59
5. Written Irish	.14	1.00	.55	.84	10.92**
6. English Reading	.85	.54	.90	.44	.70
7. Oral English	.88	.48	.91	.42	.28
8. Written English	.69	.73	.77	.63	.77
9. Mechanical Arithmetic	.63	.78	.75	.67	1.40
10. Problem Arithmetic	.02	1.01	.31	.95	4.75*
11. Absenteeism	14.00	11.70	9.92	10.50	7.19**
12. School grade at age twelve	1.83	.57	2.20	.68	16.13***

TABLE 6.7 (contd.)

Variables	*Terminal leavers (N:65)*		*Senior-Cycle entrants (N:221)*		
	M	SD	M	SD	F
Primary school attended					
1. Catholic lay admin.	-.23	.98	-.20	.98	.03
2. Catholic religious admin.	.14	1.00	.00	1.00	1.02
3. Protestant admin.	-.97	.25	-.94	.35	.49
4. Private admin.	-.94	.35	-.86	.52	1.47
5. Number of teachers	3.88	1.17	3.70	1.10	1.31
6. All male	-.57	.83	-.27	.97	5.23*
7. All female	.17	.99	-.28	.96	10.58**
8. Mixed gender	-.60	.81	-.46	.89	1.35
9. School location	1.88	.94	2.24	.86	8.49**
10. Class size	2.71	1.54	2.33	1.46	3.29
Personal characteristics					
1. Verbal reasoning ability	98.18	12.03	107.44	14.09	23.08***
2. Gender	.45	.90	.06	1.00	7.86**
3. Satisfactory class. behav.	.13	.81	.51	.77	12.06***
4. Group leadership	-.09	.91	.08	.84	1.92
5. Health/extroversion	.16	.86	.20	.79	.15
6. Aesthetic behaviour	.08	.72	.13	.73	.24

$*p < .05$ $**p < .01$ $***p < .001$

compared to persisters, JCTLs had completed fewer primary grades by age twelve, had poorer attendance records, lower class rankings, poorer primary-school progress ratings, and had experienced greater difficulty in Irish (both in reading and writing) and in Problem Arithmetic.

Significant differences were recorded on three of the variables relating to the type of primary school the students had attended. Leavers, compared to persisters, were more likely to have attended an all-female or an urban school and not to have attended an all-male school. A closer examination of the data on school location indicated that the leaving rate at the end of junior cycle of students who had attended city primary schools was approximately twice (34.7%) that of students who had attended either town or rural primary schools (16.8%).

The difference in mean verbal reasoning ability scores in favour of the persisters was 9.26 points. Over half (55.4%) of the JCTLs scored in the 70 to 100 range as opposed to 27.1% of the persisters. At the other end of the distribution, only 7.7% of leavers scored 115 or above, as opposed to 29.4% of the persisters. There was a marked tendency for the less able in terms of verbal reasoning ability to cease school after junior cycle; a sizeable number (N:60) of students who had scored in the 70 to 100 range did, however, remain in school.

The findings relating to classroom behaviour are consistent with those for the educational-history variables. Here again, leavers had lower ratings; approximately half had been rated below average, as opposed to less than one-quarter (22.7%) of the persisters. Finally, the significant difference relating to gender is attributable to the fact that girls, as has already been stated, were over-represented among leavers; they, in fact, accounted for 72.3% of leavers (and 52.9% of persisters) at this stage.

Information on four post-primary school variables was available. Three of these relate to junior-cycle certificate examination results and the fourth to boarding-school attendance. All but two of the students in both samples had taken the ICE, while the number of DGCE candidates was very small, amounting to only 14. The ICE results for one student were not available. The pass rate for the early leaver sample on the ICE was 74.19%; for the larger persister sample, it was 91.20 percent. This difference proved to be statistically significant.[7] Leavers were three times more likely to have failed the ICE than persisters. On the DGCE, however, the difference between the pass rates for the small numbers of leavers (N:7) and persisters (N:8) who had taken the examination (71.4% for leavers and 87.5% for persisters) was not statistically significant.[8] On the overall index of performance on six ICE subjects, the mean for the JCTL sample was considerably lower than that for the persisters. The difference was statistically significant.[9] Boarders were under-represented among leavers; of the 24 students who attended boarding secondary schools, only one left school at the end of junior cycle.

An analysis to find a smaller set of variables that would maximally discriminate between the two groups resulted in the identification of 12 variables. A comparison of the two samples on a combination of these variables revealed that JCTLs, in contrast to persisters, were more likely to have attended city primary schools, to have low verbal reasoning ability scores, to have experienced difficulty in Written Irish, to have completed relatively few primary school grades by the age of twelve, and to have poor attendance records. Furthermore, though to a lesser extent, they were more likely than persisters to have attended all-female primary schools, to have been members of families of low socio-economic status, and to have made unsatisfactory progress at primary school.[10]

To what extent does knowledge about a student's achievement record at secondary school increase our understanding of the nature of the differences between junior-cycle terminal leavers and persisters? To answer this question, the previous analysis was repeated but this time a measure of level of performance on a junior-cycle examination, the Intermediate Certificate, as well as information on attendance at boarding school, were included.[11] After school location, the Intermediate Certificate Examination index proved to be the best discriminator of the variables used in this analysis; that is, terminal leavers and persisters differed more on these two variables than on any of the remaining variables.[12]

Vocational School

For most vocational-school students, the junior-cycle examination appears to have signalled the end of formal full-time education. At this juncture, 68 of the 90 students attending vocational school, i.e., three out of every four students, left school. Somewhat over half (N:38) of these students had spent three years in post-primary school before taking the Intermediate Certificate Examination. For those (N:30) who took only the Day Group Certificate Examination, the junior-cycle period in most cases amounted to two years of full-time post-primary schooling.

Comparison with the total sample

In all, more than one in eight of the original sample left a vocational school at the end of the junior cycle. A comparison of these junior-cycle terminal leavers with the overall sample indicates that, on most variables, the two samples were quite similar, both in terms of their means and distributions. On four of the variables, however, the vocational junior-cycle terminal leavers could not be considered representative of the overall sample. These variables were socio-economic status, number of children in family, class place, and verbal reasoning ability (Table 6.8).

On socio-economic status, approximately half (51.5%) of the leavers had been classified in the semi-skilled and unskilled categories. In contrast, the percentage of the overall sample in these two categories was considerably less at 36.2 percent. At the other end of the distribution, early leavers were under-represented in the professional and intermediate-professional categories; a total of 17.6% of them were in these two highest categories, as against 31.2% of the overall sample.

Early leavers tended to be members of families which had approximately one child more (M = 6.60 vs. 5.65) than the overall average. Thus, their families tended to be large; almost half the leavers (48.5%) were members of families which had seven or more children, whereas approximately one in three (32.8%) of the students in the original sample came from families of this size.

In terms of rank in class while at primary school, a total of 85.3% of JCTLs had been classified in the middle 40% or the next lowest 20% of their classes. Leavers were under-represented in the top 30% of their classes; 10.3% had been rated in this category, compared with 34.7% of the overall sample.

On the final variable, verbal reasoning ability, a 5-point mean difference was recorded between the two samples. Part of this difference may be attributed to the sizeable percentage of early leavers (33.8%) who had scored below 90 (vs. 23.2% for the overall sample) on the test. Among the high verbal reasoning ability scorers (110+), the percentage of early leavers (11.8%) was considerably below that for the overall sample (27.0%).

Similar results to those obtained in the case of secondary-school students were found when the ICE and DGCE examination performances of junior-cycle terminal leavers from vocational schools were compared with the performances of the overall sample. On the ICE, 65.8% of the vocational junior-cycle terminal leavers (N:38) had passed, compared with 84.8% of the overall sample,[13] while on the DGCE, 64.8% of these terminal leavers (N:56) were successful, compared with 69.4% for the overall sample.[14]

TABLE 6.8
Statistics on Primary-School Variables for Vocational Junior-Cycle Terminal Leavers and Overall Sample

Variables	*Terminal leavers (N:68)*		*Overall sample (N:500)*		*Standard score difference*	*Goodness of fit (p)*
	M	SD	M	SD		
Home background						
1. Socio-economic status	2.37	1.09	2.80	1.13	-.38	Sig.*
2. Number of children	6.60	2.98	5.65	2.74	.35	Sig.*
3. Modified ordinal position	66.96	23.35	62.79	26.53	.16	N.S.
4. Father living	.97	.17	.95	.23	.09	N.S.
5. Mother living	.97	.17	.98	.15	-.07	N.S.
Educational history						
1. Class place	2.84	.75	3.06	1.05	-.21	Sig.***
2. School progress	.66	.48	.75	.43	-.21	N.S.
3. Irish Reading	.26	.97	.42	.91	-.18	N.S.
4. Oral Irish	.35	.94	.34	.94	.01	N.S.
5. Written Irish	.09	1.00	.21	.98	-.12	N.S.
6. English Reading	.74	.68	.80	.60	-.10	N.S.
7. Oral English	.76	.65	.81	.59	-.08	N.S.
8. Written English	.53	.85	.60	.80	-.09	N.S.
9. Mechanical Arithmetic	.59	.81	.60	.80	-.01	N.S.
10. Problem Arithmetic	.09	1.00	.07	1.00	.02	N.S.
11. Absenteeism	19.29	17.16	14.54	14.61	.33	N.S.
12. School grade at age twelve	1.87	.57	1.95	.71	-.11	N.S.

TABLE 6.8 (contd.)

Variables	*Terminal leavers (N:68)*		*Overall sample (N:500)*		*Standard score difference*	*Goodness of fit (p)*
	M	SD	M	SD		
Type of school attended						
1. Catholic lay admin.	.12	1.00	-.06	1.00	.18	N.S.
2. Catholic religious admin.	-.15	1.00	-.07	1.00	-.08	N.S.
3. Protestant admin.	-.97	.24	-.95	.31	-.06	N.S.
4. Private admin.	-1.00	.00	-.92	.39	-.21	N.S.
5. Number of teachers	3.68	1.04	3.69	1.10	-.01	N.S.
6. All male	-.26	.97	-.29	.96	.03	N.S.
7. All female	-.53	.85	-.30	.98	-.23	N.S.
8. Mixed gender	-.21	.99	-.42	.91	.23	N.S.
9. School location	2.18	.94	2.14	.90	.04	N.S.
10. Class size	2.57	1.68	2.46	1.56	.07	N.S.
Personal characteristics						
1. Verbal reasoning ability	95.01	14.07	100.15	15.46	-.33	Sig.*
2. Gender	-.24	.98	.00	1.00	-.24	N.S.
3. Satisfactory class. behav.	-.13	.88	.10	.91	-.25	N.S.
4. Group leadership	-.10	.92	.01	.89	-.12	N.S.
5. Health/extroversion	.31	.84	.12	.83	.23	N.S.
6. Aesthetic behaviour	.03	.68	.05	.72	-.03	N.S.

$^{*}p < .05$ $\quad$ $^{***}p < .001$

Comparison of leavers and persisters
Did students who left vocational school at the end of junior cycle (N:68) differ from students (N:23) who elected to commence the senior-cycle course in a vocational school? Given the small number of persisters, it is statistically inappropriate to carry out overall comparisons of the groups (Tatsuoka, 1970). When the samples were compared on each of the primary school measures separately, however, none of the differences was found to be statistically significant.

The two groups were also compared in terms of performance on junior-cycle examinations. Of the total of 54 leavers who had taken the DGCE, 35 (64.8%) passed the examination, while 12 of the 16 (75%) who commenced a senior-cycle course in vocational school had passed. The difference in the pass rates was not statistically significant.[15] On the second junior-cycle examination, the ICE, the pass rate for the 38 leavers who had taken this examination was 65.8% while for those in the senior cycle who had taken the ICE (N:18), the rate was 83.3%. In this instance, the difference in pass rates was not statistically significant either.[16]

Senior-Cycle Early Leavers

Altogether, 244 students or 48.8% of the original sample embarked on the two-year senior-cycle course leading to the Leaving Certificate Examination. Approximately 90% of these students remained in school and took the LCE, with the result that the number of senior-cycle leavers was quite small (N:22). Despite the fact that the vast majority (90.6%) of senior-cycle students attended secondary school, most of the leavers came from vocational schools.

Secondary School

The number of students who commenced the senior-cycle course in secondary school was 221. All but nine of these students sat for the LCE. Thus, the senior-cycle drop-out rate among secondary students was very low (4.1%).

Comparison with the total sample
A series of comparisons of the senior-cycle early leavers and the overall sample on each of the primary-school variables revealed that the leavers

could not be considered untypical of the total sample of students on any of the measures. There was a difference between the groups on ICE performance, however. While the overall pass rate of the 335 students who took the ICE was 84.7%, the pass rate for the senior-cycle leavers was only 55.6 percent. The difference was statistically significant.[17] None of the early leavers had taken the DGCE.

Comparison of leavers and persisters
Due to the small size of the leavers' sample, it was inappropriate to carry out overall comparisons of the two groups. None of the differences between leavers and persisters on the individual primary-school variables was significant. The pass rate for the persisters on the ICE was 92.8% compared with 55.6% for the leavers. In this case, the difference was statistically significant.[18]

Vocational School

We have already seen that at the end of the junior cycle there was a major exodus of students from vocational schools. The number (N:23) that commenced senior cycle amounted to approximately one-quarter of the number that completed junior cycle. This small number was reduced still further during the senior-cycle years by the withdrawal from school of 13 students, giving a drop-out rate of 56.5% at this level.

Comparison with the total sample
The 13 students who dropped out of vocational school could not be considered untypical of students in the overall sample except on two primary-school variables related to students' gender and the gender composition of students in primary school. None of the senior-cycle leavers had attended an all-female primary school, which is not surprising since our data on gender indicate that 12 of the 13 students were boys. Eight of the 13 leavers had taken the ICE; five had passed. This passing rate was not significantly different from the passing rate of ICE candidates in the total sample (84.78%).[19] On the DGCE, six of the nine students who had taken the examination had passed it, giving a pass rate of 66.7%, which is very similar to that for students in the total sample of students who had taken this examination (69.4%).

Comparison of leavers and persisters
Comparisons between leavers and persisters in the senior cycle in

vocational schools revealed significant differences on three variables — Oral Irish, attendance at an all-female primary school, and gender. Seven of the 13 leavers had been rated by their teachers as having experienced difficulty with Oral Irish, compared to one of the 10 persisters. On the other two variables, the findings to a great extent reflect the fact that all but one of the leavers were boys, whereas boys and girls were equally represented among the persisters.

The pass rate for leavers who had taken the ICE (N:8), i.e., 62.5%, was poorer than that of the 10 persisters, all of whom had passed the examination. The difference is statistically significant.[20] On the second junior-cycle examination, the DGCE, which had been taken by eight of the persisters (six passed) and nine of the leavers (six passed), the difference in pass rates was not significant.[21]

Conclusion

The vast majority of the students in our sample of 500 transferred to a post-primary school on completing their primary-school education. However, 37 students, or 7.4% of the overall sample, terminated their formal education at this point. This figure would probably have been lower if we had collected our data after the raising of the school-leaving age to 15 years, rather than shortly before it. However, the primary-school terminal leavers, though they are now a disappearing genre, are of more than historical interest in that they constitute a group of students who drop out of school at the first available opportunity.

Of the 461 students who went to a post-primary school, just under half (222) completed the full post-primary course to the Leaving Certificate Examination. A total of 235 left school without taking this examination. (A further four students of the original sample do not figure in these totals; two died and two emigrated shortly after commencing post-primary school.)

A large number of students (133 or almost 27% of the original sample) left school on completing the junior cycle; approximately three-quarters of these (101) had taken the Intermediate Certificate Examination, while the remaining quarter (31) had taken only the Day Group Certificate Examination.

Quite a large number (80 students or 16% of the original sample) did not stay in post-primary school long enough to take either the Day Group or Intermediate Certificate Examination. When combined with the primary-school terminal leavers, this means that over 23% of the sample of 500 left school without having sat for a public examination.

Once students embarked on a senior-cycle course, drop-out rate was low. Of the 244 students who commenced studies for the Leaving Certificate, only 22 left school without taking the examination.

Drop-out rates were higher at all stages in vocational than in secondary school. During the junior cycle, of the 128 students who had enrolled in vocational school and the 13 others who had transferred there from secondary school, 50 (or 35.7%) dropped out of full-time education before taking a public examination, while this was true for only 30 (or 9.5%) of those enrolled in secondary school.

At the end of the junior cycle, the contrast between secondary- and vocational-school students was even more stark. A total of 22.6% of secondary-school students left school at this stage as against 75% of vocational-school students.

The drop-out rate of secondary-school students during the senior cycle reduced to 4.1%, but at 56.5%, it remained high for vocational-school students.

At each stage at which students left school, we examined a range of characteristics of the students to see if they differed from the original sample and from those who stayed on at school. These characteristics related to students' home background, personal characteristics, their educational history while at primary school, the type of primary school they had attended, and where appropriate, their performance on public examinations taken in post-primary school.

Students who left the system early differed from the overall sample of students on a wide range of characteristics — personal, home background, and scholastic. Students who did not proceed to any kind of post-primary school, compared to the overall population, had lower verbal ability scores, showed poorer scholastic progress in primary school on a variety of indices, had poorer school attendance records at primary school, and came from larger families of relatively low socio-economic status.

Students who left vocational school during or at the end of the junior cycle also tended to differ from the overall population in a similar fashion on a variety of variables, particularly verbal reasoning ability, socio-economic status, as well as rank in class and school progress while at primary school. However, verbal reasoning ability and socio-economic status played little role in differentiating drop-outs from secondary schools from the overall population. They did however, along with a number of primary-school educational-history variables, serve to differentiate drop-outs from stay-ins in the secondary school up to the

Intermediate Certificate Examination. After this examination, the personal and family-background characteristics of a student were not related to a student's perseverance in either secondary or vocational schools. As students proceed through the post-primary school, public examination performance (on the Intermediate Certificate) tends to take over from the primary-school achievement measures as a predictor of retention in the system.

The type of primary school attended by the student played a relatively minor role in our analyses. It was of some significance, however, after students had taken the Intermediate Certificate Examination; at this stage, secondary-school leavers were more likely to have attended a city primary school than a town or rural one, perhaps reflecting better prospects for employment in urban areas. Further, early leavers at this stage were more likely to be girls than boys, perhaps again a reflection of employment opportunities.

FOOTNOTES

1 In the comparisons between early leavers and persisters, the following analyses were carried out. At the outset, through the use of multivariate analysis of variance, it was established whether or not there were overall differences between the two groups. If such an overall difference was found, a series of comparisons was then carried out between the two groups on each of the primary-school variables to identify those variables on which the leavers and persisters differed by a statistically significant amount. This involved a series of one-way analyses of variance. A discriminant analysis was then carried out to build a single new variable which would maximize the difference between the two groups. Since this type of variable is generally difficult to interpret due to the fact that it is made up of a large number of variables (31 in this instance), a number of the variables of lesser importance from the point of view of discrimination were dropped. Deleting these variables served the interests of parsimony, in that it helped to select considerably fewer variables without compromising our ability to discriminate between early leavers and persisters. The final step in the analyses involved classifying a student as either an early leaver or as a persister on the basis of his/her score on the new variable. The purpose of classifying the students was to determine the effectiveness of the new discriminating variable. If a large proportion of misclassifications occurred, then the variables selected to make up the new variable would have to be considered poor discriminators.

2 Wilks' Lambda = .839; $\chi^2 = 52.70$; $df = 31$; $p < .01$

3 First of all, by means of a stepwise discriminant analysis (Nie *et al.*, 1975) it was determined that a subset of 11 variables could discriminate between the two groups almost as well as the full set of variables. A new discriminating variable (i.e., a discriminant function) based on these 11 variables was created (Table 6.9). The Wilks criterion determined the number of variables in the reduced model.

TABLE 6.9
Standardized Discriminant Function Coefficients: Secondary Junior-Cycle Early Leavers and Persisters

Variables	*Standardized coefficients*
1. Socio-economic status	.48
2. Written Irish	.42
3. All female	.42
4. Satisfactory classroom behaviour	.38
5. Lay administration	.29
6. Unsatisfactory progress	.28
7. School grade at age twelve	.26
8. Health/extroversion	.21
9. Aesthetic	-.17
10. Number of children in family	-.28
11. Oral Irish	-.47
Group Means (Centroids)	
Leavers (N:30)	-1.26
Persisters (N:287)	.13

The order of entry of the 11 variables was as follows: 1) satisfactory classroom behaviour; 2) socio-economic status; 3) all-female primary school; 4) Written Irish; 5) Oral Irish; 6) number of children in family; 7) Catholic lay administration; 8) grade achieved at age twelve; 9) school progress; 10) health/extroversion; 11) aesthetic behaviour. A variable which correlated highly with satisfactory classroom behaviour, the first variable entered, would not have been entered second, since it would not have added much to our ability to discriminate between the two samples; the dimension or trait it measured would, to a great extent, have been already taken into account by the first variable. Thus, it would appear that socio-economic status measures something which is independent of satisfactory classroom behaviour.

The coefficients in the final column of Table 6.9, irrespective of the sign before them, indicate the relative importance of the associated variable to the general variable or function. The four largest positive weights (.48 for SES, .42 for Written Irish and for all-female primary school, and .38 for satisfactory school behaviour) are considerably larger than the remaining positive weights. Similarly, the negative weight with the largest absolute value (Oral Irish) is considerably larger than the remainder of the negative weights. Due to the relatively large absolute values of the weights attaching to these five variables, it is reasonable to focus attention on them.

The means for the early leavers and persisters on the new variables indicate that persisters scored higher (0.13) than leavers (-1.26). The meaning of the new variable or function is interpreted in the light of coefficients and sample means. A student with a low score on the function, i.e., an early leaver, was more likely to have come from a low socio-economic background, to have experienced difficulty in Written Irish, not to have attended an all-female primary school (i.e., had attended an all-male or mixed-gender school), and to have received a low rating for satisfactory classroom behaviour.

The remaining sizeable coefficient, -.47 for Oral Irish (the fifth variable entered), is rather difficult to interpret since the mean score for the persisters (.50) was greater than that for the leavers (.40). In this instance, Oral Irish appears to serve as a suppressor variable, that is, as a predictor which "shows no, or low, correlation with the criterion, provided it correlates well with a variable which does correlate with the criterion" (McNemar, 1969, p. 210). The inclusion of the suppressor variable increases the multiple correlation and enhances the effectiveness of prediction.

The total discriminatory power of the function was estimated to be .141 which indicated that the function exhibited a relatively low degree of differentiation between the two groups.

How accurate was the function in classifying students according to their secondary-school junior-cycle status? The computed classification table is presented in Table 6.10. Correct classifications or 'hits' are italicized. Of the total of 317 secondary junior-cycle students, 232 or 73.2% were classified correctly as leavers or persisters. Most of the misclassified students were persisters who had been classified as leavers (N:74). This, in effect, means that in terms of the 11 variables used in the analysis, the misclassified persisters were more like leavers than the correctly-classified secondary persisters.

It is of interest to note that when the full set of 31 variables was used to compute the discriminant function and to classify the students, the percentage of correctly-classified students was the same. This finding serves to underline the efficiency of using an appropriate subset of variables to discriminate instead of the full battery of variables.

TABLE 6.10

Secondary Junior Cycle: Prediction of Group Membership on the Basis of Function Scores

	Predicted group	
Actual group	*Early leavers*	*Persisters*
Early leavers (N:30)	*19*	11
Persisters (N:287)	74	*213*

4 Wilks' Lambda = .731; χ^2 = 38.47; *df* = 31; N.S.
5 χ^2 = 4.09; *df* = 1; $p < .05$.
6 Wilks' Lambda = .755; χ^2 = 75.41; *df* = 31; $p < .001$
7 χ^2 = 12.67; *df* = 1; $p < .001$
8 χ^2 = 0.60; *df* = 1; N.S.

9 $F = 41.46$; $df = 1, 274$; $p < .001$

10 A subset of 12 variables was identified which served the interests of parsimony and helped to discriminate between the two groups almost as well as the original set of 31 variables. The discriminatory power of the function was .242. The new variable, along with its associated coefficients for each of the 12 original variables, is presented in Table 6.11. Junior-cycle terminal leavers (M = -.99) scored lower than senior-cycle entrants (M = .29) on the new variable. The location of the primary school attended by students proved to be the most effective discriminator. Students with a low score on the function (i.e., JCTLs), compared to persisters, were likely to have attended city primary or small schools; they were also likely to have had relatively low verbal reasoning ability scores, to have experienced difficulty in Written Irish, to have completed relatively few primary school grades by the age of twelve, and to have had poorer attendance records. Furthermore, though to a lesser extent, they were more likely than persisters to have attended all-female primary schools, to have been members of families of low socio-economic status and to have made unsatisfactory progress at primary school.

TABLE 6.11

Discriminant Function Coefficients Based on Primary-School Variables: Secondary School Students Who Leave School After Completing Junior Cycle and Senior-Cycle Entrants

Variables	*Standardized coefficients*
1. School location	.84
2. Number of teachers	.37
3. Verbal reasoning ability	.36
4. Written Irish	.36
5. School grade at age twelve	.34
6. Socio-economic status	.25
7. School progress	.25
8. Private administration	.18
9. Health/extroversion	-.18
10. All female	-.25
11. Oral Irish	-.27
12. Absenteeism	-.31
Group Means (Centroids)	
Junior-cycle terminal leavers (N:65)	-.99
Senior-cycle entrants (N:221)	.29

The accuracy of the 12-variable function in classifying the students as either leavers or persisters was determined. The function was found to have classified correctly 75.4% of the leavers and 74.7% of the persisters, giving an overall 'hit' rate of 74.8 percent.

11 Since the vast majority of the students had taken the ICE and relatively few the DGCE, it was decided to use an index of performance on the ICE as a variable in the analysis and to exclude students who had taken the DGCE only while at secondary school (N:2). Because the index was based on examination performance on the student's six best ICE subjects, a total of eight further students who had taken fewer than six subjects was excluded. (Four of these students, in fact, had attended a secondary school which completed the junior-cycle course but did not present students for the ICE.) Thus, this analysis is based on a slightly smaller sample (276 rather than 286 students) than the previous comparison of JCTLs and persisters. The following statistics were computed. Wilks' Lambda = .702; $\chi^2 = 91.15$; $df = 33$; $p < .001$. The discriminatory power of the function based on 31 primary and 2 post-primary measures was .2948, an increase of .0532 over the previous analysis based on the primary-school measures alone. Thus, an additional 5.32% of the variation in the discriminant function could be attributed to the two additional measures.

12 A subset of 14 variables was identified which discriminated between the two groups almost as well as the full set of variables. The function or new variable which was computed, apart from the addition of the ICE index, was quite similar to that presented in Table 6.12. Attendance at boarding school did not contribute to the function.

TABLE 6.12

Discriminant Function Coefficients Based on Primary and Post-Primary Variables: Secondary School Students Who Leave School After Completing Junior Cycle and Senior Cycle Entrants

Variables	*Standardized coefficients*
1. School location	.60
2. Intermediate certificate index	.57
3. School grade at age twelve	.41
4. Number of teachers	.40
5. Written Irish	.34
6. Irish Reading	.22
7. Socio-economic status	.19
8. Attendance at boarding school	-.02
9. Absenteeism	-.15
10. School progress	-.17
11. Mechanical Arithmetic	-.21
12. Written English	-.22
13. All female	-.38
14. Oral Irish	-.39
Group Means (Centroids)	
Senior-cycle entrants (N:214)	.33
Junior-cycle terminal leavers (N:62)	-1.15

13 $\chi^2 = 8.65$; $df = 1$; $p < .01$
14 $\chi^2 = 0.31$; $df = 1$; N.S.
15 $\chi^2 = 0.58$; $df = 1$; N.S.
16 $\chi^2 = 1.84$; $df = 1$; N.S.
17 $\chi^2 = 5.57$; $df = 1$; $p < .05$
18 $\chi^2 = 14.97$; $df = 1$; $p < .001$
19 $\chi^2 = 2.93$; $df = 1$; N.S.
20 $\chi^2 = 4.51$; $df = 1$; $p < .05$
21 $\chi^2 = 0.14$; $df = 1$; N.S.

7 Examination Performance

The Department of Education awards three separate certificates at the post-primary level. Each is based on performance on a public examination and may be used by students as evidence of standards attained. Two certificates are awarded at junior cycle — one for the Day Group Certificate Examination (DGCE) and one for the Intermediate Certificate Examination (ICE). At the end of the senior-cycle course, a certificate is awarded for the Leaving Certificate Examination (LCE). Traditionally, the Day Group Certificate Examination was confined to vocational schools and was regarded as the terminal examination for the vocational system, while the Intermediate and Leaving Certificate Examinations were confined to secondary schools. At present, any of the examinations may be offered in any type of post-primary school. While that is so, the Day Group Certificate Examination remains associated primarily with the vocational sector and only a small number of students in secondary schools are presented for this examination.

Normally, students in vocational schools are expected to sit for the Day Group Certificate Examination after two years. A student may sit for the examination provided he or she has reached the age of thirteen years, has followed an approved course for at least two years, and has received a specified minimum number of hours of instruction in practical subjects. For the examination, a student is required to take examinations in Irish and in English and in one of five 'groups' of other subjects: General Commerce, Secretarial Commerce, Domestic Science (formerly Home Economics), Manual Training, and Rural Science. Other optional subjects (e.g., Languages, History) are offered (Ireland: Department of Education, 1979). The most popular groups of subjects, as indicated by the number of examination candidates, have traditionally been Manual Training and General Commerce. In general, the certificate was well regarded; to have a certificate was an advantage in obtaining employment in both the semi-state and private industrial sectors.[1]

Candidates for the Intermediate Certificate Examination must have followed an approved course of not less than three years' duration in a recognised school and must have attained the age of fourteen years.

The purpose of the examination is to testify 'to the completion of a well-balanced course of general education suitable for pupils who leave school at about 16 years of age and, alternatively, to the fitness of the pupils for entry on more advanced courses of study in a secondary or a vocational school' (Ireland: Department of Education, 1969, p. 21). Examinations are offered in about 24 subjects. Higher and lower-level papers are offered in Irish, English, and Mathematics; common-level papers are provided in other subjects. Regulations regarding the award of certificates have varied from time to time. In 1971 and 1972, the years in which many of the students in the study reported in this book sat for the examination, certificates were awarded to candidates who obtained a grade D (see p. 150) or higher in at least five subjects including Irish (Ireland: Department of Education, 1970). The most popular subjects were Irish, English, Mathematics, History and Geography, French (especially among girls), Latin, and Science (especially among boys).

For many students, the Intermediate Certificate Examination is regarded merely as a preliminary state examination to be completed two years before the more highly esteemed Leaving Certificate Examination (Greaney & Kellaghan, 1979). The purpose of the Leaving Certificate course 'is to prepare pupils for immediate entry into open society or for proceeding to further education' (Ireland: Department of Education, 1975a, p. 29). To be eligible for admission to the examination, a student must have reached the age of sixteen years and should normally have followed an approved senior-cycle course. In practice, the Leaving Certificate Examination has a two-fold purpose. Firstly, it serves as a measure of student achievement, indicating the levels of performance of a student on a series of examinations based on subject areas which have been studied at a post-primary school. Secondly, it is used as a predictor of future performance. For many decades, the results of the examination have been used by Irish society as a screening device for admission to various third-level educational institutions and careers in the public and private sectors of the economy. Since in very many instances, alternative entry routes to these institutions and careers did not exist, the examination served as a form of 'make-or-break' test which conferred 'credentials' on the successful, a kind of academic currency which might be spent in third-level educational or labour markets. Given the importance of the examination, it should not surprise us if students do little academic work which is not directly related to the examination (Madaus & Macnamara, 1970). Neither should we be surprised to find a lack of emphasis on the acquisition of oral and practical skills; such skills are not likely to be emphasized in an examination which is predominantly written in character (*ICE report*, 1975).

Examinations are offered in about 30 subjects. Separate ordinary-level and higher-level papers are set in all subjects except Music and Musicianship, Building Construction, Technical Drawing, and Engineering Workshop Theory and Practice. Common-level papers are set in these subjects. To obtain a Leaving Certificate in the past, a student was required to obtain a grade D or higher in at least five subjects including Irish; from 1975 onward, each candidate was given a certificate indicating the grades obtained in the examination.

Public examinations are set by schools' inspectors in the Department of Education and are administered once a year under the control of the Department in centres throughout the country on specified days. Completed examination scripts are returned to the Department for scoring. Scorers are usually teachers in post-primary schools who work under the supervision of Departmental inspectors. An attempt is made to ensure uniformity of marking by holding a conference of examiners to discuss the interpretation of the marking schemes. Examiners are also required to return scripts to their supervisors over regular intervals so that their standards of marking may be checked. The distribution of each examiner's grades is checked against the distribution for examiners in general. Deviations from this general distribution are checked further.

Tests of oral proficiency in a modern continental language may be held, but rarely are. An oral test, however, is compulsory in the case of Irish in the LCE; 25% of marks are awarded for this part of the examination at both higher and ordinary levels. Oral assessments in Irish are conducted by a teacher from a school other than the candidate's school. At the junior-cycle level, while the emphasis in the ICE, and to a considerably lesser extent in the DGCE, is on essay-type questions, schools may opt for oral and practical assessments in the case of a number of subjects (e.g., French, Science, and Home Economics). Where schools do not avail themselves of this option, all marks are awarded for the written examination. Candidates who select Woodwork, Metalwork, and Music are required to take practical examinations. The available evidence suggests that a minority of secondary-school students have experience of either oral or practical assessment.

In 1969, a new grading system was introduced by the Department of Education to remove the concepts of 'honours', 'pass' and 'fail' both at the LCE and ICE levels. Under the new system, a student is given one of the following grades to represent a percentage range of marks: A — 85 or over; B — 70 to 84; C — 55 to 69; D — 40 to 54; E — 25 to 39; F — 10 to 24; and No Grade — less than 10. In effect, a grade of E or lower is generally regarded as a failure. Moreover, the Department itself reports the results in three categories — C or over, D, and E or lower — thus, effectively retaining the old honours-pass-fail division.

The Intermediate Certificate Examination

Of our original sample of 500, a total of 377 students (75.4%) completed a junior-cycle course. Of these, 37 students sat for the DGCE only, while four others completed the Intermediate Certificate course but did not take the examination. A total of 336 students (67.2%) sat for the ICE in either a vocational (N:55) or secondary (N:281) school.

The students in our sample did not all take the ICE in the same year. Further, there was a considerable difference in the ages of the students at the time they took the examination. The vast majority (92.3%) were aged between 15 years one month and 17 years one month when they sat for the examination in either June 1971 (N:186) or June 1972 (N:124). The remaining students sat for the examination in 1970 (19 students aged between 14 years one month and 15 years one month), 1973 (six students aged between 17 years one month and 18 years one month), or 1974 (one student aged over 18 years one month). An examination of the verbal reasoning ability scores of the students revealed that there was a tendency for the more able students to take the ICE at an earlier age. The mean verbal ability score of the 1970 candidates was 117.05, in 1971 it was 107.65, and in 1972 and 1973 the respective means were 98.66 and 85.50. The single 1974 candidate had recorded a score of 70 on the verbal ability test.

An examination of characteristics of the ICE candidates in terms of the primary-school variables revealed that by comparison with the overall sample of 500, the ICE candidates tended to come from slightly higher SES homes and had better ratings on each of the primary-school educational-history variables and on the satisfactory classroom behaviour variable. The mean verbal reasoning score of the candidates was approximately 4.50 points above that of students in the total sample. Girls were over-represented among the examination candidates (185 girls, 143 boys). The correlation between student gender and verbal reasoning ability (-.25) for the sample of ICE candidates indicates that girls tended to have scored lower than boys on the verbal ability measure.

In 1971, the year when over half the ICE candidates in our study took the examination, the list of approved examination subjects was: Irish (Higher Course), Irish (Lower Course), English (Higher Course), English (Lower Course), Mathematics (Higher Course), Mathematics

(Lower Course), History and Geography, Latin, Greek, Hebrew, French, German, Spanish, Italian, Science (Syllabus A), Science (Syllabus B), Home Economics, Music, General and Practical Musicianship, General Musicianship, Art, Woodwork, Metalwork, Mechanical Drawing, and Commerce (Ireland: Department of Education, 1970). In vocational schools, boys were required to take either Mechanical Drawing or Art while the girls had to take either Home Economics or Commerce.

Candidates for the ICE are expected to present themselves for examination in a minimum of six subjects. Many schools, however, encourage pupils to take more than that. The majority of ICE candidates in our sample took more than the required minimum. Four candidates took examinations in five or fewer subjects (i.e., less than the minimum), 57 took six subjects, 156 took seven, 103 took eight, 12 took nine, two took 10, and one took as many as 11 subjects. (The examination records of one further student were lost.)

A list of the examination subjects taken by the 335 ICE candidates is presented for boys and girls separately in Table 7.1. Virtually all students sat for examinations in Irish, English, and Mathematics. The next most popular subject was History-Geography (one examination subject). The data indicate that a student's gender may have been an important factor in determining which subjects were studied. Girls were over-represented among the students who took French, Art, and Commerce, while boys were over-represented among students taking Science (Syllabus A), Latin, and Higher Mathematics. Four additional subjects were studied exclusively by members of one gender, excluding three subjects taken by less than 1% of the sample. All of the Home Economics students were girls, while Woodwork, Metalwork, and Mechanical Drawing were taken only by boys.

For comparative purposes, the percentage of the total number of 1971 candidates taking each examination subject is given in the final column of Table 7.1. The national results for 1971 were selected since this year corresponds to the one in which over half the candidates in our study took the examination. A comparison of the figures in the final two columns of the table reveals that the percentage of our sample which took each of the ICE subjects reflects closely the percentage of all 1971 ICE candidates which took each subject (Ireland: Department of Education, 1974).

Computing an ICE index

To what extent is performance on the Intermediate Certificate Examination predictable from earlier measures obtained while the

Number of Students Taking Intermediate Certificate Examinations in Each of 22 Subjects, by Gender

Subject	Female (N:191)	Male (N:144)	Total (N:335)	Percentage of sample	Percentage of all 1971 Candidates (N:36,402)*
Irish (Higher)	58	53	111 } 335	33.1 } 100.0	30.1 } 97.3
Irish (Lower)	133	91	224	66.9	67.2
English (Higher)	98	68	166 } 334	49.6 } 99.7	48.5 } 98.6
English (Lower)	98	79	168	50.1	50.1
Mathematics (Higher)	36	44	80 } 334	23.9 } 99.7	21.6 } 98.4
Mathematics (Lower)	153	101	254	75.8	76.8
History & Geography	177	129	306	91.3	90.8
Science (Syllabus A)	54	123	177	52.8	55.3†
French	114	63	177	52.8	56.1
Commerce	110	41	151	45.1	44.7
Home Economics	141	0	141	42.1	38.3
Latin	48	86	134	40.0	37.7
Art	85	36	121	36.1	34.1
Mechanical Drawing	0	54	54	16.1	16.4
Woodwork	0	32	32	9.6	12.0
Metalwork	0	29	29	8.7	7.5
Spanish	18	11	29	8.7	7.9
General Musicianship	14	3	17	5.1	6.2
Science (Syllabus B)	4	8	12	3.6	0.0
Italian	6	4	10	3.0	0.6
German	7	2	9	2.7	2.7
Music	2	2	4	1.2	0.5
General & Practical Musicianship	3	0	3	0.9	0.4
Hebrew	2	0	2	0.6	0.0
Greek	0	1	1	0.3	0.0

*Ireland; Department of Education, 1974.

†Includes Science (Syllabus B) candidates.

student attended primary school? If the ICE had yielded one overall index of junior-cycle achievement, it would have been relatively easy to obtain an answer to this question. Unfortunately, no single summative score or index of ICE performance is available. Instead, each student is given a certificate which lists the grades obtained on each examination paper taken by the candidate. Students in the present study took the examination in 22 different subject areas. Furthermore, in three of these subject areas, Irish, English, and Mathematics, candidates could have selected either higher or lower-level examination papers. Given the range of subjects and levels (higher or lower) that were taken by students, it would not have been possible to have examined the factors related to student achievement (ICE performance) for each examination paper in each year in which that paper was taken. The only reasonable procedure seemed to be to establish a single overall index of achievement on the ICE which could be applied to the results of every student.

In creating the ICE index, the assumption was made that the overall levels of student achievement and the marking standards in the examinations did not alter appreciably during the 1970–1974 period. The assumption of parity of grading standards in national examinations, such as the ICE, across years is widely accepted in society. In support of the assumption, it should be noted that while in some subject areas, assigned texts changed during the period, in general, students followed the same broad curriculum and much of the content in the different subject areas was quite similar from year to year. Furthermore, the procedure for setting and correcting examination papers attempted to ensure comparability of standards across years. Since very many of the schools' inspectors who set the examinations and monitored the correction of papers performed this task annually, they were in a position to check that marking standards did not differ substantially from year to year. In fairness, it should be stressed that despite such precautions, marking standards on examinations such as the ICE may fluctuate over time (cf. Madaus & Macnamara, 1970; Willmott, 1979). As a check on the comparability of ICE results for our sample, the distribution of ICE grades for 1971 and 1972, the years which accounted for over 90% of the ICE candidates in our study, were compared for each examination which was taken by 60 or more students. The grade distributions were found to be quite similar. Bearing in mind the relatively unchanging nature of the examination process and the broad interval (15 percentage points) used to report results, it was considered justifiable, in the present context, to assume that ICE grades based on different examination years could be considered reasonably comparable.[2]

A number of problems arose in attempting to create an index of overall performance on the ICE. First, there was the problem of assigning a numerical value to the letter grade used in reporting examination results. Second, differences between different levels (higher or lower) of examination would have to be taken into account. And thirdly, since the number of ICE papers taken by individual students varied, to have based the ICE index on the sum of grades awarded for all subjects taken would have resulted in an index which might have been biased in favour of students who had taken a relatively large number of subjects and might not necessarily have adequately reflected level of achievement.

Arising from these considerations, a number of decisions were made about the method of calculating an ICE index. In the first place, the weighting system for grades within each level should reflect differences in letter grades; in other words, an A should receive a higher numerical value than a B, which in turn should receive a higher weighting than a C. Secondly, the same weighting procedure should apply to all subjects at each level; for example, a grade B in Art and in French (both common-level papers) should be awarded the same numerical value. Thirdly, a letter grade awarded for a higher-level paper should receive a higher numerical value than the same letter grade awarded for a lower-level paper. The problem of equating grades from different levels was referred to a number of experienced teachers and examiners. They were instructed to indicate the correspondence they perceived between letter grades awarded for higher, lower, and common-level papers. Their judgment was that a grade of C on a higher paper would correspond to an A on a lower paper, that D (higher) would equal B (lower), that E (higher) would equal C (lower), and that F (higher) would equal D (lower). They regarded grades awarded for a common paper as corresponding approximately to similar grades on a higher paper.

In light of these considerations, an ICE index was computed for each student in the following manner. Numerical values were assigned to each examination grade in accordance with the system outlined in Table 7.2. Since an approved secondary junior-cycle course requires that a student take six subjects and, furthermore, since all but four of the 335 students in our sample had taken at least that number of subjects, it was decided to base the overall ICE index on the grades obtained by students in their six best examination results. Thus the six highest values were identified for each student and averaged to form the student's ICE index. The two students with the highest ICE index values, i.e., 8.50

TABLE 7.2
Numerical Values Assigned to Examination Letter Grades in Weighting Scheme for ICE Index

	Examination Letter Grades		
Numerical values	*On higher-level paper*	*On lower-level paper*	*On common-level paper*
9	A		A
8	B		B
7	C	A	C
6	D	B	D
5	E	C	E
4	F	D	F
3	NG	E	NG
2		F	
1		NG	

points, had each received three A grades and three B grades on the three higher-level papers and on three common-level papers. At the other extreme, the student with the lowest ICE index value, i.e., 3.67 points, had received E grades on two common-level papers and on two lower-level papers, and no grades on two further common papers.

The mean and standard deviation for the ICE index were 6.13 and .92 respectively.[3]

Correlates of performance on the ICE

Correlations were calculated (Table 7.3) between the ICE index (ICEX) and each of the home-background, educational-history, type of primary school attended, and personal-characteristic variables. These variables were also correlated with the students' results on the three most popular ICE subjects, Irish, English, and Mathematics. Separate scores for these three subjects were obtained by combining higher and lower-course grades according to the scaling scheme described in Table 7.2. In addition to the primary-school variables, two post-primary school measures were included in the analyses. These were type of post-primary school attended (secondary or vocational) and boarding-school status (whether or not the student was attending a boarding school).

The correlations between the home-background and the ICE indices are quite small. Number of children in family is the only variable to correlate significantly with each of the four ICE indices. Students from smaller families tended to do slightly better on the examinations than students from larger families. Although the correlations are statistically significant, in no case do they account for more than 6% of the variation in the ICE indices. Perhaps the most interesting finding concerns the relationship between socio-economic status and the ICE indices. With the exception of the one for Mathematics (.17), the correlations are not significant.

Virtually all of the correlations between the educational-history variables and the ICE measures are statistically significant. Class place (a student's rank in class in primary school) has the highest correlations with the ICEX and the three subject indices. The relationships between assessments of scholastic progress of students at primary school and performance on the ICE show a certain amount of subject specificity. Thus, apart from class place, indices of students' scholastic progress in Irish while at primary school have the highest correlations with ICE Irish, while indices of progress in Mathematics have the highest correlations with ICE Mathematics. This relationship does not hold for English, however. While almost all of the correlations between the primary-school subject ratings and ICE performance are significant, each accounts independently for relatively little (usually less than 10%) of the variation in any of the Intermediate Certificate indices.

In general, the relationships between the type of primary school which students had attended and the ICE indices are weak. None of these variables correlate significantly with ICEX. However, attendance at a Catholic religious primary school correlates positively (.12) with performance in Irish on the Intermediate Certificate Examination, while attendance at a Protestant primary school correlates negatively (-.15); in both instances the relationship is slight. Students who had attended town and rural primary schools tend to score slightly higher on the Irish examination than students who had attended urban schools. Students who had attended larger primary schools tend to fare slightly better on the English examination in the ICE than students who had attended smaller schools. Attendance at an all-male primary school was positively correlated (.26) and at an all-female primary school negatively correlated (-.27) with performance on ICE Mathematics.

Among the set of primary-school variables, verbal reasoning ability is unquestionably the single best predictor of ICE performance. Scores on this test correlate .52 with the overall ICE index and .54 with the Mathematics index. The second best predictor of ICE performance is satisfactory classroom behaviour. This personality variable, which reflects

TABLE 7.3
Correlations Between Intermediate Certificate Examination Results and Primary and Post-Primary Measures

Variables	*ICEX* N:331	*Irish* N:330	*English* N:332	*Math* N:330
Home background				
1. Socio-economic status	.10	.05	.08	.17**
2. Number of children	-.24***	-.16**	-.14*	-.18***
3. Modified ordinal position	.01	-.03	-.03	.03
4. Father living	.01	-.03	-.01	-.04
5. Mother living	-.06	-.03	-.05	.00
Educational history				
1. Class place	.45***	.40***	.42***	.40***
2. School progress	.22***	.27***	.21***	.26***
3. Irish Reading	.28***	.35***	.25***	.17***
4. Oral Irish	.23***	.29***	.24***	.11*
5. Written Irish	.26***	.26***	.30***	.16**
6. English Reading	.18***	.16**	.12*	.18***
7. Oral English	.15**	.09	.10	.16**
8. Written English	.19***	.14*	.21***	.16**
9. Mechanical Arithmetic	.20***	.14*	.16**	.25***
10. Problem Arithmetic	.33***	.20***	.31**	.39***
11. Absenteeism	-.13*	-.11*	-.15**	-.11*
12. School grade at age twelve	.16**	.06	.16**	.17**

TABLE 7.3 (contd.)

Variables	*ICEX* N:331	*Irish* N:330	*English* N:332	*Math* N:330
Type of school attended				
1. Catholic lay admin.	-.03	-.05	-.09	-.07
2. Catholic religious admin.	.01	.12*	.06	.05
3. Protestant admin.	-.04	-.15**	-.05	.05
4. Private admin.	.09	-.04	.09	.05
5. Number of teachers	.07	.07	.12*	.03
6. All male	.07	.02	-.03	.26**
7. All female	-.05	.02	.09	-.27**
8. Mixed gender	-.02	-.04	-.07	.01
9. School location	.08	.11*	.00	.07
10. Class size	-.02	-.01	.01	.02
Personal characteristics				
1. Verbal reasoning ability	.52***	.45***	.49***	.54***
2. Gender	-.10	-.01	.06	-.33***
3. Satisfactory class. behav.	.46***	.42***	.40***	.38***
4. Group leadership	.13*	.06	.19***	.17**
5. Health/extroversion	.01	-.01	.09	.06
6. Aesthetic behaviour	.04	.04	.07	.01
Post-primary characteristics				
1. Secondary/Vocational	-.19***	-.18***	-.22***	-.22***
2. Boarding/Non-boarding	-.22***	-.21***	-.16**	-.20***

$^{*}p < .05$ $^{**}p < .01$ $^{***}p < .001$

such characteristics as the student's keenness, curiosity, and concentration while at primary school, correlates .46 with the overall ICE index and to a slightly lesser extent with performance on the three subject indices. With one exception, the correlations between gender and the ICE indices are not statistically significant. The exception is Mathematics; the correlation between performance on this subject and gender (-.33) indicates that girls do less well than boys. Finally, there is a slight though significant correlation between students' group leadership ability on the one hand and ICEX and ICE English and ICE Mathematics on the other.

The correlation between verbal reasoning ability and the ICE indices indicates that students with high scores on this variable tend to get relatively high scores on the ICE, while students with low verbal ability scores get low examination scores. Strong supporting evidence for this conclusion may be found in Table 7.4. On virtually all of the higher and lower papers, students who had been awarded the higher letter grades tended to have relatively high verbal reasoning scores. For example, the mean verbal ability scores of students who obtained B-grades in Higher English and in Higher Mathematics were 119.7 and 118.8 respectively while mean scores for students who obtained D-grades in these examinations were 107.3 in each instance. This positive relationship between students' verbal ability scores and ICE performance applied also to most of the popular common-level subject papers. Latin and, in particular, Art were the most notable exceptions to this trend.

The data in Table 7.4 are of special interest in light of the procedure used earlier to equate higher, lower, and common-level papers. In general, they support the conclusions that a grade of C on a higher paper corresponds to a grade of A on a lower paper and, to a lesser extent, that common grades should be equated with higher grades. The latter conclusion is more valid for History-Geography, Science A, French, and Latin than for Commerce, Home Economics, and Art; the grade levels in terms of verbal reasoning ability for these last three subjects correspond much more closely to lower than to higher grades.

Each of the two post-primary school characteristics which we considered correlates significantly with the ICE measure (Table 7.3). By comparison with vocational-school students, secondary-school students tend to score higher on the ICEX and on the Irish, English, and Mathematics indices. Similarly, boarding school students tend to score slightly higher than non-boarding students on these measures.

So far we have examined the relationships between our indices of Intermediate Certificate Examination performance and a series of

TABLE 7.4
Intermediate Certificate Examination Grades Obtained by Students of Varying Levels of Verbal Reasoning Ability

Mean Verbal Reason-ing Ability Score	On higher-level paper			On lower-level paper			On common-level papers						
	Irish	*English*	*Math*	*Irish*	*English*	*Math*	*Hist./ Geog.*	*Science A*	*French*	*Commerce*	*Home Economics*	*Latin*	*Art*
120		B	B										
118	B												
116			C				B	B				A, C	
114		C							C			B	
112	C			A		A		C	B				
110							C	D				E	C
108		D	D			B			D		B	D	
106	D				B	C				B			
104				B			D			C	C		
102				C	C				E				E
100									F				D
98				D	D	D, E		E		D, E			
96							E					F	
94				E				F			D		
92											E		
90						F	F						
88					E								

Note: Mean verbal reasoning scores were not calculated for grade categories which had 6 or fewer students. The subjects listed represent the most popular papers (see Table 7.1).

individual variables. However, we know that many of these individual variables are themselves inter-related. There is much to be said for taking whatever relationships may exist among such predictor variables into account when examining their relationship to a criterion such as performance on the Intermediate Certificate Examination. Further, if we confine ourselves to correlations between pairs of variables, we cannot estimate the cumulative value of the predictor variables in predicting a criterion. Taken together, a group of predictors might be much more effective than any single predictor. The use of multiple regression analysis allows us to take into account inter-relationships between variables as well as to estimate the cumulative power of a set of combined variables to predict a criterion.

We looked first at the relationship between the set of primary-school measures and the overall index of performance on the ICE (ICEX). In effect, this analysis sought to determine the proportion of the overall variation in students' scores on the ICEX that could be explained by information obtained about the students at least three years before they sat for the examination. The results of the analyses reveal that, taken *together*, the primary-school variables account for 54.74% of the variation in ICEX scores. Furthermore, over 35% of this variation can be attributed to four measures: verbal reasoning ability (which accounts for 27.26%), satisfactory classroom behaviour (which accounts for an additional 5.67%), class place (accounting for an additional 1.73%), and school progress (accounting for an additional 1.51%). Thus, students with relatively high scores in the ICEX tend to have high verbal reasoning ability and satisfactory classroom behaviour scores and are likely to have had high class rankings and to have received positive satisfactory progress ratings while in primary school.

Similar analyses were carried out to determine the extent of the relationship between the primary-school variables and performance on each of the three major ICE subjects, Irish, English, and Mathematics. In the case of Irish,[4] 39.76% of the variation is accounted for by the primary-school variables. Of this total, 30% is accounted for by five variables: verbal reasoning ability (18.90%), satisfactory classroom behaviour (6.19%), grade achieved by age twelve (3.28%),[5] Protestant administration (1.74%), and school location (1.55%). Thus, a student with a high score in Irish tended to have scored highly on the verbal reasoning test and to have received relatively high ratings on satisfactory classroom behaviour. To a considerably lesser extent, attendance at a non-Protestant and non-city primary school contributes to a relatively high score on the Irish examination.

The primary-school variables account for 36.30% of the variation on the English ICE index, which is slightly less than that accounted for in the case of Irish. Again, verbal reasoning ability proves to be the most important variable, accounting for 24.22% of the variation. It is followed in turn by class place (4.18%) and attendance at an all-female primary school (1.03%). Together, these three variables account for 29.42% of the total variation that can be attributed to the primary-school variables. Thus, relatively high scores on the English index were obtained by students with relatively high verbal reasoning scores who had received above-average class rankings, and had attended all-female primary schools.

The primary-school variables account for more variation in ICE Mathematics (51.26%) than in either Irish or English. A subset of four measures account for over 40% of the variation: verbal reasoning ability (29.18%), gender (7.63%), place in class (3.28%) and Problem Arithmetic (1.61%). Thus, a high level of performance in Mathematics in the ICE was associated with relatively high verbal reasoning ability, being male, having had a relatively high place in class while at primary school, and not having had difficulty with Problem Arithmetic while at primary school.

The number of students taking the ICE who had attended a boarding school was small (N:27). The performance of these students on the overall ICE index and also in Irish, English, and Mathematics was compared with the performance of the much larger sample of non-boarding students. The purpose of this comparison was to determine if attendance at this type of post-primary school was significantly related to examination performance after the differences between the two samples on the primary-school variables had been taken into account. In other words, did attendance at boarding school explain unique portions of the variation in ICEX and in the indices of performance in Irish, English, and Mathematics? We found that attendance at boarding school did in fact account for a small but unique portion (2.43%) of the variation in ICEX.[6] Furthermore, boarding-school attendance accounted for unique portions of the variation in each of the ICE Irish (1.30%),[7] English (1.01%),[8] and Mathematics (2.74%),[9] indices. In each instance, attendance at a boarding school was associated with superior student performance on the Intermediate Certificate Examination.

We saw in Chapter 3 that vocational schools tended to attract students who, by comparison with secondary-school students, had scored lower on the verbal reasoning ability test and had received poorer achievement ratings in primary school. Given this background, it is not surprising that vocational students fared less well on the ICE than their secondary-school counterparts. It could be argued that the failure of vocational-school students to do as well as the secondary students on the ICE simply reflected initial differences in ability and achievement between the two samples. Alternatively, it might be argued that attendance at a vocational school further adversely affected students' chances of doing well on the ICE. Thus, it was important to attempt to determine whether or not attendance at a vocational, as opposed to a secondary school, was in itself significantly related to performance on the ICE (i.e., after the initial differences between vocational and secondary-school students had been taken into consideration). In analytic terms, the issue concerned the extent to which attendance at a vocational (as opposed to a secondary) school explained a unique portion of the variation in student performance on the Intermediate Certificate Examination.

The results of our analyses show that type of post-primary school attended does not account for a unique portion of the variation in students' scores on the overall measure of performance on the ICE.[10] Further, the type of post-primary school attended does not contribute uniquely to variation in students' scores on either the English[11] or Irish[12] indices of ICE performance. In the case of Mathematics, however, type of post-primary school attended does account for a small but unique portion of the variation (0.70%) in students' scores on the examination index.[13] Students who had attended secondary school tended to score slightly higher than vocational-school students on the Mathematics examination even after the differences between the two samples in terms of primary-school variables had been taken into account.

Among ICE candidates, the correlation (–.25) between student gender and verbal reasoning ability indicated that boys (N:146) had scored higher than girls (N:189) on the verbal ability test. The difference between the means for boys (M:108.23) and for girls (M:101.52) is statistically significant.[14] Given this difference and the fact that verbal reasoning ability is correlated (.52) with the ICEX, it seems reasonable to expect that boys would perform better than girls on the ICE. However, the difference between the mean ICEX scores for boys (6.23) and for girls (6.05) is not significant.[15] When the effects of differences in verbal ability between the two samples are taken into account, the correlation between student gender and ICEX (–.07) is again not significant. Stated another way, knowledge about a student's gender does not help to explain or account for variation in ICE performance as measured by the ICEX.

The relationships between gender and the Irish, English, and Mathematics indices were also examined. The correlation between gender and performance in Irish (-.01) is extremely small; it is still only .02 when verbal ability is taken into account. Neither correlation is significant. The correlation between gender and English performance is .06; controlling for verbal ability it is .11. The latter correlation is significant; after controlling for differences in verbal ability, girls tended to score slightly higher than boys on the ICE English index. Finally, the correlation between gender and Mathematics is -.33, which is significant and indicates that boys performed better than girls. When the effects of verbal reasoning ability are taken into account, the correlation between gender and Mathematics remains significant (-.33).

Number of ICE subjects taken

Apart from the stipulation that a student's junior-cycle course must include a minimum of six examination subjects, no guidelines are offered as to the number of subjects a student should take in the Intermediate Certificate Examination. In many cases, school policy, staffing and timetabling concerns dictate the number of subjects which are available to students. In other instances, able students are encouraged to take additional subjects. Concern is sometimes expressed over the number of ICE subjects taken by some students. It has been argued, for example, that students who take eight or nine subjects have less time to devote to each subject than students in other schools who take six or seven subjects, and as a result the former students cannot be expected to perform as well as the latter. In our sample, of those who sat for six or more ICE subjects (N:331), 82.8% sat for more than the minimum number of examination papers. The correlation between the number of subjects taken and performance on the ICE, as measured by the ICEX, was significant (.34). Thus it would appear that, compared to students who take relatively few subjects, those who take a lot tend to have better results on their best six subjects. It might be argued that brighter students, in terms of verbal reasoning ability, take more subjects and that the correlation between the number of subjects taken and performance on the ICE simply reflects the significant relationship (.52) that exists between verbal reasoning ability and ICEX. Our data, however, do not support the argument that the relationship between the number of subjects taken and performance on the ICE can be attributed to verbal ability. The correlation between number of subjects taken and verbal reasoning ability is very small and is not statistically significant (.04).

The Leaving Certificate Examination

Of the original sample of 500, a total of 377 (75.4%) completed a junior-cycle course in either a secondary (N:287) or a vocational school (N:90). At this stage, 65 students in secondary school and 68 in vocational school left school. During the subsequent two-year senior-cycle course, an additional 9 secondary and 13 vocational students left, leaving a total of 222 (212 secondary, 10 vocational) candidates for the Leaving Certificate Examination. Thus, a total of 44.4% of the original sample completed the senior-cycle course.

Over 90% of the students sat the LCE either in 1973 or 1974. Slightly over half (129, i.e., 58.1%) took the examination in June 1973, at which time their ages ranged from 17 years one month to 18 years one month. In 1974, a total of 73 (32.9%) students aged between 18 years one month and 19 years one month sat for the examination. Of the remainder, ten (4.5%) were aged over 19 years one month when they took the examination in 1975, and nine (4.1%) had taken it as early as 1972 when they were aged between 16 years one month and 17 years one month. The year in which one student took the examination was not known. There was a slight tendency for the more able students in terms of verbal reasoning ability to take the LCE at an earlier age. As evidence of this, it was found that the mean verbal ability score of the 1972 candidates was 114.67; for the 1973, 1974, and 1975 candidates, the respective mean scores were 109.36, 104.19, and 94.70.

As a group, the LCE candidates tended to be members of families that were above average in terms of socio-economic status. They had slightly fewer brothers and sisters (.50) than students in the overall sample. Their primary-school educational-history records were superior, especially in terms of number of grades covered by age 12, overall school progress rating, class rank, and performance in different subject areas, especially in Written Irish. Furthermore, their ratings on satisfactory classroom behaviour were substantially superior to those recorded by the overall sample. Their overall mean verbal reasoning ability score (107.29) was more than 7 points greater than that of the overall sample. Finally, their pass rates on both the ICE and the DGCE were superior to the corresponding rates for all ICE and DGCE candidates.

The *Rules and programme for secondary schools* (Ireland: Department of Education, 1975a) specify that the approved course for recognized senior pupils must include not less than five subjects, of which one must be Irish. Under certain circumstances (e.g., diplomats' children), a modern continental language may be substituted for Irish. The Department of Education recommends strongly that, since high standards are set in the LCE, 'pupils should not be presented in too many subjects — not more than seven in any case' (Ireland: Department of Education, 1973, p. 29). In the present study, the majority (87.8%) of the 222 candidates, took seven or fewer subjects. More specifically, one student (0.5%) took four subjects, ten (4.5%) took five subjects, 72 (32.4%) took six subjects, and 112 (50.5%) took seven subjects. A total of 27 (12.2%) students presented themselves for more than the recommended number of subjects; of this total, 23 (10.4%) took eight subjects while four others (1.8%) took as many as nine subjects. The mean verbal reasoning scores of students who took examinations in five (106.10), six (105.08), and seven (107.37) subjects were similar. Considerably higher mean verbal reasoning scores were recorded by the relatively small number of students who had taken either eight (M:112.09) or nine (M:125.75) subjects. Within the two largest categories of students, i.e., those who took six subjects and those who took seven subjects, the difference in mean verbal ability scores was not statistically significant.[16]

The fifteen most popular examination subjects in the LCE among the students in our sample are listed in Table 7.5. The table also presents details of the national LCE results for 1973, the year when over half of the present sample took the examination. The data indicate that all but one student in our sample took both Irish and English as subjects in the examination. Mathematics and Geography proved to be the next most popular subjects. It is interesting to note that the percentage taking Mathematics is down by approximately 10% from the corresponding percentage for the ICE (cf. Table 7.1). Less than half the students sat for any one of the remaining subjects. The results for 15 additional LCE subjects, each of which, with the exception of Spanish (N:15), attracted fewer than ten students are omitted from the table.

Some examinations were more popular among girls than among boys. These included Home Economics (which was taken exclusively by girls), Art, Biology, and French. On the other hand, more boys than girls took examinations in Mathematics, Economics, Physics, Higher-level History, and Ordinary-level Latin. Over 18% of girls did not take Mathematics at all.[17] The small number of girls (N:2) who took Higher Mathematics is particularly noteworthy. Although the number of boys (N:20) who took this subject was also small, a boy was ten times more likely than a girl to do so.

Since a number of third-level educational institutions require that a student takes at least one (and in some instances all) of the three subjects, Irish, English, and Mathematics, the high percentage taking these

TABLE 7.5
Number of Students Taking Leaving Certificate Examinations in Each of 15 Most Popular Subjects, by Gender

Subject	*Female (N:116)*	*Male (N:106)*	*Total (N:222)*		*Percentage of sample*		*Percentage of all 1973 candidates (N:25,280)**	
Irish (Higher)	41	32	73	222	32.9	100.0	30.2	97.2
Irish (Lower)	75	74	149		67.1		67.0	
English (Higher)	49	40	89	221	40.1	99.6	36.6	98.8
English (Lower)	67	65	132		59.5		62.2	
Mathematics (Higher)	2	20	22	198	9.9	89.2	9.4	87.1
Mathematics (Lower)	93	83	176		79.3		77.7	
Geography (Higher)	43	35	78	151	35.1	68.0	38.3	70.2
Geography (Lower)	39	34	73		32.9		31.9	
History (Higher)	16	25	41	99	18.5	44.6	20.4	43.6
History (Lower)	34	24	58		26.1		23.2	
French (Higher)	27	14	41	99	18.5	44.6	20.5	46.7
French (Lower)	41	17	58		26.1		26.2	
Latin (Higher)	23	22	45	77	20.3	34.7	17.6	34.8
Latin (Lower)	7	25	32		14.4		17.2	
Biology (Higher)	23	14	37	55	16.7	24.8	14.2	25.1
Biology (Lower)	13	5	18		8.1		10.9	

TABLE 7.5 (contd.)

Subject	*Female (N:116)*	*Male (N:106)*	*Total (N:222)*		*Percentage of sample*		*Percentage of all 1973 candidates (N:25,280)**	
Home Econ. (Higher)	21	0	21	52	9.5	23.5	11.8	27.4
Home Econ. (Lower)	31	0	31		14.0		15.6	
Economics (Higher)	6	20	26	44	11.7	19.8	8.4	16.8
Economics (Lower)	7	11	18		8.1		8.4	
Art (Higher)	12	3	15	44	6.8	19.9	9.2	22.4
Art (Lower)	22	7	29		13.1		13.2	
Accounting (Higher)	9	12	21	43	9.5	19.4	7.5	19.4
Accounting (Lower)	13	9	22		9.9		11.9	
Chemistry (Higher)	8	22	30	42	13.5	18.9	10.0	18.3
Chemistry (Lower)	4	8	12		5.4		8.3	
Business Org. (Higher)	1	7	8	37	3.6	16.7	6.2	21.1
Business Org. (Lower)	18	11	29		13.1		14.9	
Physics (Higher)	0	18	18	35	8.1	15.8	6.0	11.5
Physics (Lower)	3	14	17		7.7		5.5	

*Ireland: Department of Education, 1975b.

subjects is understandable. In many instances, we suspect that within a particular school, a student's choice of other LCE subjects and subject levels (higher or ordinary courses) may be quite limited and may be determined by staffing and time-tabling factors. In other instances, knowledge concerning the difficulty of certain subjects and the amount of study required to prepare for the examinations probably influences both the selection of individual subjects and the level at which the course is taken. Where choices do exist, factors such as student interest and knowledge of entry requirements for particular career or third-level courses of studies no doubt play important roles in the selection both of subjects and subject levels. For example, students must have taken Irish at higher level and English and Mathematics at either higher or ordinary level before they can be considered for admission to a college of education. Whatever the reason for opting for certain subjects and subject levels, the majority of LCE candidates in our sample took Irish, English, Mathematics, and Geography as examination subjects. None of the remaining 26 subjects was taken by more than 45% of the sample.

To qualify for the award of a Leaving Certificate, a student had to obtain a grade D or higher in at least five subjects or in four subjects including Irish. Of the total of 222 LCE candidates in our sample, 208 or 93.7% met the qualification requirements. This qualification or passing rate is slightly above the passing rates recorded for all students who took the examination in 1973 (91.2%) and 1974 (90.4%) (Ireland: Department of Education, 1975b).

Leaving Certificate Examination results were reported in the form of letter grades which corresponded to percentage ranges. The distribution of the letter grades awarded to the students in our sample for higher and

TABLE 7.6
Number of Students Obtaining Grades of Varying Values on all Examinations Taken for the Leaving Certificate

Grade	*Percentage range*	*Higher/Common level*	*Lower level*
A	85+	5	17
B	70-84	90	92
C	55-69	228	291
D	40-54	252	371
E	25-39	25	75
F	10-24	11	36
No Grade	- 9		1

ordinary papers is given in Table 7.6. Since the number of letter grades awarded for common-level subjects was small (N:21), they were not treated separately. Instead they were grouped with the grades for higher-level subjects. On both the higher (including common) and lower-level examination subjects, C and D were the most frequently awarded grades. In fact, C and D grades accounted for 76.4% of all grades awarded. Equally interesting was the reluctance of the examiners to award A grades. With the exception of Latin (N:1), Geography (N:2), and Art (N:2), none of the students received an A grade on any of the higher-level examination subjects. On the ordinary-level examination papers, the limited number of A grades was confined to Mathematics (N:16) and History (N:1).

Most advantageous LCE subjects

For students interested in proceeding to some form of third-level education, obtaining a pass on the LCE is not the major concern; students need to get good grades in at least six subject areas. Normally, the admission procedures to third-level educational institutions involve creating an order of merit for applicants; this is done by assigning points to letter grades awarded for the student's six best LCE results. Different third-level educational institutions use different weighting systems in creating order of merit lists. Given the degree of competitiveness and the difficulty of gaining admission to third-level educational institutions, the question of whether one particular combination of LCE subjects is more advantageous (in terms of gaining points) than another is clearly of interest. If one particular set of LCE subjects offers a greater probability of obtaining higher points than another set, then it is clearly in the student's interest, if the option is available, to select that particular set.

We cannot provide definitive evidence on this issue from the data in our study since we do not know how precisely students selected the subjects in which they took examinations. For example, if more students were awarded higher grades in Latin than in Geography can we infer that Latin is the easier subject? Or might the difference be attributable to the fact that more able students study Latin rather than Geography? Since we do, however, have data on student verbal reasoning ability and also on post-primary school achievement (ICEX), we can check the extent to which the samples of students taking different subjects are comparable on these two measures. Thus, we have some kind of basis, even if not a very satisfactory one, for comparing marking systems.

For our analyses, numerical values were assigned to letter grades for the six best Leaving Certificate Examination subjects in the following manner: on a higher or common paper, grade A = 5 points; B = 4; C = 3; D = 2; on an ordinary paper, grade A = 2 and B = 1.[18] Two separate probability indices were calculated. The first indicated the probability that a student would obtain 1 or more points in a particular subject. The data which are derived from the examination results of 222 candidates are summarized in Table 7.7. The data are confined to the 15 most popular subjects; each subject was taken by a minimum of 15% of the sample.

TABLE 7.7
Probability of Obtaining 1+ and 3+ Points on 15 LCE Subjects

Examination subjects listed in order of popularity	*1+ Points*	*N*	*3+ Points*	*N*
1. Irish	.396	222	.712	73
2. English	.416	221	.539	89
3. Mathematics	.369	198	.500	22
4. Geography	.536	151	.385	78
5. History	.485	99	.366	41
6. French	.434	99	.610	41
7. Latin	.597	77	.711	45
8. Biology	.636	55	.405	37
9. Home Economics	.423	52	.333	21
10. Economics	.477	44	.462	26
11. Art	.364	44	.733	15
12. Accounting	.465	43	.571	21
13. Chemistry	.691	42	.433	30
14. Business Organization	.270	37	.500	8
15. Physics	.486	35	.722	18

For students who were anxious to obtain at least one point from the listed LCE subjects, the most advantageous subjects were Chemistry, Biology, Latin, and Geography, while the least advantageous were Business Organization, Art, and Mathematics. Even when the analysis is confined to the most popular subjects and allowance is made for the fact that the student has Irish, English, and Mathematics, it is apparent that Latin or Geography were better 'bets' for getting at least one point than either French or History.[19]

Students competing for admission to areas of study which are highly selective would require considerably more than 1 point from most of their LCE subjects if they were to have a reasonable opportunity of gaining admission. Of necessity, they would be obliged to take a majority of higher level papers. When a more rigorous criterion than 1+ points is used, e.g., 3+ points (i.e., Grade C or better on a higher level paper), the results are somewhat different. The data which are confined to candidates for higher and common level papers indicate that the most advantageous subjects are Art, Physics, Irish, and Latin, while the least advantageous are Home Economics, History, Geography, and Biology. It is interesting to note that higher level Mathematics which was taken by a small but select proportion[20] of LCE candidates tended to receive relatively few of the higher grades (worth 3+ points). However, when a double weight is awarded for Mathematics grades obtained on higher papers, as was done by a number of universities, the probability of gaining a minimum of 3 points increases to .909.

In most instances, it will not be possible for a student to select all his or her LCE subjects from the list of subjects in Table 7.7. Apart from the obvious fact that the majority of these subjects are not offered in most schools, entry requirements to third-level institutions generally require that a student should have taken one, two, or in some cases all three of the subjects, Irish, English, and Mathematics. Obviously, this limits a student's choice. However, even in such a case it would appear that a student who takes Latin has a much better prospect of gaining a high grade than one taking either History or Geography.

Computing an LCE index

Given the fact that students could opt for different Leaving Certificate Examination subjects and also different levels in these subjects, a common index or metric of LCE performance was necessary to identify factors related to overall student performance on the examination. Since many third-level educational institutions require students to have taken six LCE subjects for admission, it was decided that the index should be based on the results of six subjects. Accordingly, indices were not computed for the small number (N:11) of students who had taken five or less subjects in the examination.

Four separate indices of LCE performance were computed to determine the effects of different weighting systems on each index. The first of these, the scaled points index, had been developed in an earlier study (Madaus, Kellaghan, & Rakow, 1975). In computing the indices, the examination grades of the student's six best LCE subject results were taken into consideration. For the first index, the scaling system used to transfer letter grades into numerical values was as follows:

on a higher paper: A = 92, B = 77, C = 62, D = 47, E = 30, F = 17; on an ordinary paper: A = 56, B = 49, C = 41, D = 33, E = 25, F = 15; took the paper but no grade given = 5 on both papers.

The second index, the *university index*, was one adopted by university colleges (Dublin and Cork). The system of scoring was as follows: higher papers, grade A = 5 points, B = 4, C = 3, D = 2; on an ordinary paper, grade A = 2 and B = 1. A double score was awarded on the higher paper in Mathematics.

The third index was based on the system used in the selection of students for admission to colleges of education. In calculating this index, students' grades in Irish, English, and Mathematics had to be included along with the best three grades from among the student's remaining LCE subjects. Each LCE grade was assigned a numerical value as follows: A = 72, B = 60, C = 48, D = 36. Numerical values for Irish and Mathematics were assigned a weight of 1.5. Numerical values of grades scored on ordinary-level papers were reduced by one-third.

The fourth and final index was computed in the same manner as the ICE index described earlier. For higher-level papers, values ranging from 9 for an A to 3 for NG (no grade) were assigned and for ordinary-level papers, values ranged from 7 for an A to 1 for NG.

Students' scores were computed for each of the four indices. Correlations between the indices indicate that there is a very high measure of agreement among them (Table 7.8). Given this, it seemed reasonable to assume that from the point of view of explaining differences in student performance on the LCE, no one index was likely to be very different from any of the remaining three. We opted to use the fourth of the indices simply because the scoring system (see Table 7.3) was the same as that which had been used to compute the Intermediate Certificate Examination index (ICEX). The label LCEX was assigned to the Leaving Certificate Examination index.

TABLE 7.8
Correlations among Indices of LCE (N:211)

	University	*College of Education*	*LCEX*
Scaled Points	.95	.97	.97
University		.97	.95
College of Education			.98

Correlates of performance on the LCE

Each of the primary-school measures of home background, educational history, type of school attended, and personal characteristics was correlated with the LCEX as well as with student scores on the three most popular LCE subjects, Irish, English, and Mathematics.[21] (For each of these three LCE subjects, letter grades were transformed into numerical values using the same procedure as had been used to compute the LCEX.) In addition to the primary-school measures, six post-primary school variables were included in the analyses. Two of these referred to characteristics of the post-primary school (whether vocational or secondary, and whether boarding or non-boarding) while the remaining four were indices of student performance on the Intermediate Certificate Examination.

A summary of the correlational analyses is presented in Table 7.9. None of the home-background variables was found to correlate significantly with the LCEX. Similarly, with one exception, none of the home background measures correlated significantly with the LC Irish, English, or Mathematics indices. The exception was size of family; students with fewer siblings tended to perform significantly better in the English examination than students from larger families.

In sharp contrast to the home background variables, each of the educational-history variables correlated significantly with the LCEX. As in the case of ICEX, place or rank in class proved to be the best of the educational-history variables in predicting LCEX and the Irish, English, and Mathematics LCE indices. Most of the primary teacher ratings of students' progress in specific subject areas correlated significantly with students' performance in the Leaving Certificate Examination, whether one used the overall index of performance in the examination or the separate subject indices. The relationships, however, were not very strong; correlations ranged from .06 to .42. Only in one case did an educational-history variable account for more than 18% of the variation in Leaving Certificate Examination performance; in the majority of cases, the proportion of variation accounted for was considerably less than 10 percent.

In general, the type of primary school which a student had attended was not related to LCE performance. The only exceptions to this were in the case of Irish. Students who had attended either Protestant, private primary, or city schools tended to score less well on the Irish LCE index than students who had not attended such schools. The size of the three correlations, although statistically significant, was small and suggests a weak relationship between the variables and LCE performance in Irish.

TABLE 7.9
Correlations Between Leaving Certificate Examination Results and Primary and Post-Primary Measures

Variables	*LCEX* N:211	*Irish* N:222	*English* N:221	*Math* N:198
Home background				
1. Socio-economic status	.10	.03	.04	.09
2. Number of children	-.13	-.10	-.18**	-.09
3. Modified ordinal position	-.02	-.02	.02	-.05
4. Father living	-.09	-.04	.02	-.03
5. Mother living	-.04	-.08	-.09	.03
Educational history				
1. Class place	.39***	.34***	.42***	.32***
2. School progress	.23***	.23***	.21***	.17*
3. Irish Reading	.24***	.26***	.23***	.19**
4. Oral Irish	.29***	.35***	.28***	.17*
5. Written Irish	.22***	.23***	.27***	.13
6. English Reading	.22**	.16*	.20**	.27***
7. Oral English	.18**	.12	.19**	.06
8. Written English	.24***	.19**	.30***	.13
9. Mechanical Arithmetic	.30***	.15*	.19**	.23***
10. Problem Arithmetic	.32***	.19**	.29***	.23***
11. Absenteeism	-.14*	-.13*	-.10	-.16*
12. School grade at age twelve	.14*	.00	.02	.12

TABLE 7.9 (contd.)

Variables	*LCEX* *N:211*	*Irish* *N:222*	*English* *N:221*	*Math* *N:198*
Type of school attended				
1. Catholic lay admin.	-.05	.07	-.04	.06
2. Catholic religious admin.	.04	.08	.06	-.03
3. Protestant admin.	-.08	-.20**	-.05	-.03
4. Private admin.	.07	-.14*	.00	-.04
5. Number of teachers	.10	.02	.07	.07
6. All male	.08	-.08	-.05	.10
7. All female	.00	.07	.09	-.11
8. Mixed gender	-.08	.01	-.04	.01
9. School location	.00	.15*	.03	-.03
10. Class size	.02	-.06	-.01	.02
Personal characteristics				
1. Verbal reasoning ability	.51***	.35***	.46***	.42***
2. Gender	-.02	.11	.07	-.05
3. Satisfactory class. behav.	.45***	.39***	.43***	.33***
4. Group leadership	.09	.05	.14*	.04
5. Health/extroversion	.02	.05	.03	.08
6. Aesthetic behaviour	.06	-.03	.10	.05
Post-primary characteristics				
1. Secondary/Vocational	-.09	-.14*	-.09	-.16*
2. Boarding/Non-boarding	-.15*	-.21**	-.13	-.09
3. ICEX	.82***	.69***	.71***	.56***
4. Irish ICE	.62***	.72***	.58***	.41***
5. English ICE	.62***	.56***	.65***	.39***
6. Math ICE	.61***	.49***	.47***	.57***

*$p < .05$

Both verbal reasoning ability and satisfactory classroom behaviour correlated significantly with the LCEX. Students who had scored highly on these variables while at primary school tended to score highly on the LCEX, while those who had not scored as well on both variables tended to have lower scores on the LCEX. Both variables also correlated significantly with the Irish, English, and Mathematics LCE indices. With the exception of group leadership, which correlated positively with the LC English index, none of the remaining personal variables (including gender) was significantly related to the LCE indices.

Not surprisingly, measures obtained on the students while at post-primary school tended to correlate more highly with the indices of LCE performance than did the primary-school measures. Boarding-school students tended to score slightly higher on the LCEX than non-boarding students. Attendance at a secondary as opposed to a vocational school did not appear to affect students' scores on the overall LCEX. However, attendance at a secondary school (as opposed to a vocational school) was related to slightly better performance in LCE Irish and Mathematics though not in English, while boarding-school attendance was related to slightly better performance in LC Irish but not in English or Mathematics.

Substantial correlations were recorded between performance on the Intermediate and Leaving Certificate Examinations. In particular, the relationships between the overall indices (ICEX and LCEX) was strong (.82). Thus, approximately 67% of the variation in students' scores on the LCEX could be accounted for by performance on the ICEX. The best subject predictor of performance in LCE Irish was ICE performance in the same subject. Similarly both English and Mathematics ICE performance proved to be the best predictors of the corresponding LCE measures. A comparison of the size of these correlations indicates that the relationship between the corresponding ICE and LCE indices was stronger for Irish (.72) than for either English (.65) or Mathematics (.57).

When the total set of primary-school variables was related to Leaving Certificate Examination performance in multiple-regression analysis, the set accounted for 40.61% of variation.[22] The three best predictors (considered together) of LCEX were, in order of entry, verbal reasoning ability (which accounted for 21.43% of the variation), satisfactory classroom behaviour (which accounted for an additional 7.30%) and grade achieved by the student at age twelve (accounting for a further 2.85%). Altogether, these three variables accounted for 31.85% of LCEX variation.

Together, the set of primary-school variables accounted for 39.84% of the variation in the Irish LCE index. The three best predictors of performance in the LC examination in Irish, accounting for 24.20% of student variation, were satisfactory classroom behaviour (which accounted for 14.36%) and verbal reasoning ability (accounting for an additional 5.23%), both of which contributed positively, and Protestant administration (adding an additional 4.62%), which contributed negatively.

Verbal reasoning ability and satisfactory classroom behaviour also featured among the set of three best predictors of the English LCE index. Verbal reasoning ability alone accounted for 20.37% of variation in this examination. Satisfactory classroom behaviour accounted for an additional 7.41% and gender for 3.92 percent. Thus, the data suggest that girls (slightly more so than boys) with high verbal ability scores and satisfactory school behaviour ratings were likely to receive relatively high scores on LCE English. Together the full set of primary measures accounted for 39.81% of variation in this index.

On the final index, LCE Mathematics, the primary measures accounted for 35.37% of variation in student scores. This percentage, although substantial, is somewhat less than that recorded for the other indices of Leaving Certificate Examination performance. Again, verbal reasoning ability was the first variable entered and accounted for 16.22% of the variation. The next two variables in the set of the three best predictors were English Reading (+4.92%) and Mechanical Arithmetic (+2.76%). Thus relatively high verbal reasoning ability, and satisfactory teacher ratings in English Reading and Mechanical Arithmetic were associated with relatively high scores on the LCE Mathematics index.

Separate analyses relating to boarding-school attendance revealed that attendance at a boarding school added a small but statistically significant amount to the proportion of variation explained by the primary-school measures in the case of LCEX (+2.10%), Irish (+2.52%) and English (+1.83%), but not in the case of Mathematics.[23]

The effects of attendance at a vocational as opposed to a secondary school on LCE performance, after initial differences on the primary-school variables had been taken into account, were also examined. Attendance at a vocational school during the senior-cycle course did not add a significant amount to the percentage of variation already accounted for by the primary-school measures in the overall LCEX, or in any of the Irish, English, or Mathematics indices.[24]

When considering the Intermediate Certificate Examination results, we found that boys who had taken the examination tended to have scored higher than girls on the verbal reasoning test (108.23 versus 101.52). After differences in verbal ability had been taken into account, however, the difference between the mean ICEX scores for boys and girls was not significant. Among the Leaving Certificate Examination candidates in our sample, boys again did significantly better than girls on the verbal reasoning test (111.58 versus 103.60).[25] As in the earlier analyses of ICE results, a separate analysis was carried out to determine if student gender was a significant factor in explaining LCE performance, after initial verbal reasoning differences between boys and girls had been taken into consideration. The results showed that it was not a significant factor in accounting for differences in scores on Mathematics.[26] Student gender, however, though not independently related to performance on our four LC indices (cf. Table 7.9) did add small but statistically significant amounts to the proportion of variation in the LCEX (+1.6%), Irish (+4.6%) and English (+4.4%) indices explained by verbal reasoning ability.[27] Thus, the data suggest that after verbal ability differences are taken into account, girls scored higher than boys on three of the four LC indices.

We have already seen that the amount of variation in the overall LCEX measure in the Irish, English, and Mathematics LCE indices which was attributable to primary-school variables alone ranged from approximately 35% (for Mathematics) to 41% (for LCEX). A number of post-primary school measures were added to the primary-school measures in regression analysis. These included indices of student performance in the overall ICE (i.e., ICEX) and in the ICE Irish, English and Mathematics examinations, as well as attendance at a boarding-school and type of post-primary school attended (secondary or vocational).[28] Information from our total set of variables — gathered at primary and post-primary levels — accounted for 71.50% of the variation on the overall LCEX.[29] This represents an increase of 30.89% over the 40.61% which was accounted for by the primary-school variables alone. Information on boarding-school attendance accounted for a slight increase beyond that accounted for by the primary-school variables; type of post-primary school attended, however, did not. The ICEX alone accounted for 65.26% of the variation in the LCEX.[30] This finding underlines the importance of students' performance on the ICE as a predictor of subsequent performance on the LCE. It is striking that prediction to this extent of performance on the Leaving Certificate Examination can be made on the basis of information obtained earlier in the primary and post-primary career of students.

The primary-school variables accounted for 38.94% of variation in the

LCE Irish index. Boarding-school attendance accounted for a small additional percentage. When the ICE Irish index was taken into consideration, the overall percentage of variation accounted for in the LCE index rose to 67.22%. On its own, the ICE Irish index accounted for 55.49% of the variation, which was substantially more than that accounted for by the primary-school variables. Similarly on LC English, the inclusion of the post-primary variables increased the proportion of variance accounted for from 39.81% for the primary-school variables to 55.27 percent. Attendance at a boarding-school again accounted for a small but significant increase in variance over the primary measures. Virtually all of the increase could be attributed to the ICE English index which alone accounted for 41.92% of the variation in LCE English. On the final LCE index, Mathematics, 35.37% of variance was accounted for by the primary-school measures. The addition of information on attendance at a boarding-school and on the type of post-primary school (secondary or vocational) attended by students did not add a significant amount to the percentage of variance accounted for. The inclusion of the ICE Mathematics index, however, did increase the percentage accounted for by an additional 10.78% to 46.15 percent. On its own, the ICE Mathematics index accounted for 30.04% of the variation in the corresponding LCE index.

Repeating the LCE

For the vast majority of students who took the LCE, the examination signified either the end of formal full-time education or took the form of an admission test to a third-level educational institution. A small minority of the students in our sample (N:13), however, fell into neither of these two categories. These were students who elected to repeat the examination. Admissions criteria to universities and colleges of education allowed students to take the LCE more than once; points for admission were based on a student's best grades for six subjects from a combination of two sittings. Given this system of accumulating points, it would seem reasonable for a student who was very keen to qualify for admission to a third-level institution to repeat the LCE. This would apply particularly to students who failed by a narrow margin to gain admission or to qualify for a grant on the first attempt, as well as to those who felt that their first performance on the examination did not adequately reflect their true potential.

In our study, the LCE second-sitting results were not available for one of the 13 students who repeated the examination. At the outset, it should be stressed that we do not know why individual students repeated the examination. However, since the students who repeated had relatively good grades from the first sitting, we suspect that they took the examination a second time to improve their points total with a view to qualifying for positions in third-level institutions. In fact, nine of the 12 were eventually admitted to a third-level school on the basis of their LCE points. We do not know, however, if they qualified for the institutions or faculties of their choice.

The mean number of subjects taken by the 12 students on the second sitting was 5.33 (SD = 2.31). The number of subjects ranged from as few as two to as many as nine. Four students took one subject and one student took two subjects which they had not taken on the first LCE sitting. Mathematics was the subject taken most frequently in the repeat examination; it was taken by 11 of the 12 students for whom we have results. Two of the 11 students took the higher-level paper. English and Geography were taken by eight students and Irish was taken by seven. A total of 12 other subjects was taken by four or fewer students.

Students' grades on the repeat examination were compared with their original grades using the scoring system outlined in Table 7.2. A total of 58 subject papers were repeated. On 38 of these, an improvement of one or more points was recorded. No improvement was recorded for 16 papers, while in the case of the four remaining papers, grades obtained on the resit were lower than initial grades. Overall, the students improved their scores by an average of 1.07 points. Among the four most repeated subjects, the mean improvement in score was 1.14 for Geography, 1.13 for English, 0.73 for Mathematics, and 0.71 for Irish.

To gain admission to most third-level institutions, the important question concerns the effect that repeating the LCE has on a student's *total* number of points based on his or her six best results derived from two sittings. Of the 12 students for whom initial and repeat LCE grades were available, 10 had taken at least six subjects on the first attempt. The mean number of points based on the six best LCE subjects for the 10 students was 35.00 (SD = 3.63). On the repeat examination, the mean score increased by five points to 40.00 (SD = 3.41). It is of interest that eight of the 10 subsequently graduated from third-level educational institutions, five of them with honours degrees.

Number of LCE subjects taken

The Department of Education recommends that students should not take more than seven subjects in the LCE. In the present study the majority (87.8%) of the LCE candidates took seven or fewer subjects, while 27 (12.2%) took eight or more subjects. The correlation between number of subjects taken and LCEX was .38. The correlation is clearly significant. Even after controlling for differences in verbal reasoning ability the correlation (.33) between number of subjects taken and LCEX is still significant.

Conclusion

Three out of four students completed a junior-cycle course in post-primary school by taking either the ICE or the DGCE. Two out of every three students in our sample sat for the ICE. Girls were in the majority among ICE candidates. Most students were either 15 or 16 years of age and took more than the recommended minimum number of six subjects. The vast majority took Irish, English, and Mathematics. Girls, in comparison with boys, were more likely to have taken French, Art, Commerce, and Home Economics, while boys were more likely to have opted for Science, Latin, Higher Mathematics and a number of trade-related subjects. The mean verbal reasoning score of the ICE candidates was approximately 4.5 points above the national mean.

After a further two years in post-primary school, almost 45% of the students sat for the LCE. At this stage, the number of girls slightly exceeded the number of boys. These students were approximately 17 years of age and had, on average, scored seven points above the national mean on the verbal reasoning test taken some six years previously. Most students sat for the Irish, English, and Mathematics examinations, though the proportion of girls taking Mathematics had decreased from the ICE. More girls took French, Art, and Commerce, while more boys took Physics, History, Higher Mathematics, and Latin. Grades C and D accounted for over three-quarters of all the grades awarded for higher-, common- and lower-level papers. Four measures or indices of student achievement were used at both the ICE and LCE levels. At each level, these provided measures of overall performance on the student's best six examination subjects, and also separate measures of performance on the Irish, English and Mathematics papers.

In general, student home background, as measured by father's occupation, was not a factor in explaining student performance on either the ICE or the LCE. Students from smaller families, however, tended to perform better on the ICE and also on the English LCE.

Virtually all the achievement-related primary-school measures correlated significantly with performance on both the overall ICE and LCE indices as well as with the separate measures of performance on the

Irish, English and Mathematics examinations. Of the 12 achievement-related variables, class place in primary school proved to be the best predictor of student performance on the two major post-primary state examinations. In general, however, the correlations were small (averaging approximately .21).

Not surprisingly, the type of primary school a student had attended was not generally related to student performance on either the ICE or the LCE. By comparison with students who had attended other types of primary schools, however, students who had attended Protestant primary schools generally did less well on the Irish examinations at both the ICE and LCE levels. Furthermore, students who had attended urban primary schools did not receive as high grades on the Irish papers as students from rural schools.

Verbal reasoning ability and satisfactory classroom behaviour (i.e., being keen to get on, having an enquiring mind, being able to work intently) were identified as the two best primary-school predictors of student performance on the ICE and LCE. Although ICE boys as a group had scored higher than girls on the verbal ability measure, their superiority was not reflected in level of performance on the ICE, except for Mathematics. Indeed, after allowance was made for differences in verbal reasoning ability between boys and girls, girls tended to score slightly higher on ICE English. At the LCE level, after initial verbal ability differences had been taken into account, girls tended to do better than boys on the overall LCE index and also on the English and Irish examinations. These findings suggest that girls tend to do comparatively well under the ICE and LCE systems.

Information obtained about students when they were at primary school accounted for slightly over half of the variation in student performance on the overall ICE index and on the ICE Mathematics index, and for slightly less than 40% of the variation on the Irish and English ICE papers. The same set of measures accounted for approximately 40% of variation on the overall LCE index, and on the LCE Irish and English indices and for a slightly smaller proportion of the variation on the LCE Mathematics index.

Numbers of students attending either boarding or vocational schools, especially at the LCE level, were small. After other factors, such as verbal ability, home background, and primary school achievement had been taken into account, attendance at a boarding school was positively related to performance on each of the ICE measures and on three of the four LCE measures. In each instance, the contributions were small but statistically significant. On the other hand, after initial differences between students had been taken into consideration, attendance at a secondary school as opposed to a vocational school did not contribute uniquely to performance on the ICE measures (with the exception of Mathematics) or to performance on the LCE measures.

Overall performance on the ICE correlated very highly (.82) with overall performance on the LCE. At the subject level, the correlations between ICE and LCE subjects were .69 for Irish, .71 for English, and .56 for Mathematics. The combined set of primary and post-primary school measures accounted for over 70% of the variation on the index of overall performance on the LCE.

The majority of ICE candidates took either seven or eight subjects, while the majority of LCE candidates opted for either six or seven subjects. Students who opted for more subjects tended to have scored well on the verbal ability test. It is of interest that, even after these differences in verbal ability had been taken into account, students who had taken most subjects recorded better results on their six best subjects than students who took somewhat fewer subjects.

Finally, a small number of students (N:13) opted to repeat the LCE. While the overall mean improvement in their LCE results tended to be small, it generally resulted in a gain in points which would have improved the student's chances of entering third-level education.

FOOTNOTES

1 In the present study, the number of candidates for each of the five 'groups' of subjects was small. Manual Training was taken by 38 candidates; each of the remaining four 'groups' was taken by fewer than 20 candidates. Because of the small sizes of the samples, analyses similar to those used with the ICE and LCE results could not be carried out on the DGCE results.

2 In 1970, 1971, and 1972 the percentages of ICE candidates who qualified for the award of an Intermediate Certificate (i.e., who obtained a grade D or higher in at least five subjects, including Irish) were 73.4%, 73.2%, and 76.0% respectively (Ireland: Department of Education, 1974).

3 It is recognised that an alternative weighting system would have produced somewhat different results. Two other indices were computed. In the first of these, common-level grades were given numerical values one point lower than the corresponding grades for higher-level papers; in the second, like grades from different paper levels were treated as equal (e.g., higher-, lower- and common-level A grades were each assigned the same value). The correlation between the adopted ICE index and the one that differed from it the most, i.e., the second alternative, was .95.

4 Irish indices were computed in accordance with the weighting system outlined in Table 7.2.

5 Grade at age twelve acted as a suppressor variable.
6 ICEX: $F = 13.97$; $df = 1,298$; $p < .001$
7 Irish: $F = 6.55$; $df = 1,298$; $p < .05$
8 English: $F = 4.81$, $df = 1,299$; $p < .05$
9 Mathematics: $F = 17.84$; $df = 1,299$; $p < .001$
10 ICEX: $F = 0.01$; $df = 1,298$; N.S.
11 English: $F = 0.52$; $df = 1,299$; N.S.
12 Irish: $F = 0.01$; $df = 1,298$; N.S.
13 Mathematics: $F = 4.33$; $df = 1,299$; $p < .05$
14 $F = 20.41$; $df = 1,333$; $p < .001$
15 $F = 3.06$; $df = 1,329$; N.S.
16 $F = 1.26$; $df = 1,182$; N.S.
17 An interesting aspect of the data in Table 7.5 is the difference between the numbers of students taking higher and ordinary-level papers in different subject areas. After taking into account minimum requirements for a particular choice of career or third-level college, a student with a choice of subject areas within a school may find it advantageous to select some subjects rather than others. Additional points are awarded in the admissions procedures of many third-level institutions for grades obtained on LCE higher and common papers. Given the differential reward system for subjects taken at different levels, discrepancies in the proportions of students taking higher- as opposed to ordinary-level papers in individual subject areas are of interest. In our sample, the percentage of students in a particular subject area taking higher course papers varied from 71.4% in Chemistry, 67.7% in Home Economics, and 67.3% in Biology to 11.1% in Mathematics, 21.6% in Business Organization and 32.9% in Irish.
18 An alternative scoring system which corresponds to one used earlier in this study (see Table 7.2) was also used and yielded substantially similar results.
19 Based on LCE results for the 15 most popular subjects, the probability of passing either the higher-, lower- or common-level papers was .959 for Irish, 1.000 for English, .919 for Mathematics, 1.000 for Geography, .939 for History, .980 for French, .935 for Latin, .964 for Biology, 1.000 for Home Economics, .977 for Economics, .977 for Art, 1.000 for Accounting, .905 for Chemistry, .919 for Business Organization, and .971 for Physics.
20 The mean verbal reasoning ability score for the higher-level Mathematics students was 122.23; the mean for the ordinary-level students was 106.62.
21 Indices were computed in each of the three major subject areas for all students who had taken Irish or English or Mathematics. The overall LCE index, i.e., LCEX, was computed only for students (N:211) who had taken a minimum of six LCE subjects.
22 For the regression analyses, the sample size was reduced somewhat (by 28 in the case of LCEX analyses) due to the adoption of the listwise deletion procedure for missing data. Hence, the degrees of freedom used in these analyses may differ slightly from those reported earlier.
23 LCEX: $F = 5.48$; $df = 1,150$; $p < .05$
Irish: $F = 6.56$; $df = 1,150$; $p < .05$
English: $F = 4.70$; $df = 1,150$; $p < .05$.
Mathematics: $F = 3.62$; $df = 1,150$; N.S.
24 LCEX: $F = 0.01$; $df = 1,150$; N.S..
Irish: $F = 0.47$; $df = 1,150$; N.S.
English: $F = 0.04$; $df = 1,150$; N.S.
Mathematics: $F = 1.33$; $df = 1,150$; N.S.

25 $F = 18.98$; $df = 1{,}209$; $p < .001$
26 $F = 0.83$; $df = 1{,}195$; N.S. (Partial correlation = .07)
27 LCEX: $F = 4.70$; $df = 1{,}208$; $p < .05$ (Partial correlation = .15)
Irish: $F = 12.05$; $df = 1{,}219$; $p < .01$ (Partial correlation = .23)
English: $F = 12.83$; $df = 1{,}218$; $p < .001$ (Partial correlation = .24).
28 Since the primary and post-primary measures share attributes, the total percentage of variation accounted for is less than the sum of the individual percentages accounted for by the primary and post-primary measures separately.
29 This analysis refers only to students who had taken a minimum of six LCE subjects.
30 The ICE indices for English, Irish, and Mathematics were not included in this regression analysis. Similarly, in each of the three remaining analyses for LCE Irish, English, and Mathematics, only one ICE measure, i.e., the corresponding ICE subject variable, was included.

8 Higher Education

At the end of the senior-cycle course in post-primary school, students either leave full-time education or seek admission to one of a number of third-level or higher educational institutions. In Chapter 7, we saw that 222 students (or 44.4%) of our original sample completed the senior cycle in a post-primary school by taking the Leaving Certificate Examination. At this stage, 158 (31.6% of the original sample) left school. The remaining 64 (12.8% of the original sample) enrolled in a third-level educational institution. This latter figure is close to the 11.8% of 19-year-olds who were in receipt of full-time third-level education in 1974–75 (Ireland: Department of Education, 1977). Details of the enrolment figures are presented in Table 8.1.

TABLE 8.1
Numbers of Students in Sample Attending Varying Types of Higher-Education Institutions

Type of Institution	*N*
University	36
College of Education	11
Regional Technical College	6
College of Technology	2
Domestic College	2
National Institute of Higher Education	1
Seminary	2
College of Pharmacy	1
College of Art	1
National Electronics Institute	2
	64

Practically all the third-level students in our sample had attended secondary schools. In fact, only three had taken the LCE while attending a vocational school; these enrolled in a regional technical college. None of the entrants to a university or a college of education, which together comprised 73.4% of the third-level sample, had completed the senior cycle in a vocational school.

Higher-Education Students And The Original Sample

In this section we compare the sample of higher-education students with the original sample. The purpose of the comparison is to identify variables on which the two samples differ. For each variable, a goodness of fit test was applied to the distribution of scores of students who proceeded to higher education, to determine if the scores could be considered representative of the distribution for the original sample. Table 8.2 contains the mean scores of the higher-education students and the mean scores of the original sample as well as the difference between the means expressed in standard-score format.

The largest home-background difference (and the only one that is statistically significant) occurs in the case of socio-economic status. The mean on this variable for the higher-education sample differs by slightly more than one-half a standard deviation from the mean of the original sample. It is clear that higher-education entrants tended to come from higher SES levels. Students whose fathers' occupations had been classified as professional or intermediate professional were over-represented. Whereas students from these two SES categories amounted to 31.2% of the original sample, they made up 57.8% of students entering higher education. At the other extreme, students from the two lowest SES categories (partly-skilled and unskilled) were under-represented, accounting for 17.2% of the higher-education group as opposed to 36.2% of the original sample.

A clear-cut pattern, reflecting differences in achievement, emerges when the score distributions for the higher-education and original samples are compared on the set of educational-history variables. Students who subsequently enrolled in higher-education institutions were regarded by their primary-school teachers as showing higher levels of achievement than students in general in the original sample. Over half of the students who subsequently entered third-level education (54.7%) had been ranked by their teachers in the top 30% of their classes, while less than 5% were considered to have made unsatisfactory progress at primary school, compared to 25% of the original sample. Further, relatively few of the higher-education students had, according to their primary-school teachers, experienced difficulty in any of the eight basic areas of the school curriculum (Table 8.2). In Problem Arithmetic, for

TABLE 8.2

Means (and Standard Deviations) on all Variables for Students Proceeding to Higher Education and for Students in Total Sample, Together with Standard Score Differences

Variables	*Higher education students (N:64)*		*Total sample (N:500)*		*Standard score difference*	*Goodness of fit (p)*
	M	SD	M	SD		
Home background						
1. Socio-economic status	3.42	1.01	2.80	1.13	.55	Sig.***
2. Number of children	4.92	2.50	5.65	2.74	-.27	N.S.
3. Modified ordinal position	61.73	29.81	62.79	26.53	-.04	N.S.
4. Father living	.92	.27	.95	.23	-.13	N.S.
5. Mother living	.97	.18	.98	.15	-.07	N.S.
Educational history						
1. Class place	3.64	1.07	3.06	1.05	.55	Sig.***
2. School progress	.95	.21	.75	.43	.47	Sig.***
3. Irish reading	.81	.59	.42	.91	.43	Sig.***
4. Oral Irish	.75	.67	.34	.94	.44	Sig.***
5. Written Irish	.66	.76	.21	.98	.46	Sig.***
6. English reading	.97	.25	.80	.60	.28	Sig.*
7. Oral English	.97	.25	.81	.59	.27	Sig.*
8. Written English	.91	.43	.60	.80	.39	Sig.**
9. Mechanical Arithmetic	.94	.35	.60	.80	.43	Sig.***
10. Problem Arithmetic	.69	.73	.07	1.00	.62	Sig.***
11. Absenteeism	9.66	7.32	14.54	14.61	-.33	Sig.*
12. School grade at age twelve	2.42	.66	1.95	.71	.66	Sig.***

TABLE 8.2 (contd.)

Variables	Higher education students (N:64) M	Higher education students (N:64) SD	Total sample (N:500) M	Total sample (N:500) SD	Standard score difference	Goodness of fit (p)
Type of school attended						
1. Catholic lay admin.	-.25	.98	-.06	1.00	-.19	N.S.
2. Catholic religious admin.	.00	1.01	-.07	1.00	.07	N.S.
3. Protestant admin.	-.97	.25	-.95	.31	-.06	N.S.
4. Private admin.	-.78	.63	-.92	.39	.36	Sig.**
5. Number of teachers	3.84	1.04	3.69	1.10	.14	N.S.
6. All male	-.09	1.00	-.29	.96	.21	N.S.
7. All female	-.41	.92	-.30	.98	-.11	N.S.
8. Mixed gender	-.50	.87	-.42	.91	-.09	N.S.
9. School location	2.16	.86	2.14	.90	-.01	N.S.
10. Class size	2.45	1.34	2.46	1.56	-.01	N.S.
Personal characteristics						
1. Verbal reasoning ability	115.63	12.45	100.15	15.46	1.00	Sig.***
2. Gender	-.13	1.00	.00	1.00	-.13	N.S.
3. Satisfactory class. behav.	.81	.75	.10	.91	.78	Sig.***
4. Group leadership	.16	.80	.01	.89	.17	N.S.
5. Health/extroversion	.15	.76	.12	.83	.04	N.S.
6. Aesthetic behaviour	.12	.66	.05	.72	.10	N.S.

*$p < .05$ **$p < .01$ ***$p < .001$

example, the subject area which appears to have caused difficulty for most students (46.4% of the total sample), as few as 15.6% of the higher-education group had been perceived as having experienced difficulty. The rate of progress in primary school of the subsequent higher-education students, as measured by number of classes or grade levels completed, was also superior. By age twelve, only two (i.e., 3.1%) of them had not completed fifth grade, compared to 21.8% of the total sample, while 39.1% had completed primary school as opposed to 17.4% of the total sample. Finally, the school-attendance record of the higher-education students differed significantly from that of the original sample. The average number of days missed by higher-education students in a year was approximately one week less (4.88 days) than the mean of all students in the original sample.

On nine of the ten variables relating to the type of primary school students had attended, the distributions for the higher-education students could not be considered different from the corresponding distribution for the overall sample. The one exception related to students who had attended private primary schools (N:7) who were over-represented (10.9%) among the sample of higher-education students, having accounted for only 4% of the original sample.

By far the largest difference in standard score (1.00) between the two samples was found for verbal reasoning ability. The mean score of the higher-education students (115.63) corresponded to the 84th percentile on the distribution of verbal ability scores in the overall sample. In other words, 84% of the original sample scored at or below the verbal reasoning score recorded by the average third-level education student. Looking more closely at the data, we find that as few as 7% of the higher-education sample had scored below 100 on this measure. At the other end of the distribution, 64% had scored above 110 (compared to 27.0%) of the overall sample). It should not be inferred from the over-representation of students with high verbal reasoning ability scores in the higher-education sample that the majority of students with high verbal ability scores entered third-level education. In fact, as few as 30.0% of students who had scored 110 or more on the verbal ability tests subsequently enrolled in a higher-education institution. If, however, we use 120 instead of 110 as the cut-off point, the percentage of students with such a score going on to higher education rises to 43.6.

Verbal ability differences among the three largest groups within the higher-education sample were examined. University students (N:36) scored highest (M:119.3; SD:11.2) and were followed in turn by college of education students (N:11; M:115.9; SD:11.9), and regional college students (N:6; M:101.2; SD:14.6). Given the small sample sizes, these data should be interpreted with considerable caution.

In addition to verbal reasoning ability, higher-education students could be distinguished from the original sample in terms of how teachers had rated their classroom behaviour. The former tended to have received much more positive teacher ratings on this variable than did students in the overall sample. The difference in their favour was apparent at each level of the distribution. For example, 37.5% of higher-education students had been rated at the highest level of the distribution (i.e., had scores greater than 1.00) while only 16.6% of the total sample had received ratings at this level.

Higher-Education Students And Leaving Certificate Terminal Leavers

Next we look at differences between the group of students who enrolled in full-time higher education courses and the larger group of students who left school after taking the LCE. In these analyses, in addition to the primary school variables, three post-primary school variables were included (type of post-primary school attended, whether the school was boarding or non-boarding, and students' performance on the LCE as measured by LCEX).[1]

Having established that the two samples differed *overall* from one another,[2] a series of comparisons was carried out on each of the primary and post-primary variables to identify the measures on which the higher-education and LCE terminal students differed from one another by a statistically significant amount. A summary of the comparisons is presented in Table 8.3. Significant differences were recorded on six of the educational history variables, on one relating to type of primary school attended, on two personal characteristic variables, and on one of the post-primary variables. None of the differences on the home-background variables was statistically significant.

Higher-education students, by comparison with LCE terminal leavers, tended to have been ranked higher in their classes in primary school and to have completed more grades by the age of twelve. While neither group had been considered by their teachers to have experienced any great degree of difficulty in the basic curricular areas, fewer of the subsequent higher-education students had experienced difficulties in Oral Irish, Written English, Mechanical Arithmetic, and Problem Arithmetic. Higher-education students were more likely to have attended an all-male primary school than LCE terminal leavers.

TABLE 8.3
Means (and Standard Deviations) on all Variables for Students Proceeding to Higher Education and for Leaving Certificate Terminal Leavers

	Higher education students (N:62)		*LCE terminal leavers (N:148)*		
Variables	M	SD	M	SD	F
Home background					
1. Socio-economic status	3.40	1.02	3.13	1.05	3.07
2. Number of children	4.94	2.46	5.22	2.48	.59
3. Modified ordinal position	61.90	29.24	61.16	27.17	.03
4. Father living	.92	.27	.96	.20	1.41
5. Mother living	.97	.18	.97	.16	.04
Educational history					
1. Class place	3.65	1.09	3.28	.99	5.49*
2. School progress	.95	.22	.87	.34	3.00
3. Irish Reading	.81	.60	.64	.78	2.43
4. Oral Irish	.77	.64	.49	.88	5.46*
5. Written Irish	.65	.77	.51	.86	1.09
6. English Reading	.97	.25	.88	.48	1.92
7. Oral English	.97	.25	.89	.45	1.53
8. Written English	.90	.43	.70	.71	4.23*
9. Mechanical Arithmetic	.94	.36	.68	.74	6.96**
10. Problem Arithmetic	.68	.74	.19	.99	12.29***
11. Absenteeism	9.61	7.43	10.78	12.03	.50
12. School grade at age twelve	2.42	.67	2.10	.64	10.62***

TABLE 8.3 (contd.)

Variables	*Higher education students (N:62)* M	SD	*LCE terminal leavers (N:148)* M	SD	F
Type of school attended					
1. Catholic lay admin.	-.26	.97	-.18	.99	.31
2. Catholic religious admin.	.03	1.01	-.02	1.00	.12
3. Protestant admin.	-.97	.25	-.92	.40	.80
4. Private admin.	-.81	.60	-.89	.45	1.28
5. Number of teachers	3.82	1.05	3.61	1.12	1.56
6. All male	-.06	1.01	-.35	.94	3.91*
7. All female	-.42	.92	-.20	.98	2.21
8. Mixed gender	-.52	.86	-.45	.90	.25
9. School location	2.16	.85	2.28	.85	.91
10. Class size	2.44	1.35	2.30	1.52	.38
Personal characteristics					
1. Verbal reasoning ability	115.79	12.62	103.95	12.91	37.29***
2. Gender	-.16	.99	.12	1.00	3.53
3. Satisfactory class. behav.	.82	.75	.39	.76	14.22***
4. Group leadership	.15	.79	.05	.84	.65
5. Health/extroversion	.14	.75	.22	.81	.39
6. Aesthetic behaviour	.12	.67	.11	.73	.08
Post-primary characteristics					
1. Secondary/Vocational	1.05	.22	1.04	.20	.06
2. Boarding/Non-boarding	1.84	.37	1.91	.28	2.42
3. LCEX	6.48	.84	5.07	.93	106.6***

Note: The actual number that enrolled in higher education was 64 and the number of LCE terminal leavers was 158; these numbers are reduced in this table because of missing data.

*p < .05 ***p < .01 ***p < .001

Marked differences between the two samples were recorded on the verbal ability and satisfactory classroom behaviour variables. There was about a 12-point difference between the means of the two groups on the verbal ability test. About one-third of the LCE terminal leavers scored below 100 on this measure, compared to 10.9% of the higher-education group, while slightly more than one-third (35.6%) of the former had scored 110 or greater compared to about two-thirds (64.1%) of the latter. Within the higher-education group, verbal reasoning scores ranged from a low of 88 to a high of 140.

Both higher-education students and LCE terminal leavers tended to have received positive ratings from teachers for their classroom behaviour. However, the higher-education students had been rated more positively. Approximately 37% of them had been rated in the two highest or most positive categories on the variable as compared to approximately 22% of the LCE terminal leavers; at the other end of the distribution, approximately 11% of the higher-education students had received negative ratings as opposed to 27% of the LCE terminal leavers.

A stepwise discriminant analysis procedure identified the index of overall level of student achievement on the LCE (LCEX) as the major discriminator between higher-education students and LCE terminal leavers; the former had the higher scores. A measure of the superiority of the higher-education students may be gleaned from the fact that although the number of LCE terminal leavers was considerably more than twice the number of higher-education students, the actual number of higher-education students who obtained six or more points on the LCEX (N:49) exceeded the number of LCE terminal leavers scoring at or above this level. Within the higher-education sample, group differences were again in evidence on the LCEX. Mean scores on the LCEX of the university students (M = 6.77; SD = 0.61) and of the college of education students (M = 6.88; SD = 0.53) were quite similar. Both means were considerably higher than the mean score recorded by regional technical college students (M = 5.36; SD = 0.67).

Indices of student performance on the ICE and on the three LCE subjects were not included in the previous analysis. However, a series of separate comparisons of higher-education students and LCE terminal leavers on four indices of ICE performance and on the three subject indices of LCE performance was carried out. The results clearly support our findings on the LCEX (Table 8.3). On each of the seven indices of examination performance, higher-education students scored higher than the students who left school after taking the LCE (Table 8.4). In each instance, the difference was statistically significant.

TABLE 8.4
Means (and Standard Deviations) on Public Examinations (Intermediate and Leaving Certificates) for Higher-Education Students and Leaving Certificate Terminal Leavers

	Higher-education students			*Leaving Certificate terminal leavers*			
Examination	N	M	SD	N	M	SD	F
ICEX	59	7.09	.73	157	6.14	.79	64.41***
ICE Irish	60	6.65	1.15	158	5.61	1.24	31.80***
ICE English	60	6.43	.95	158	5.23	1.10	31.72***
ICE Mathematics	59	6.54	1.26	157	5.02	1.45	50.75***
LCEX	62	6.48	.84	148	5.07	.93	106.60***
LCE Irish	64	6.27	1.22	157	5.05	1.07	53.60***
LCE English	63	6.10	1.28	157	4.91	1.19	42.68***
LCE Mathematics	63	5.78	1.21	134	4.51	1.41	38.05***

***$p < .001$

From the larger set of primary and post-primary variables used in the above analysis to discriminate between higher-education students and LCE terminal leavers, a subset of seven variables was identified in a further analysis which discriminated between the two groups almost as well as the full set of 34 measures. The latter analysis revealed that the higher-education student, in contrast to the LCE terminal student, was likely to have had a relatively high LCEX score. To a much lesser extent, the student was likely to be male and to have had relatively high ratings for achievement while still at primary school.[3]

The Use Of A Points System For Selection For University

University entrants comprise the largest subgroup among third-level students in Ireland. Most students qualify for admission to university on the basis of their performance on the Leaving Certificate Examination; a small proportion gain admission on the basis of a separate matriculation examination set by a university. The use of LCE results for selection by Irish universities has given rise to some debate. Faced with the problem of having to limit admission to any course for which the demand exceeds the number of places available, individual faculties within universities may decree that an applicant has to obtain a minimum number of points based on the LCE (or on the university matriculation examination) in order to gain admission. While much public interest has focussed on the sharp annual increase in the number of points required for entry into some university faculties, relatively little attention has been paid to the scoring system from which the points are derived or to the appropriateness of the LCE for the purpose for which it is being used.[4]

There are two questions which may be asked about the selection procedures used by third-level educational institutions which our data might address. The first acknowledges the rather arbitrary basis of points systems employed for selection and asks if the use of different systems would result in the identification of the same or different sets of students. The second question deals with the predictive validity of the LCE and points systems based on it, i.e., the extent to which the examination results predict a student's future level of performance within the university. Do students who obtain a large number of points on the basis of their LCE performance have better university academic records than students who have fewer points?

To obtain an answer to our question about the effects on student selection of different points procedures, the LCE results of the sample of 222 students who had completed the senior cycle were used as a basis for calculating points according to four different systems. The systems, details of which were given in Chapter 7, were (1) Scaled points (SP); (2) University College points (UC); (3) College of Education points (CE) and (4) LCEX. On the basis of these systems, four different indices of LCE achievement were calculated for each student in our sample. Scores on the indices were very highly correlated (cf. Table 7.8).

Students were ranked from high to low on each of the four indices to determine the extent to which the use of different points systems would result in the identification of the same or different sets of students in a competitive situation. We decided to select the top 50 students on each index. Due to the fact that more than one student received identical scores on the same index (e.g., two students tied for 50th place on the SP index and 10 students tied for the 42nd place on the LCEX), the numbers selected were the top 51 students on the SP index, the top 53 on the UC index, the top 50 on the CE index, and the top 52 on the LCEX. If the different points systems or indices had yielded identical rank orders, then the top 50 candidates under the Scaled Points system would also have emerged as the top 50 under the other systems. However, as the data in Table 8.5 show, despite the high intercorrelations among the indices, the different points systems resulted in some students being admitted on the basis of one particular system and not being admitted when another system is adopted. Altogether, 43 candidates (69.4%) would qualify, whichever index was used.[5]

TABLE 8.5
Numbers Qualifying for Admission to University Using Four Different Points Systems

Criterion	*N*
Would qualify only on one index	10
Would qualify on two of the indices	3
Would qualify on three of the indices	6
Would qualify on each of the four indices	43

The second question of interest relating to the use of the LCE and points systems based on it to select students for university concerns the predictive validity of the examination. At the outset, it should be pointed out that if selection is based on a criterion, such as performance on the LCE, our ability to examine the predictive capability of the selection instrument is limited, since students who fail to score above the qualifying mark in almost all instances have no opportunity of being assessed on a criterion variable (such as performance in a final university examination). Thus, predictive validity studies are confined to those limited number of students who survive a cut-off point. Furthermore, the higher the cut-off point on the predicting instrument, the less is the likelihood of establishing a significant relationship between the predictor and the criterion due to the restriction in variance in the scores of successful candidates. For this reason we would expect the LCE points of students in a highly selective faculty such as Medicine not to correlate as highly with final examinations marks as would the points of students in less restrictive faculties such as Arts and Commerce. In the case of our study, there was an added limitation. Since the number of students in our sample is small, students could not be divided in analysis by university, faculty, or year of study. If such a division had been possible, it is virtually certain that the correlations between the points systems and subsequent academic performance would have been substantially increased.[6]

Bearing these reservations in mind, we may examine the relationship between the four points systems described above and the subsequent academic performance of the 36 students in our sample who gained admission to university.[7] Three criteria of academic performance in university were used. The first was the number of years taken by a student above the minimum normally required to complete a degree course. Since four of the students left university without graduating and two others did not complete their degree requirements by the end of the data-collection period, our sample size was reduced to 30. Eight of these students required one additional year to complete the required course work. The correlation between LCEX and number of additional years (-.22) indicated that the relationship between student performance on the LCE as measured by LCEX and number of additional years required to complete a degree course was negative but not statistically significant. Similarly, none of the correlations between number of extra years and the other three indices of LCE achievement was statistically significant.

A second criterion of undergraduate achievement was the number of times a student was required to repeat an examination. Again, the analysis was confined to the 30 students who had graduated. Of this total, 17 had not repeated any examination; four repeated once; six repeated twice; two repeated three times, while one student repeated as many as four times. (One of the two students still studying when our study terminated had also repeated four times; one of the students who did not complete the degree course had repeated once and another had repeated twice.) Again, the correlation between LCEX and this measure of university achievement was negative but not significant (-.10). None of the other three LCE indices correlated significantly with number of repeats either. Interestingly enough, the verbal ability of students, assessed when they were 11 years of age, did correlate negatively and significantly (-.39) with the number of repeat examinations students had taken at university.

The third and final criterion of undergraduate achievement was the level of the degree awarded the student. Of the 30 students, 19 were awarded pass degrees, six obtained Second Class Honours, Grade II degrees and five received Second Class Honours, Grade I degrees. A correlational analysis revealed no significant relationship (.08) between LCEX (or any of the other LCE indices) and level of final degree. A closer examination of the data yielded confirmatory evidence. For instance, six of the top one-third of the students on the LCEX got pass degrees, while among the honours graduates, seven of the 11 had scored in the bottom two-thirds on the LCEX.

Conclusion

A total of 222 students (44.4%) from the original sample of 500 completed senior cycle in a post-primary school. Of these, 71.8% (or 31.6% of the original sample) immediately left school, while 28.8% (12.8% of the original sample) went to a third-level educational institution. All except three of the latter had attended secondary school.

Not surprisingly, students who proceeded to a third-level educational institution differed from the original sample from which they were drawn on a number of background, personal, and achievement-related variables. The greatest difference between the groups was in their verbal reasoning ability; third-level students had a mean score of 115.6 on a verbal reasoning test as against 100.2 for the total sample — a difference of one standard deviation. The groups also differed in socio-economic background: students in the original sample were more likely to go to a third-level institution if they came from a higher socio-economic background.

Higher-education students also differed from the total sample on a number of variables relating to their scholastic progress while at primary school. This was true of variables based on teachers' perceptions of the students' progress as well as of more objective measures, such as school attendance and grade achieved by age twelve. On all variables, the future higher-education students exhibited superior scholastic performance.

The higher-education students also differed from students who completed their education with the Leaving Certificate, though the differences here were not as great as those between the higher-education students and the original sample. Again, a difference appeared on the verbal reasoning test; the mean score for those proceeding to higher education was 115.79, while the mean for the Leaving Certificate terminal leavers was 103.95. There were also differences between the groups on a number of variables relating to achievement in the primary school.

The major difference between the groups, however, was not on characteristics of the students when they were at primary school but on their Leaving Certificate performance. The performance of higher-education students was superior to that of Leaving Certificate terminal leavers on the overall LCE index as well as on the individual subjects, English, Irish, and Mathematics. The important role played by the Leaving Certificate Examination in differentiating between the groups can hardly be regarded as surprising since the examination represents the major and, in some instances, the only admission test to higher-education.

Gender also was a factor differentiating between higher-education students and Leaving Certificate terminal leavers. Boys were more strongly represented among those who went on to higher education than among terminal leavers; they accounted for 56.3% of the higher-education entrants and for 43.7% of the terminal leavers. Among the LCE candidates, the percentage of girls in full-time education (52.7%) had exceeded the percentage of boys (47.3%). This situation was reversed among the higher-education students.

It is of interest that higher-education students and Leaving Certificate terminal leavers were not differentiated in terms of socio-economic status. Selection on this basis which, as we saw operated throughout the junior cycle post-primary years, did not operate at the point of entry to higher education.

A number of interesting differences were noted between students attending different types of higher-education institutions. The mean verbal ability level of university students was similar to that of college of education students and was higher than the mean of regional technical college students. On the Leaving Certificate Examination, university and college of education students performed similarly, while regional technical college students again occupied the lowest position.

Finally, we gave some consideration to the use of points' systems based on performance on the Leaving Certificate Examination. We found inter-correlations between actual and possible systems to be high. However, differences between the systems were sufficient to result in the selection of different sets of students by different systems. Our finding that no relationship existed between students' performance on the Leaving Certificate Examination and a number of indices of subsequent performance at university should be interpreted cautiously since the size of our university sample was extremely limited.

FOOTNOTES

1 The variable LCEX was computed only for those students who had taken at least six subjects in the examination; this led to a slight reduction in number in both the LCE and higher-education samples. Seven additional post-primary measures could have been included in the overall comparison. These were the ICEX and the indices for the Irish, English, and Mathematics examinations at both ICE and LCE levels. The multivariate analysis which was used to compare the two samples required the deletion of any case for which there were missing data. Had the seven variables been included, the total size of both samples would have been reduced by 39 due to the fact that this number of students had not taken one or more of these examinations. Furthermore, and much more important, had these variables been included, certain biases would have been introduced into the overall data due to the deletion effect. For instance, since some of the mathematically weaker girls did not take Mathematics as an LCE subject, the deletion of students who had not taken Mathematics could have biased the data on many of the other variables. Accordingly, it was decided to limit the initial comparison of the two samples to three post-primary variables, one of which, LCEX, was highly correlated with the omitted post-primary measures.

2 Wilks' Lambda = .577; χ^2 = 104.97; df = 34; $p < .001$

3 The discriminant function coefficients which were derived from the subset are presented in Table 8.6. The LCEX is clearly the most important contributor to the function. A student with a high score on the function (i.e., a higher-education student) was likely to have had a relatively high LCEX score; to a lesser extent, the student was likely to be male and to have received relatively high ratings for achievement while at primary school.

TABLE 8.6
Standardized Discriminant Function Coefficients: Higher Education Students and LCE Terminal Leavers

Variables	*Order of entry*	*Standardized coefficients*
1. LCEX	1	.94
2. School grade at age twelve	2	.23
3. Type of post-primary school	4	.18
4. Class place	5	.18
5. Verbal reasoning ability	6	.17
6. Modified ordinal position	7	.12
7. Gender	3	-.20
Group Means (Centroids)		
Higher-education students (N:62)		1.23
LCE terminal leavers (N:148)		-.51

The function derived from the full set of variables was used to classify students as either 'typical' higher-education students or 'typical' LCE terminal leavers. The purpose of this procedure was to identify the likely group membership (Higher Education or LCE Terminal Leaver) of a student when the only information known was the student's scores or ratings on the primary and post-primary school variables. Table 8.7 summarizes the outcome of the classification analysis. Altogether 80.5% of the combined samples were classified correctly. The incorrect classifications indicate that 20.9% of the LCE terminal leavers were more like the higher-education students than other LCE terminal leavers. Similarly, 10 (or 16.1%) of the higher-education students would seem to have been more at home with LCE terminal leavers than with their own group.

TABLE 8.7
Numbers of Actual and Predicted (On the Basis of Discriminant Functions) Students Proceeding to Higher Education and Leaving School Following the Leaving Certificate Examination

	Predicted group	
Actual group	*Higher education*	*Terminal leaver*
Higher education	*52* (83.9%)	10 (16.1%)
Terminal leaver	31 (20.9%)	*117* (79.1%)

Students' performance on the LCE, as measured by the LCEX, was clearly the major difference between the students in the higher-education and LCE terminal samples. Indeed, a separate discriminant analysis revealed that the discriminatory power of a function based on LCEX alone was 33.46%, i.e., 80% of the discriminatory power of the 34 variable function was attributable to LCEX. In addition, through the use of this single-variable function, 75.24% of the students were classified correctly as either higher-education students or LCE terminal leavers.

Finally, while the LCEX was the major discriminator, it would still have been possible to discriminate between the two samples on the basis of the primary and remaining post-primary school variables. When LCEX was excluded from the analysis, verbal reasoning ability proved to be the major discriminator between higher-education students and LCE terminal leavers.

4 An additional weighting for Mathematics is employed in some points systems (e.g., for admission to University College Dublin and University College Cork). This has been justified on the basis that Mathematics is considerably more difficult and time-consuming than other LCE subjects. The President of University College Dublin, Dr T. Murphy, stated that this argument had been made to the universities by the Irish Mathematics Teachers' Association, which claimed that failure to give some additional incentive in terms of points would result in fewer students taking the higher Mathematics course (Murphy, 1978). It might also be argued that the higher paper in Mathematics yields a better measure of a student's general ability than other LCE subject areas. However, there is some evidence to indicate that the relationship

between general ability and performance on the higher Mathematics paper is actually not as strong as that between ability and performance in other subject areas. For example, Madaus *et al.* (1975) found that the correlation between a measure of general ability (The Primary Mental Abilities Test) and Chemistry and Physics was higher than the correlation between the same measure of general ability and Mathematics (higher or ordinary).

Arising from the additional weighting for higher Mathematics, the subject has become particularly important for applicants for those university faculties which require the highest number of points — namely, Medicine, Veterinary Medicine, Dentistry, Engineering, and Architecture. Since the proportion of boys taking higher-level Mathematics (Ireland: Department of Education, 1977) is considerably greater than the proportion of girls (almost 3.5:1 in 1976), boys as a group have a pronounced advantage under this points system. Interestingly enough, in one large-scale study, the correlation between student gender and performance on either higher or ordinary Mathematics was not found to be statistically significant (Madaus *et al.*, 1975).

5 It can be argued that the comparison of university and college of education indices is not altogether appropriate since students tend to emphasize subject areas that are likely to maximize the possibility of their qualifying for the third-level educational institution of their choice. To illustrate this point, a student who is anxious to gain admission to a university is more likely to select and to devote more time to higher Mathematics than, for example, to English. On the other hand, the potential college of education student is likely to concentrate on Irish and Mathematics.

6 Higher correlations were reported by Moran & Crowley (1978/79) between LCE points and average first-year marks in six separate faculties. Using a technique which set an upper limit to the correlation between LCE points and first-year marks, they reported R^2s (coefficient of squared multiple correlation) of .15 for Arts, .32 for Commerce, .33 for Law, .28 for Medicine, .49 for Science and .51 for Engineering.

7 A similar analysis was carried out in an earlier study (Greaney, 1979) which included a sample of high-ability students as well as the sample of students used in the present study.

9 A Meritocratic View of Equality

In definitions of equality of opportunity in terms of access which are based on a meritocratic principle, a student's level of ability or achievement is taken into account. According to such definitions, the educational system should distribute its benefits to accord with the distribution of educationally relevant attributes in the population, and one of these attributes is 'ability'. We saw in Chapter 1 that, in Ireland, some official statements indicated that ability or aptitude should be a consideration in determining the distribution of benefits. What was meant by ability in such statements was not always clear and, indeed, the whole nature of ability in the context of equality of opportunity is a matter of controversy. In analyses throughout this book, we repeatedly identified verbal reasoning ability as a student characteristic that was strongly related to school progress; it correlated with the post-primary destination of students, with their perseverance in the system, and with their performance on examinations. In the light of these relationships, it can be argued that verbal reasoning ability may be taken as an index of a more general scholastic ability defined as 'whatever it is on the basis of which the [educational] system distributes its benefits' (Green, 1980, p. 51).

The major question we seek an answer to in this chapter is: to what extent does the Irish system of education distribute its benefits on the basis of ability, which we may regard as an educationally relevant attribute? We already know from analyses which have been reported earlier in this book that ability is related to the scholastic success of students. Our task in this chapter will be to identify more precisely the extent to which students of high ability survive or fail to survive in the system and the extent to which ability overrides the influence of gender and socio-economic status, variables which, in the meritocratic view, should not be related to educational progress. We shall not consider the location (urban-town-rural) of the primary school which students attended since this variable did not emerge in our earlier analyses as being of great importance in determining the scholastic careers of students. As far as socio-economic background is concerned, we shall attempt to determine if the principle of favouring students of high ability applies equally to students in all socio-economic groups. Similarly, in the case of gender, we wish to determine if the principle applies equally to boys and girls. Finally, we shall consider possible interactions between socio-economic background, gender, and ability in relation to students' progress in the system.

To answer the questions we have posed for this chapter, it is necessary to decide on an operational definition of high ability and to identify students who meet the criterion. Any definition of high ability will be arbitrary to some extent, both in the measure that is used and in the cut-off point that is accepted. We decided to take as our criterion measure the Drumcondra Verbal Reasoning Test for the reasons outlined above, and the cut-off point on this measure which we accept as indicative of relatively 'high ability' was the mean standard score of students who eventually passed the Leaving Certificate Examination. That level was a score of 107.6. It seemed reasonable to expect that students with scores at this level, or above, had the necessary 'ability' to cover the course-work required for the Leaving Certificate and to pass the examination. In examining the scholastic progress of the group we shall provide data on students with scores less than the cut-off point (i.e., scores of less than 108 on the verbal reasoning test) for comparative purposes.

Ability And Retention In The System

Approximately one third of students (N:159, or 32.2%) in our sample had verbal reasoning scores of 108 or greater. It is clear that not all these students survived even to the Leaving Certificate level; this is obvious from a consideration of the percentages of students who were in full-time education at varying points in the educational system (Table 9.1). While the vast majority of more able students (95%) completed the junior cycle, only 72% completed the senior cycle. Thus, 28% of students who, on the basis of their verbal reasoning scores, had the ability to pass the Leaving Certificate Examination, did not get as far as taking the examination. 'More able' students did, however, show a higher rate of perseverance at all stages in the system than 'less able' ones (Table 9.1). While 95% of the high scorers survived to the end of junior cycle, only 67.5% of less able students did. Again 71.7% of the former completed the senior-cycle course, while only 32.2% of the latter did. Finally, 28.9% of high scorers entered a third-level institution, while only 5.4% of the low scorers reached this level.

TABLE 9.1
Percentages of Students of Different Levels of Ability at Varying Points in the System, by Socio-Economic Status

	*Number**		*Entering post-primary school*		*Completing junior cycle*		*Completing senior cycle*		*Entering third-level*	
Socio-economic status	VR 108+ N	VR < 108 N	VR 108+ %	VR <108 %	VR 108+ %	VR < 108 %	VR 108+ %	VR < 108 %	VR 108+ %	VR <108 %
Professional/intermediate professional	66	88	100.0	96.6	100.0	84.1	86.4	52.3	37.9	13.6
Skilled	63	97	100.0	92.8	92.1	70.1	61.9	28.9	22.2	2.1
Partly-skilled	21	68	100.0	89.7	85.7	69.1	57.1	32.4	19.0	4.4
Unskilled	9	82	100.0	75.6	100.0	45.1	66.7	14.6	33.3	1.2
Total	159	335	100.0	89.0	95.0	67.5	71.7	32.2	28.9	5.4

*Six students who died or emigrated are not included in the analyses described in this chapter. Thus, the total on which analyses are based is 494 rather than 500 students.

Ability, Socio-Economic Status, and Retention in the System

Students with verbal reasoning scores of 108 or greater were to be found in all socio-economic groups (Table 9.1).[1] However, they were not distributed equally across the groups, proportions varying markedly from group to group; 42.9% of students from professional and intermediate professional homes had verbal reasoning scores of 108 or greater, while the percentage for students from skilled homes was 39.4, that for students from partly-skilled homes, 23.6, and that for students from unskilled homes, 9.9. It is clear from these data that by the age of 11 years, children from higher socio-economic groups have an obvious advantage in terms of verbal reasoning ability.

However, the general pattern in which more able students survive longer than less able ones holds for all socio-economic groups and at all points in the system. For example, the probability that a student from a professional/intermediate professional background would complete the Leaving Certificate cycle was .86 if the student had a verbal reasoning score of 108 or greater, but only .52 if his/her score was less than 108. Similarly, the respective probabilities for higher and lower ability students from an unskilled background were .67 and .15.

The contribution of ability to survival is further underlined by the fact that at any given point in the system, the survival rate for more able students, whatever social class they belong to, is always greater than the survival rate for less able students, whether those students come from the same or from another socio-economic class. For example, students from partly-skilled backgrounds have the lowest probability (.19) among students of high ability of entering third-level education; however, that is still higher than the highest probability among less able students (.14 for students from professional/intermediate professional backgrounds).

These data all indicate that verbal ability is an important variable for student survival in the system, and to some extent overrides social-class membership. However, this does not mean that one's socio-economic background does not also play a role in the survival process. If socio-economic background were irrelevant, drop-out, and its reciprocal, survival, would be spread equally across socio-economic groups. But we know from the results of analyses in preceeding chapters that this is not likely to be so and an examination of the data in Table 9.1 confirms that indeed it is not. With only one exception, the higher the socio-economic status of a more able student, the greater are his/her chances of survival in the system.[2] Students from the professional/intermediate professional group fare best, while ones from partly-skilled and unskilled backgrounds have the poorest survival rates.

Differences in survival rates in the educational system related to socio-economic background increase as one proceeds from lower to higher levels in the system. All students with verbal reasoning scores of 108 or greater enter post-primary school. By the completion of junior cycle, class differences are already in evidence, however, particularly differences between the professional and partly-skilled groups. While all students from the former group complete a junior cycle, only 85.7% of more able students from partly-skilled backgrounds do so. By the end of senior cycle, there has been a further widening of the gap. At this stage, 86.4% of students with a high verbal ability score from a professional or intermediate professional home are still in the system, but only 57.1% of more able students from a partly-skilled home are. The proportion of more able students from a professional/intermediate professional background who enter third-level education is twice that of students from a partly-skilled background.

Differential rates of survival related to socio-economic background also operate for the less able group of students (i.e., those with verbal reasoning scores less than 108). Again, students from the professional/intermediate professional group do best at all points in the system. On the basis of the proportions of students from each socio-economic background who actually survived in our study, we can say that the probability of a student from a professional/intermediate professional background completing junior cycle is .84, almost twice that for a student from an unskilled background (.45). The probability of the student from a professional background completing senior cycle is .52, while that for the student from an unskilled background is .15. Thus, in the case of less able students, as was the case with more able ones, social-class differences in survival become greater the higher one goes in the educational system. While the chances of a student of lower ability from a high socio-economic background (professional/intermediate professional) entering a post-primary school are approximately 1.3 times better than those of a student from a low socio-economic background (unskilled), the difference in the chances of the two completing junior cycle has increased to almost 1.9 and, by the end of senior cycle, the difference is approximately 3.6. Although a student of lower ability is unlikely to enrol in third-level education, such a student is 11.3 times more likely to do so if he/she comes from a high socio-economic background than if he/she comes from a low socio-economic background.

A comparison of the participation rates of more and less able students indicates that differences in survival related to socio-economic status are greater for less able than for more able children. The greatest difference in survival between the classes is to be found between the highest and lowest socio-economic groupings for less able children at the point of entry to third-level education; we have just seen that the student of lower ability from a professional/intermediate professional home is more than 11 times more likely to enter a third-level institution than is a student from an unskilled background. The largest difference between classes for more able children also occurs at third level. However, it is a much smaller difference. Students of high ability from professional homes are only twice as likely to enter a third-level institution as are students from a partly-skilled background.

The differential between the survival rates of students of the two levels of ability is less for students from upper socio-economic backgrounds than it is for students from lower socio-economic backgrounds. For example, a more able student from a professional/intermediate professional background is almost 1.7 times more likely to complete the senior-cycle course than is a less able student from the same background, but an able student from a skilled background is 2.2 times more likely to complete senior cycle than a less able student from the same background. At the point of entry to third-level education, the difference is considerably greater. A student from a professional/intermediate professional background is 2.8 times more likely to enter third-level education if he/she falls in the more able category than if he/she falls in the less able group. But a more able student from a skilled background is 10.6 times more likely to enter third-level education than a less able student from the same background. Thus, we may conclude that the probability of a student staying in the educational system is more dependent on the student's ability if he or she comes from a relatively low socio-economic background than if he or she comes from a relatively high socio-economic background. In other words, the student from a high socio-economic background is less dependent on ability for survival in the system than is a student from a low socio-economic background. Without a relatively high level of ability, the low socio-economic student has little hope of obtaining all the benefits of the system; the student of high socio-economic status, on the other hand, is more likely to be able to draw on resources other than ability to ensure survival in the system.

Finally, it is of interest to ask if the chances of survival of more able students are greater in a secondary school than in a vocational school. Unfortunately, the small number of students of this level of ability who enrolled in a vocational school precludes us from answering this question definitively. Of the 333 students who went to a secondary school, 141 (or 43.2%) had a verbal reasoning score of 108 or greater, while of the 128 vocational-school entrants, only 18 (or 14.1%) had such a score. These figures confirm our earlier finding about differences in the mean verbal reasoning ability of secondary-school and vocational-school entrants. They also indicate that students who in terms of ability are likely to pass the Leaving Certificate Examination are more likely to choose a type of school with a long tradition of preparing students for that examination.

The answer to our question regarding probability of survival in the two types of post-primary school is that the educational prospects of a more able student are better in a secondary than in a vocational school. Of the students of high ability who went to secondary school, 80.1% stayed until the Leaving Certificate Examination, which meant that a student of this level of ability entering a secondary school had a probability of .80 of staying to the Leaving Certificate (Table 9.2). Of the small number of more able students who commenced their post-primary education in a vocational school, on the other hand, only one completed the Leaving Certificate course; the probability of a student of this level of ability completing the course in a vocational school was .06 (Table 9.3). Thus, a student with a verbal reasoning score of 108 or more was about 14 times more likely to get to the Leaving Certificate if he or she went to a secondary school rather than to a vocational school.

A comparison of the survival rates of more able with less able students is possible on the basis of the data in Table 9.2 for secondary schools and Table 9.3 for vocational schools. Again we stress that the data on more able students in vocational schools are extremely limited.

In secondary schools, the chances of surviving to the Leaving Certificate level are about one and a half times better for more able than for less able students. When it comes to entrance to a third-level institution, the advantage of the more able student is even greater. Such a student is about four times more likely than a less able student to go to a third-level institution. In vocational schools, more able students have a better survival rate than less able ones up to the end of junior cycle. After that point, however, the less able students have slightly higher survival rates.

From the data we have considered, we would clearly expect to find changes in the ability and social-class composition of schools from the point of entry to post-primary school to entry to third-level education. The data in Table 9.4 (represented graphically in Figure 9.1) provide details on the percentages of more and less able students from different

TABLE 9.2
Percentages of Students of Different Levels of Ability at Varying Points in Secondary School, by Socio-Economic Status

	Number entering school		*Completing junior cycle*		*Completing senior cycle*		*Entering third-level*	
Socio-economic status	VR 108+ N	VR <108 N	VR 108+ %	VR <108 %	VR 108+ %	VR <108 %	VR 108+ %	VR <108 %
Professional/intermediate professional	63	71	100.0	90.1	90.5	62.0	39.7	15.5
Skilled	58	58	91.4	86.2	67.2	44.8	24.1	1.7
Partly-skilled	14	35	92.9	88.6	85.7	54.3	28.6	5.7
Unskilled	6	25	100.0	60.0	83.3	36.0	50.0	4.0
Total	141	189	95.7	84.7	80.1	51.9	32.6	7.9

TABLE 9.3
Percentages of Students of Different Levels of Ability at Varying Points in Vocational School, by Socio-Economic Status

Socio-economic status	*Number entering school*		*Completing junior cycle*		*Completing senior cycle*		*Entering third-level*	
	VR 108+ N	VR <108 N	VR 108+ %	VR <108 %	VR 108+ %	VR <108 %	VR 108+ %	VR <108 %
Professional/intermediate professional	3	14	100.0	71.4	0.0	14.3	0.0	7.1
Skilled	5	32	100.0	56.3	0.0	6.3	0.0	3.1
Partly-skilled	7	26	71.4	61.5	0.0	11.5	0.0	3.8
Unskilled	3	37	100.0	59.5	33.3	8.1	0.0	0.0
Total	18	109	88.9	60.6	5.6	9.2	0.0	2.8

TABLE 9.4
Number of Students from Each Socio-Economic Background as a Percentage of all Students of Similar Ability Participating in Education at Varying Levels

	Entering post-primary		*Completing junior cycle*		*Completing senior cycle*		*Entering third-level*	
Socio-economic status	VR 108+ (N:159) %	VR <108 (N:298) %	VR 108+ (N:151) %	VR <108 (N:226) %	VR 108+ (N:114) %	VR <108 (N:108) %	VR 108+ (N:46) %	VR <108 (N:18) %
Professional/intermediate professional	41.5	28.5	43.7	32.7	50.0	42.6	54.3	66.7
Skilled	39.6	30.2	38.4	30.1	34.2	25.9	30.4	11.1
Partly-skilled	13.2	20.5	11.9	20.8	10.5	20.4	8.7	16.7
Unskilled	5.7	20.8	6.0	16.4	5.3	11.1	6.5	5.6
Total	100.0	100.0	100.0	100.0	100.0	100.0	99.9	100.1

social-class backgrounds in school through the period of second-level education. The first obvious feature of the table and figure is the increase in the proportion of more able students (verbal reasoning scores of 108+) relative to the proportion of less able ones. At entry to post-primary school, more able students constitute 34.8% of the total number of students. On completion of junior cycle, that proportion had increased to 40.1%; by the end of senior cycle, it was 51.4%, while for entrants to third-level education, it was 71.9 percent. Again, we see a clear illustration of the tendency in the system to retain students of relatively high scholastic ability.

The second feature of the data in Table 9.4 and Figure 9.1 is the tendency for the proportion of students of high socio-economic status to increase over time and the proportion of students of low socio-economic status to decrease. This happens for both the more able and less able groups, reflecting the trends we have repeatedly noted of high SES students to persevere in the system and of low SES students to drop out. In the case of more able students, those from professional/intermediate professional homes make up 41.5% of the more able students entering post-primary school. Their representation increases, however, to 43.7%

FIGURE 9.1
Numbers of Students at Various Stages of Education by Socio-Economic Background and level of Ability

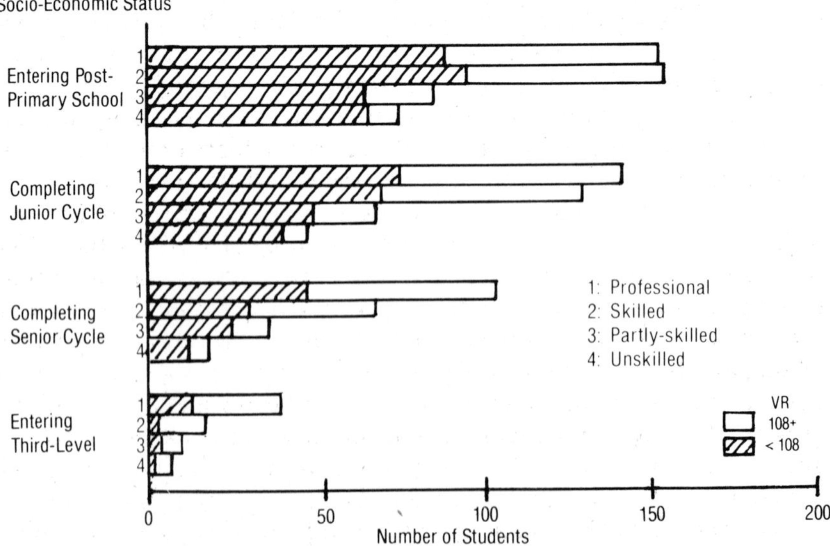

by the end of junior cycle, to 50.0% by the end of senior cycle, and to 54.3% for entrants to third-level education. By contrast, the representation of the other socio-economic groups (with the exception of the small unskilled group) falls off. In the case of more able students from partly-skilled backgrounds, for example, it drops from 13.2% at entry to post-primary school to 10.5% on completion of senior cycle, and to 8.7% on entry to third-level education.

This pattern is reflected more strikingly in the case of less able students. For the less able, the relative advantage of students from professional/intermediate professional homes is even greater than in the case of the more able. Students from such homes more than double their representation among less able students in the system from entry to post-primary school to entry to third-level education (from 28.5% to 66.7%). At the other extreme, the proportion of less able students from unskilled homes is reduced from 20.8% to 5.6% over the same period.

Ability, Gender, and Retention In The System

In the group of students with verbal reasoning scores of 108 or greater, there is a greater proportion of boys (57.2%) than of girls (42.8%) (Table 9.5).

Survival rates for boys and girls of high ability were similar throughout the post-primary school (Table 9.5). All boys and girls of this level of ability went to a post-primary school and almost all completed junior cycle (94.5% of boys and 95.6% of girls). The percentage completing senior cycle dropped for both genders — to 71.4 for boys and to 72.1 for girls. At the point of entry to third-level education, boys had an advantage. Almost a third (31.9%) of boys of high ability went on to third-level education, while only a quarter (25%) of girls did.

Differences in survival in the educational system between less able boys and girls (that is, with verbal reasoning scores less than 108) consistently favour girls (Table 9.6). For such students, the probability that a girl will remain in the educational system is higher at all points in the system than it is for a boy. It first appears at entry to post-primary school, at which point 90.7% of girls are represented as against 86.9% of boys. By the end of junior cycle that gap has been widened to 72.0% for girls and 62.1% for boys, while at the end of senior cycle, it is 36.8% for girls and 26.8% for boys. On entry to third-level education, the gap is considerably narrowed, but not quite closed; six percent of girls and less than five percent of boys in the less able group find their way into a third-level institution.

TABLE 9.5
Percentages of More Able Students (VR = 108+) Who Survive in the Educational System, by Socio-Economic Background and Gender

Socio-economic status	*Number*		*Entering post-primary*		*Completing junior cycle*		*Completing senior cycle*		*Entering third-level*	
	M	F	M	F	M	F	M	F	M	F
			%	%	%	%	%	%	%	%
Professional/intermediate professional	36	30	100.0	100.0	100.0	100.0	83.3	90.0	41.7	33.3
Skilled	37	26	100.0	100.0	91.9	92.3	64.9	57.7	21.6	23.1
Partly-skilled	13	8	100.0	100.0	84.6	87.5	53.8	62.5	23.1	12.5
Unskilled	5	4	100.0	100.0	100.0	100.0	80.0	50.0	60.0	0.0
Total	91	68	100.0	100.0	94.5	95.6	71.4	72.1	31.9	25.0

TABLE 9.6
Percentages of Less Able students (VR < 108) Who Survive in the Educational System, by Socio-Economic Background and Gender

Socio-economic status	Number		Entering post-primary		Completing junior cycle		Completing senior cycle		Entering third-level	
	M	F	M %	F %	M %	F %	M %	F %	M %	F %
Professional/intermediate professional	42	46	97.6	95.7	83.3	84.8	52.4	52.2	11.9	15.2
Skilled	46	51	95.7	90.2	67.4	72.5	23.9	33.3	2.2	2.0
Partly-skilled	27	41	77.8	97.6	51.9	80.5	18.5	41.5	0.0	7.3
Unskilled	38	44	71.1	79.5	39.5	50.0	7.9	20.5	2.6	0.0
Total	153	182	86.9	90.7	62.1	72.0	26.8	36.8	4.6	6.0

Ability, Socio-Economic Status, Gender, And Retention In The System

In the preceding pages, we considered the role of ability, first in relation to socio-economic status and then in relation to gender, for survival in the educational system from entry to post-primary school to entry to third-level education. It only remains for us to consider interactions between ability, socio-economic status, and gender. Since we have already considered the general trends for gender and socio-economic status, at this point we need only consider statistics which seem to deviate somewhat from those trends.

None of the deviations within any socio-economic group is very great. While the trend for more able students from higher socio-economic backgrounds to survive longer in the system than similar students from lower socio-economic backgrounds does of course involve disadvantage, for the most part, such disadvantage does not interact with gender (Table 9.5). Within socio-economic classes, the survival rates of more able boys and girls are almost identical up to the completion of junior cycle. Some differences between the genders begin to appear at the senior-cycle level. This difference is exhibited in the slight tendency for girls from higher socio-economic backgrounds to have a higher probability of completing senior cycle (.90) than boys (.83), while at the lower socio-economic levels, the position is reversed: more able boys from unskilled backgrounds are more likely (.80) to complete senior cycle than are girls (.50). At third level, more able girls from professional/intermediate professional homes lose their advantage; the probability of a boy from this background entering third-level education is .42, while that for a girl is .33. Boys of high ability from partly-skilled and unskilled homes are much more likely to go to a third-level institution than are girls of similar ability from a similar background.

Differences in level of school attainment between boys and girls within socio-economic groups for less able students in general favour girls throughout the period of post-primary education (Table 9.6). Such differences become apparent for students from partly-skilled and unskilled homes at the point of entry to second-level education and continue to the completion of senior cycle. At third-level, the numbers involved are very small; differences appear to be slight and inconsistent.

Conclusion

In this chapter we focussed on a group of students, the members of which had a relatively high level of ability, defined in terms of their performance on a standardized test of verbal reasoning ability (a standard score of 108 or greater on the Drumcondra Verbal Reasoning Test). We found that such students exhibited something more than twice the retention rate of students who were less able, by the end of their post-primary schooling. However, not all more able students remained in the system until the Leaving Certificate Examination, even though in terms of their verbal reasoning scores they at least equalled the mean level of performance of students who passed that examination. Almost 30% of the more able students in our sample failed to complete the senior-cycle course in a post-primary school.

While students with high levels of ability were spread across all socio-economic groups, they were not spread evenly. There was a much higher proportion of more able students in the higher than in the lower socio-economic groups. Thus, it would appear, problems associated with differences in participation in the post-compulsory period of schooling have their origins at a much earlier stage. This finding has considerable implications for a policy of equality of opportunity.

More able students stay longer in the educational system than less able ones in the case of all socio-economic groups, indicating the role of ability for survival in the system. But it is not an unqualified role. For survival, even for more able students, varies with socio-economic background. While 86% of such students from professional/intermediate professional backgrounds survive to the Leaving Certificate level, the percentage surviving to this level of students from skilled backgrounds is 62, for students from partly-skilled backgrounds it is 57, and for the small number of students from unskilled backgrounds, it is 67. The higher one goes in the system, the greater the difference in survival rate between the classes becomes. Thus, the greatest differential appears at the point of entry to third-level education. The proportion of students from professional/intermediate professional backgrounds (38%) entering third-level education is almost twice that of students from partly-skilled backgrounds (19%).

Among comparatively less able students (i.e., those who had scored less than 108 on the verbal reasoning test), differences in survival rates within the system related to socio-economic status were more pronounced than among more able students. Our data suggest that for survival within the educational system the student of low ability is much more likely to be dependent on socio-economic status than his/her more able counterpart. For example, for lower ability students, the proportion from the upper socio-economic status levels who completed senior cycle was approximately 3.5 times greater than the proportion from the lowest socio-economic status level. Furthermore, while low ability students were unlikely to enrol in third-level educational institutions, such students were 11 times more likely to do so if they came from high social class backgrounds rather than from an unskilled background.

The proportion of more able boys in our sample was greater than the proportion of more able girls. There was, however, little difference in the survival rates of such boys and girls during the period of post-primary education. A more able boy was more likely than a girl of similar ability to proceed to third-level education. We found no evidence of marked interactions between gender and socio-economic status for more able students. There were some indications, however, that among students from lower socio-economic backgrounds, the probability of a more able girl surviving in the post-compulsory section of the system was less than that of a more able boy.

Overall, our findings indicate that, even though the educational system favours more able students more than it does less able ones, there is a considerable loss of more able students from the system. Further, the loss occurs at all socio-economic levels. While a consideration of the proportions from each socio-economic group which are lost to the system points to a greater loss among lower than among higher socio-economic groups, in terms of the absolute number of students lost, the figures are similar for professional/intermediate professional and partly-skilled groups. The absolute number lost from the unskilled group is the smallest, while students from skilled backgrounds fare worst both in proportional and in absolute terms.

FOOTNOTES

1 In the analyses in this chapter, the professional and intermediate professional groups are combined because of the small number of students in the former.

2 The one exception to this trend is the case of more able students from unskilled backgrounds who, after the completion of junior cycle, but not up to that point, show higher survival rates than students from skilled and partly-skilled backgrounds. This finding must be treated with caution since it is based on a very small number of students from unskilled backgrounds.

10 Occupations

Many factors help to determine a person's occupation. Among the more obvious ones are geographical location, economic conditions, gender, home-background, personality factors, level of school attainment, and indeed luck (cf. Jencks *et al.*, 1972). Of these, school attainment seems particularly important; the correlation between occupational level and years of education in the United States has been found to range from .60 (Blau & Duncan, 1967) to .65 (Jencks *et al.*, 1972). No empirical data of this nature are available for Ireland; however, level of school attainment is perceived by the general public in the country as an important factor in determining occupational level (Fontes *et al.*, 1980).

The reasons for the relationship between schooling and occupational achievement are not clear. One view is that the skills acquired at school are needed to carry out the tasks of jobs, and that the higher the level of occupation the more education and training needed. At any rate, there appears to be a general tendency for employers to prefer workers with more rather than with less education and this is so whether or not the additional educational requirements are really necessary for the discharge of the duties of an occupation. Level of school attainment can be used in a rather arbitrary way to limit the number admitted to an occupation, a course of training, or education. In this context, educational credentials, which have the advantage of appearing fair and objective, often make good rationing devices (Collins, 1979; Jencks *et al.*, 1972). Given this situation, a shortage of occupational opportunities (as in times of recession) may lead to an increased emphasis on the acquisition of credentials.

While educational credentials are often viewed as a means for increasing one's employment opportunities, anticipation of the number of years one may have to spend in school can deter students from getting the necessary qualifications. Students who leave school early may do so more on account of their dislike for school and their perceptions of the type and amount of school expected of them rather than because they are attracted by a particular job opportunity. Such students may well settle for any job which becomes available.

In this chapter we examine the relationship between students' first occupations on leaving school and information which was obtained about the students while they were still at primary school and, where applicable, at the post-primary and higher-education levels. The first information about students we look at is general level of educational attainment (i.e., the highest point reached by a student in the educational system) and we examine how that level is related to a student's subsequent occupational status. Secondly, relationships between information about students obtained when they were at primary school and the students' subsequent occupational status are described. Thirdly, we consider relationships between post-primary variables and occupational status; the analyses in which these relationships are examined include a description of the relationship between different levels of student achievement (as measured by students' performance on the Intermediate and Leaving Certificate Examinations) and future occupational status for students with the same level of educational attainment (i.e., students with similar amounts of schooling). Lastly, we compare the students' first occupation with those of their fathers to ascertain the extent of occupational mobility.

To obtain data for these analyses, a questionnaire was mailed to each student's school to obtain information on the student's destination on leaving school. If a student had commenced working immediately, schools were asked to state the place of the student's employment and to supply a detailed description of the type of work involved in the employment. If the school was unable to supply this information, or if the student had not commenced work immediately, the student was contacted directly. Employment details were obtained for 478 (i.e., 95.6%) of the original sample. It was not possible to obtain information on a further 20 students, six of whom had emigrated.[1] A further two students had died while still at school.

Occupations were categorized according to the classification system of the British Census (Great Britain: Registrar General, 1956) with certain modifications, as had been done earlier in classifying the occupations of students' fathers. The following categories were used: (a) higher professional, administrative, and managerial, and farmers with over 150 acres; (b) intermediate professional, administrative, and managerial, and farmers with over 30 but less than 150 acres; (c) skilled occupations; (d) partly-skilled occupations, and farmers with 30 acres or less; and (e) unskilled occupations.[2] The reader is reminded that occupational status (JOBSES) of students described in this chapter refers to students' first occupation after leaving school. Once that information was obtained, the collection of data ceased. Thus we do not know if individuals changed their occupations and if they did, whether those changes resulted in a raising, a lowering, or a maintenance of status. Neither do we know if students who found jobs continued in employment.

School Attainment And Occupational Status

A measure of school attainment was created for each of the 478 people for whom occupational status was known. A hierarchy of seven levels of school attainment was identified: (1) primary-school terminal leaver (PSTL), (2) junior-cycle early leaver (JCEL, i.e., a leaver from a post-primary school who did not take a Day Group or Intermediate Certificate Examination), (3) junior-cycle terminal leaver (JCTL, i.e., a leaver from a post-primary school who sat for the Day Group or Intermediate Certificate Examination), (4) senior-cycle early leaver (SCEL, i.e., a leaver from a senior cycle in a post-primary school who did not take the Leaving Certificate Examination), (5) senior-cycle terminal leaver (SCTL, i.e., a student who took the Leaving Certificate Examination), (6) higher-education early leaver (HIEDEL, i.e., a student who commenced study in a higher-education institution but did not complete the course), (7) higher-education terminal leaver (HIEDTL i.e., a student who completed a course in a third-level institution). The numbers of students in our sample in each of these attainment categories for whom occupational information was available are presented in Table 10.1.

An examination of the data in Table 10.1 reveals that for each level of school attainment (defined as the last level of the educational system reached by a student), the larger frequencies are to be found approximately along a diagonal which extends from the upper right-hand corner of the table downwards towards the lower left-hand corner, clearly indicating that level of occupational status tends to rise with the amount of education a student has received. In fact, the correlation between occupational status and the level of education attained by a student (.61) is considerably larger than any of the other correlations which we considered between occupational status and students' background characteristics (home background, personal, or educational characteristics).

The bar-chart in Figure 10.1 provides an over-view of the data on school attainment and occupational status. The bars in the chart indicate that as level of school attainment increases, so does mean level of occupational status.

TABLE 10.1
Numbers of Students Achieving Each Occupational Level by Level of School Attainment

	Occupational status					
Level of school attainment	*Higher profes-sional*	*Inter. profes-sional*	*Skilled*	*Partly-skilled*	*Un-skilled*	*Total*
1. Primary-school terminal leaver	0	2	9	17	8	36 *7.5%*
2. Junior-cycle early leaver	0	2	42	29	5	78 *16.3%*
3. Junior-cycle terminal leaver	0	5	96	19	6	126 *26.4%*
4. Senior-cycle early leaver	1	2	13	3	1	20 *4.2%*
5. Senior-cycle terminal leaver	6	35	92	20	1	154 *32.2%*
6. Higher-education early leaver	2	3	2	0	0	7 *1.5%*
7. Higher-education terminal leaver	14	39	4	0	0	57* *11.9%*
Total	23 *4.8%*	88 *18.4%*	258 *54.0%*	88 *18.4%*	21 *4.4%*	478 *100%*

*Two students who were nearing completion of degree courses at the time of the final data collection have been included in this category.

To look more closely at the relationship between level of school attainment and occupational status, we carried out a series of comparisons of students of varying levels of attainment.

Primary-school terminal leavers and post-primary school entrants
Information on occupational status was obtained for 36 of the 37 primary-school terminal leavers and for 442 of the 461 post-primary school entrants. The results of a statistical analysis[3] revealed that the occupational-status levels of the post-primary school entrants were superior to those of the primary-school terminal leavers.[4]

FIGURE 10.1
Occupational Status of Students by Their Level of School Attainment

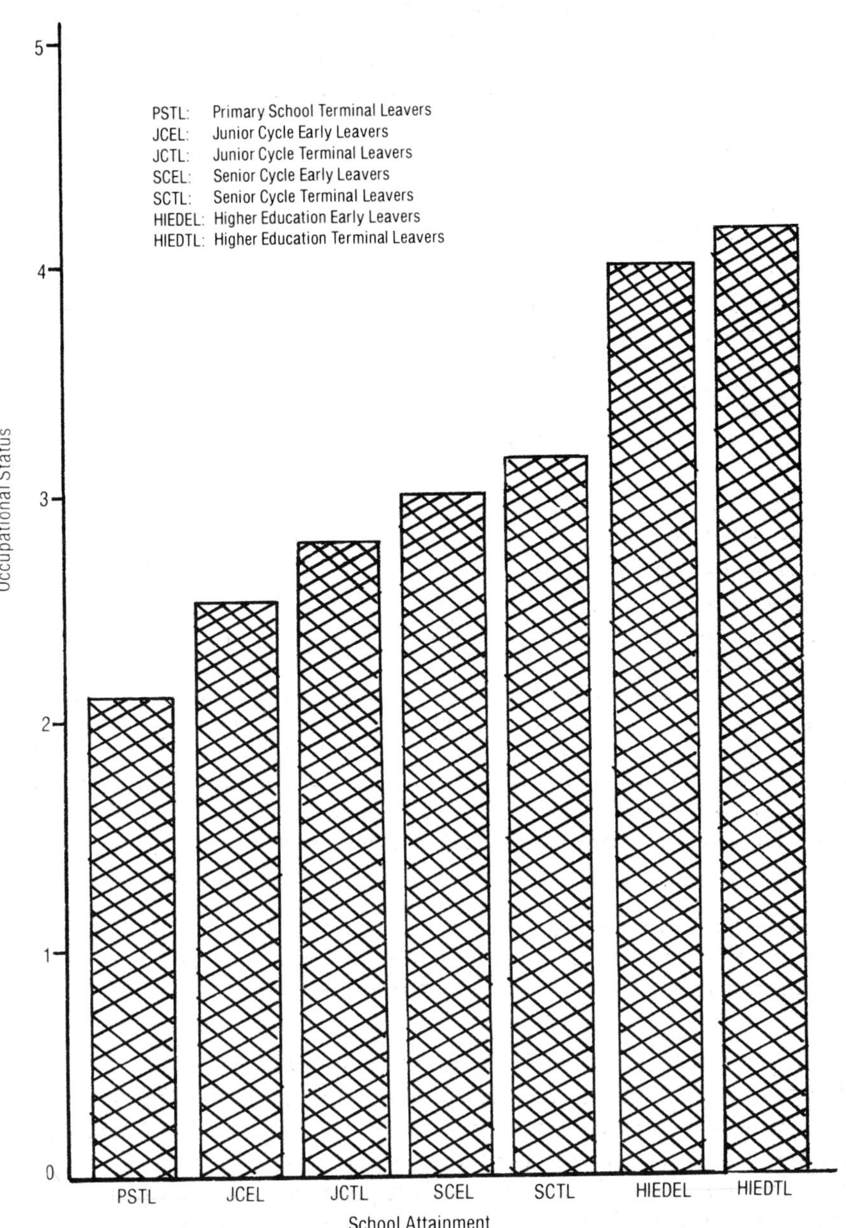

Junior-cycle early leavers and students who completed junior cycle

Occupational status data were obtained for 87 of 90 students who completed junior cycle in a vocational school and for 49 of the 50 students who had left vocational school before completing the junior cycle. A comparison of the two samples in terms of subsequent occupational status indicated that those who completed junior cycle subsequently obtained higher-status occupations than students who had left school during the course of junior cycle. The difference was statistically significant.[5]

A similar comparison was made between 277 of the 287 students who had completed junior cycle in a secondary school and 29 of the 30 students who had left school without taking a junior-cycle certificate examination. (Occupational status data could not be obtained for 10 students who completed the junior cycle and for one who failed to complete it.) The results of this comparison indicate that students who had completed the junior cycle in a secondary school also tended to have the higher-status occupations. The difference between the two samples in terms of occupational status was statistically significant.[6]

Junior-cycle terminal leavers and senior-cycle entrants

Data on occupational status were obtained for 22 of the 23 students who had commenced a senior-cycle course in a vocational school and for 66 of the 68 who elected to leave school at this stage. A comparison of the two groups revealed that those who had enrolled in the senior-cycle course tended to have higher-status occupations than leavers. Again the difference was statistically significant.[7]

Over three-quarters of the secondary-school students remained in school after completing junior cycle. Of the total of 221 former senior-cycle students in secondary school, occupational status information was obtained for 216. Similar information was obtained for 60 of the 65 students who left secondary school at the end of the junior cycle. A comparison of these two samples on the occupational-status measure showed that those who had persisted in secondary school tended to achieve higher-status occupations.[8]

Senior-cycle early leavers and students who completed senior cycle

The number of students who had enrolled in a senior-cycle course in a vocational school was small (N:23). During the two years of the senior-cycle course, 13 students left school without taking the Leaving Certificate Examination. Information on occupational status was obtained for 12 of the early leavers and for all of the 10 students who completed the course. At this level, no significant relationship in occupational status was found between the two groups.[9]

Of the total of 221 students who had commenced the senior-cycle course in a secondary school, only nine left school without sitting for the Leaving Certificate Examination. Information on the occupational status of 208 of the 212 who completed senior cycle and on eight of the nine early leavers was obtained. Given the sizes of the two samples, it was not surprising to find that there was not a significant difference in occupational status between the two groups.[10]

Senior-cycle terminal leavers and third-level entrants

A total of 64 of the 222 students who completed senior cycle enrolled in third-level educational institutions. Occupational status data were obtained for each of these students as well as for 154 of the 158 senior-cycle terminal leavers. Statistical analysis revealed that the occupational status levels of third-level entrants tended to be superior to those of the senior-cycle terminal leavers. A closer examination of the data showed that intermediate or higher professional status occupations were achieved by 58 (90.6%) of the third-level entrants compared with 41 (26.6%) of the senior-cycle terminal leavers.[11]

Primary-School Correlates Of Occupational Status

Two home-background variables (socio-economic status and number of children in family) correlate significantly with students' subsequent occupation; the largest is between socio-economic status and occupation (r = .32) (Table 10.2).[12] However, even this relationship is not very strong, indicating that many students took up occupations which, in terms of socio-economic status, differed from those of their parents.

The correlation (–.11) between the number of children in a student's family and the student's occupational status on leaving school suggests that higher occupational status tends to be associated with slightly below average family size. However, the value of the correlation is small, indicating that relatively high status occupations were not achieved exclusively by students who had been members of small families. In fact, students from large families were to be found in each occupational status. For example, 11.7% of students classified in professional and intermediate professional occupations had been members of families of nine or more children. A similar percentage (12.4) of those in skilled occupations came from families of this size.

Each of the twelve educational-history variables correlated significantly with occupational status. The largest correlation (.31) was recorded for the grade the student had attained by the age of 12. Thus, there was a slight tendency for students who had completed relatively more grades by age 12 to achieve a higher occupational status than students who had covered fewer grades. The relationships between the other educational-history variables and the later occupational status of students convey a similar picture; there was a slight but consistent tendency for the students with the more positive ratings for achievement in the primary school to achieve higher-status occupations. For example, 72.1% of those who achieved occupations of professional and intermediate professional status had been rated as not having had difficulty in Problem Arithmetic, while only 33% of those who entered partly-skilled and unskilled occupations had received this rating.

In general, the type of primary school which a student had attended was not related to future occupation. There were some exceptions to this. There was a relatively small, though significant, correlation (.16) between occupational status and attendance or non-attendance at a private school. Put another way, 44.4% of students who had attended private primary schools and over half (54.3%) of those who had attended national schools entered skilled occupations. However, over half (55.6%) of the private-school students entered professional occupations, compared to 21.9% of students who had attended non-private primary schools. At the other extreme, none of those who had attended private primary schools took up a partly-skilled or unskilled occupation, while almost one-quarter of those who had attended other types of primary school were in these two categories. There were also significant, though small, correlations between occupational status and two other indices of the type of primary school which the student had attended. Students who had attended either lay-administered or mixed gender primary schools tended to achieve lower-status occupations.

Of all the primary-school variables, verbal reasoning ability had the highest correlation with future occupation. The magnitude of the correlation (.40) indicated that there was a moderate tendency for occupational status to increase concomitantly with verbal reasoning ability scores (cf. Table 10.3). Slightly over three-quarters (76.6%) of those entering professional occupations had scored above 100 on the verbal ability measure, as opposed to somewhat over half (54.3%) of those entering skilled occupations, and approximately one-third (33.0%) of those entering partly-skilled and unskilled occupations.

A student's rating for satisfactory classroom behaviour correlated about as highly ($r = .33$) as socio-economic status with occupation.

TABLE 10.2
Correlations Between Occupational Status and Other Variables

Primary Variables (N:478)

Home background		**Type of School Attended**	
1. Socio-economic status	.32***	1. Catholic lay admin.	-.11*
2. Number of children	-.11*	2. Catholic religious admin.	.05
3. Modified ordinal position	-.07	3. Protestant admin.	-.03
4. Father living	-.07	4. Private admin.	.16***
5. Mother living	-.05	5. Number of teachers	.05
		6. All male	.01
		7. All female	.09
Educational history		8. Mixed gender	-.11*
1. Class place	.27***	9. School location	.00
2. School progress	.24***	10. Class size	.00
3. Irish Reading	.16***		
4. Oral Irish	.19***	**Personal Characteristics**	
5. Written Irish	.19***	1. Verbal reasoning ability	.40***
5. Written Irish	.20***	2. Gender	.08
6. English Reading	.09	3. Satisfactory classroom behaviour	.33***
7. Oral English	.10	4. Group leadership	.08
8. Written English	.16***	5. Health/extroversion	.08
9. Mechanical Arithmetic	.17***	6. Aesthetic behaviour	.11*
10. Problem Arithmetic	.28***		
11. Absenteeism	-.21***		
12. School grade at age twelve	.31***		

Post-Primary Characteristics

Type of school attended for junior-cycle (N:364)	-.21***
Type of school attended for senior-cycle (N:218)	-.04
Boarding school for senior-cycle (N:216)	-.27***
ICEX (N:320)	.41***
LCEX (N:208)	.47***

Overall level of education

School attainment (N:478)	.61***

*$p < .05$ ***$p < .001$

TABLE 10.3
Numbers of Students at Varying Levels of Verbal Reasoning Ability by Occupational Status Achieved

	Occupational status					
Verbal reasoning ability	*Higher profes-sional*	*Inter. profes-sional*	*Skilled*	*Partly-skilled*	*Un-skilled*	*Total*
65-79	0	3	19	20	4	46 *9.6%*
80-89	1	6	33	17	7	64 *13.4%*
90-99	1	15	66	20	5	107 *22.4%*
100-109	4	30	74	22	3	133 *27.8%*
110-119	6	20	41	8	1	76 *15.9%*
120-129	6	9	24	1	1	41 *8.6%*
130-139	5	4	1	0	0	10 *2.1%*
140-149	0	1	0	0	0	1 *0.2%*
Total	23 *4.8%*	88 *18.4%*	258 *54.0%*	88 *18.4%*	21 *4.4%*	478

Among high scorers (N:80) on the satisfactory classroom behaviour measure (i.e., 1.00 to 2.99), 38.8% entered professional occupations, 53.8% went to skilled occupations, and 7.5% to partly-skilled or unskilled occupations. On the other hand, among the low scorers (−1.00 to −2.99) on this measure (N:57), as few as 7% were employed in professional occupations, 49.1% were in skilled occupations, and 43.9% were in semi-skilled or unskilled occupations.[13]

A statistically significant though small correlation (.11) was recorded between the measure of aesthetic behaviour and occupation. This would seem to suggest that, on balance, students who achieved relatively high-status occupations tended to have been perceived by their teachers in primary school as being somewhat above average in their sense of appreciation of beauty.

Altogether, the set of primary-school variables account for 28.5% of the variation in occupational status. Most of this variation (22.6%) is accounted for by three variables: verbal reasoning ability, socio-economic status, and satisfactory classroom behaviour.

Post-Primary School Correlates Of Occupational Status

Of the 331 students who had taken six or more ICE subjects, information on occupation was obtained for 320. The correlation (Table 10.2) between the index of overall Intermediate Certificate Examination performance (ICEX) and occupational status (.41) was statistically significant, indicating that students with relatively high scores on the ICEX tended to enter relatively high-status occupations. When we examine the mean occupational status achieved by students with different levels of ICEX scores, we see that occupational status rose for successively higher levels of the ICEX (Table 10.4). There was one exception to this trend: the occupational-status level of the small number of students (N:13) who had scored in the highest ICEX category was lower than that of those in the second-highest category.

TABLE 10.4
Means (and SDs) on Occupational Status Index of all ICE Examinees for Varying Levels of Performance on the Intermediate Certificate Examination (ICEX)

ICEX score	N	*Occupational status* M	SD
-4.8	24	2.58	.78
4.9–5.8	112	3.07	.68
5.9–6.8	116	3.21	.76
6.9–7.8	55	3.82	.75
7.9–	13	3.69	.75
Overall	320	3.24	.80

In a separate analysis of the occupational destinations of students who left school on completing the junior cycle (junior-cycle terminal leavers), we found that the leavers with higher ICEX scores tended to acquire jobs with higher occupational status ratings (Table 10.5).[14]

Similar relationships were found between Leaving Certificate

TABLE 10.5
Means (and SDs) on Occupational Status Index of Junior-Cycle Terminal Leavers for Varying Levels of Performance on the Intermediate Certificate Examination (ICEX)

ICEX score	N	*Occupational status* M	SD
-4.8	17	2.47	.72
4.9-5.8	45	2.87	.50
5.9-6.8	28	2.82	.48
6.9-7.9	5	3.20	.45
Overall	95	2.80	.56

Examination performance and occupational status. Information on occupation was obtained for 208 of the 211 students who had taken six or more LCE subjects. The correlation between the overall index of Leaving Certificate Examination performance (LCEX) of these students and their subsequent occupational status (r = .47) was statistically significant. An examination of the mean scores for occupational status achieved by students of varying levels of performance on the LCEX also reveals that occupational status increases for each successive level of LCEX performance (Table 10.6). The size of the mean occupational-status difference between successive LCEX levels increases as one moves from the lower to the higher LCEX levels. This finding is not surprising since LCE students who score in these higher levels would have qualified for admission to colleges of higher education. Presumably, part of the increase reflects the bonus or advantage of higher education, rather than LCE performance per se, for the subsequent occupational status of students. In support of this view, we find that when the analysis is confined to students who did not proceed to third-level education (N:146), the relationship between LCEX and subsequent occupational status is not statistically significant (Table 10.7).[15]

TABLE 10.6
Means (and SDs) on Occupational Status Index of all ICE Examinees for Varying Levels of Performance on the Leaving Certificate Examination (LCEX)

LCEX score	N	*Occupational status* M	SD
-4.9	73	3.11	.74
5.0–5.8	56	3.34	.77
5.9–6.8	55	3.75	.70
6.9+	24	4.25	.68
Overall	208	3.47	.82

TABLE 10.7
Means (and SDs) on Occupational Status Index of Senior-Cycle Terminal Leavers for Varying Levels of Performance on the Leaving Certificate Examination (LCEX)

LCEX score	N	*Occupational status* M	SD
-4.9	6	3.07	.11
5.0–5.8	45	3.22	.77
5.9–6.8	29	3.38	.68
6.9-	3	3.00	.00
Overall	146	3.18	.72

Three indices of the type of post-primary school which students had attended were correlated with occupational status. One was the type of school (secondary or vocational) which students who completed the senior cycle had attended at the junior-cycle level. The second was the type of school (secondary or vocational) which students who completed the senior cycle had attended at that level. The third measure distinguished between senior-cycle students in boarding and non-boarding schools. Analyses revealed (Table 10.2) that attendance at a secondary school rather than at a vocational school at junior level was significantly related to subsequent occupational status ($r = -.21$). Whether a student attended a secondary or a vocational school at senior level, however, was not related to occupational status (r = –.04). The statistically significant correlation for attendance during junior cycle is probably due to the fact that over three-quarters of those who had been in secondary school at this stage continued in school, while less than one-quarter of vocational-school students remained at school after completing the junior cycle. At the senior-cycle level, the number of vocational students who completed the course was too small (N:10) to have an impact on the correlation with occupational status. Attendance at boarding school during senior cycle was positively and significantly related to subsequent occupational status (r = –.27).

Occupational Mobility

In considering the correlation between students' home background and their future occupational status, we noted that the magnitude of the correlation indicated that many students took up occupations at a level which differed from the level of their fathers' occupations. In some cases, students had higher social-status occupations than their fathers; in other cases, they had lower ones. In this section, we examine the extent of such mobility — both upward and downward — and factors associated with it.

At the outset, a number of points should be borne in mind. Firstly, since our student occupational data are based on initial occupation, it seems reasonable to assume that we are underestimating the level of later occupational status. Factors such as change in occupation, on-the-job training and experience, and seniority tend to result in increased occupational status. Secondly, our analyses are based on relatively small samples by comparison with other studies of social mobility. However, they include women as well as men, which many studies do not.

An examination of the data in Table 10.8 shows that the initial occupations of a total of 258 students (54.0%) were classified as skilled. Fewer than 10% were classified in the two extreme categories, professional or unskilled. A total of 175 (36.6%) students had improved on their fathers' occupations by at least one socio-economic status level, while the occupational level of 117 (24.5%) had dropped below that of their fathers. The remaining 186 (38.9%) maintained the level of their fathers' occupations. Overall, the mean socio-economic status level for sons and daughters (M = 3.01; SD = .87) represents a significant increase over the corresponding mean for their fathers (M = 2.79; SD = 1.13).[16] Part of the overall increase can be attributed to the fact that the number

TABLE 10.8
Numbers (and Percentages) of Students Achieving each Occupational Level by Level of Fathers' Occupation: Total Sample

	Fathers' occupations					
Students' occupations	*Higher professional*	*Inter. professional*	*Skilled*	*Partly-skilled*	*Unskilled*	*Total*
Higher professional	3 *13.0%*	8 *34.8%*	10 *43.5%*	1 *4.3%*	1 *4.3%*	23 *4.8%*
Intermediate professional	6 *6.8%*	47 *53.4%*	13 *14.8%*	15 *17.0%*	7 *8.0%*	88 *18.4%*
Skilled	3 *1.2%*	61 *23.6%*	105 *40.7%*	48 *18.6%*	41 *15.9%*	258 *54.0%*
Partly-skilled	2 *2.3%*	16 *18.2%*	16 *18.2%*	23 *26.1%*	31 *35.2%*	88 *18.4%*
Unskilled	0 *0.0%*	2 *9.5%*	10 *47.6%*	1 *4.8%*	8 *38.1%*	21 *4.4%*
Total	14 *2.9%*	134 *28.0%*	154 *32.2%*	88 *18.4%*	88 *18.4%*	478

of fathers in the lowest category, i.e., the unskilled (N:88), far exceeds the number in the highest (professional) category (N:14). Because of this, it was virtually inevitable that the number who raised their status would have exceeded the number experiencing a decline in status. In fact, if the two extreme categories of fathers' occupation are excluded, slightly more students (N:106) experience a decrease rather than an increase in status (N:95).

The children of farmers present particular problems when it comes to considering occupational mobility. Those problems arise in part from the tradition of migration from rural areas (Raftery, in press) but they also arise from the way in which farmers were categorized in our scheme of occupational status. It will be recalled that the status of farmers was determined on the basis of the acreage of their farms as well as on the basis of their occupations, something which did not apply, of course, to non-farmers. The procedure of taking acreage into account in assigning farmers to a socio-economic level revealed an anxiety we had about the amount of variance covered by the term farmer. However, while we felt that all farmers, whatever their size of holding, could not be considered as belonging to a single socio-economic level, we were not sure that the categorization we adopted was entirely satisfactory or that the way in which we matched the three groups of farmers which we formed to other occupations in our socio-economic hierarchy accurately reflected the relative socio-economic levels of the three groups. While there were problems in all analyses involving the socio-economic status of farmers in our study, they are accentuated in analyses in which mobility from one occupational category to another is the topic of interest.

With these reservations in mind, we carried out analyses of occupational mobility which were confined to the sons and daughters of farmers. These analyses revealed that 38.3% of sons had experienced a decrease on their fathers' occupational status; that is a much higher percentage than that recorded for any other sub-sample in the present study. Further, the percentage of farmers' daughters who retained their father's occupational status (24.6%) was considerably lower than that of other sub-samples, while the percentage of farmers' daughters who experienced a decrease in status (41.0%) was also much larger than for other groups. We do not know if these changes are to be interpreted as real changes in status or whether they are reflections of the problems relating to occupational classification which we discussed above. Weight is added to the latter interpretation when we consider that, in our classification scheme, a son of a farmer with 50 acres of relatively poor land who became a skilled tradesman would be deemed to have experienced a decrease in occupational status. Certainly, our findings for farmers' children differ from those for other groups. While the issue of the mobility of farmers' children obviously deserves further attention, we decided not to include such children in further analyses because of the nature of our preliminary findings which might be due to problems arising from their socio-economic classification. Thus, the remaining analyses of occupational mobility in this chapter are confined to the 370 sons and daughters of non-farmers.

Results for the non-farming group were quite similar to those reported for the total sample: 38.9% improved on their father's occupation, while the percentages which maintained or dropped occupational status levels were 40.0 and 21.1 respectively.

A separate index of mobility, i.e., occupational structural mobility was computed. This index measured the extent to which the occupational distribution of the sons and daughters differs from that of their fathers. In computing this index all of the occupational mobility as well as the size of the movements across occupational categories are taken into consideration. The extent of inter-generational mobility in occupational structure conveyed by our data is relatively low by international standards (cf. Raftery, in press).[17]

TABLE 10.9
Numbers (and Percentages) of Students Achieving each Occupational Level by Level of Fathers' Occupation: Non-Farm Sample

Students' occupations	*Fathers' occupations*					
	Higher profes-sional	*Inter. profes-sional*	*Skilled*	*Partly-skilled*	*Un-skilled*	*Total*
Higher professional	2 *10.0%*	6 *30.0%*	10 *50.0%*	1 *5.0%*	1 *5.0%*	20 *5.4%*
Intermediate professional	6 *10.3%*	26 *44.8%*	12 *20.7%*	7 *12.1%*	7 *12.1%*	58 *15.7%*
Skilled	3 *1.4%*	36 *17.1%*	102 *48.6%*	28 *13.3%*	41 *19.5%*	210 *56.8%*
Partly-skilled	1 *1.6%*	5 *8.1%*	15 *24.2%*	10 *16.1%*	31 *50.0%*	62 *16.8%*
Unskilled	0 *0.0%*	1 *5.0%*	10 *50.0%*	1 *5.0%*	8 *40.0%*	20 *5.4%*
Total	12 *3.2%*	74 *20.0%*	149 *40.3%*	47 *12.7%*	88 *23.8%*	370

Changes in occupational status from father to child in the non-farming sample are made up largely of an increase (from 149 to 210) in the number in the skilled category and a corresponding decrease in the number in the unskilled category (from 88 to 20) (Table 10.9). The numbers in the professional categories remained fairly constant. Given the large increase in service sector employment in Ireland over the period 1950–80, this result is somewhat surprising. It is, of course, likely that many of those who commenced work in the skilled category may subsequently have moved upwards into the professional categories. Viewed from the perspective of mobility across the professional/non-professional divide (defined in this instance as the divide between intermediate professional and skilled), the data reveal that, in terms of occupational status, many children of professional parents have moved downwards for their first job and that very few (13.4%) of children of non-professional parents commence work with a professional job.

Upward occupational mobility among non-farmers appears to have been more prevalent among girls (42.5%) than among boys (35.6%) (Table 10.10). Further, the overall difference in occupational structure between fathers and children is higher for girls than for boys.[18] A very large proportion of girls were classified as skilled. While only 69 of the fathers' occupations were skilled, 112 (i.e., 63%) of our sample of girls entered skilled occupations. At the same time, the number of girls in the unskilled category decreased from 46 to two. The changes in occupational classification were not as pronounced in the case of the boys; a total of 98 fathers and 80 sons were classified as skilled and 42 fathers and 18 sons as unskilled. Girls were also more likely to be more mobile across the professional/non-professional divide than boys; in particular, daughters of professional fathers were more downwardly mobile than sons. The high representation of girls in the skilled category (63.0%) can be attributed to the fact that our occupational classification system assigns such traditionally popular female occupations as secretary, typist, sales assistant, and telephone operator to the skilled category; relatively few female occupations were in the partly-skilled category and even fewer were in the unskilled category. The distributions of occupations which we obtained serve to underline the difficulty of making valid assertions about social mobility, especially in the case of females.

TABLE 10.10
Percentages of Students Exhibiting Occupational Mobility by Gender and Level of Ability (Non-Farm Sample)

		Direction of mobility		
	N	*No change* %	*Upward* %	*Downward* %
Girls	179	39.7	42.5	17.9
Girls 108+ VA*	49	49.0	30.6	20.4
Girls<108 VA	130	36.2	46.9	16.9
Boys	191	40.3	35.6	24.1
Boys 108+ VA	76	40.8	34.2	25.0
Boys<108 VA	115	40.0	36.5	23.5

*VA = Verbal ability.

A consideration of the role of level of ability in occupational mobility led us to conclude that girls who scored below 108 on the verbal reasoning measure (i.e., the mean verbal reasoning score of students who passed the LCE) experienced the highest level of occupational mobility

— higher than boys and higher than girls with higher scores (Table 10.10).[19] A closer examination of the data reveals that the fathers of 60 (46.2%) of the girls in the 'below 108' verbal ability group had been classified as semi-skilled or unskilled (compared to 16.3% of the 108+ category). For this relatively large number of girls, upward occupational mobility was almost inevitable. Of the 60 girls, 55 experienced an increase in occupational status — 32 of them to the skilled category. On the other hand, the fathers of 18 (36.7%) of the girls in the 108+ verbal ability category had professional or intermediate professional occupations (compared to 18.5% of the 'below 108' category). Clearly among these girls there was little or no room for upward occupational mobility. A total of nine of this sample experienced downward mobility — eight of them, not surprisingly, to the skilled occupational category.

TABLE 10.11
Numbers of Girls who Achieved Varying Levels of Socio-Economic Status, by Level of Ability (Non-Farm Sample)

	Verbal ability	
Socio-economic status	108+	<108
Professional/Intermediate professional	18 (36.7%)	24 (18.5%)
Skilled	23 (46.9%)	46 (35.4%)
Partly-skilled/Unskilled	8 (16.3%)	60 (46.2%)

Our data reveal that almost half the combined male and female city samples experienced no change in status compared to approximately one-third of the town and rural (non-farm) samples. In terms of upward mobility, students from rural (non-farm) backgrounds experienced the greatest degree of upward occupational mobility (49.3%); somewhat less upward mobility (41.9%) was experienced by the town sample (most notably by the males) while the overall city sample recorded the lowest degree of upward mobility (29.7%).[20]

To date, many studies of occupational mobility have been confined to samples of city males and the results have been interpreted as providing national indices of occupational mobility (cf. Raftery, in press). However, our data (Table 10.12) suggest that the pattern of

TABLE 10.12
Percentages of Students Exhibiting Occupational Mobility, by Location and Gender

		Direction of mobility		
Location	N	*No change* %	*Upward* %	*Downward* %
City				
Total	158	48.7	29.7	21.5
Male	82	47.6	30.5	22.0
Female	76	50.0	28.9	21.1
Town				
Total	86	33.7	41.9	24.4
Male	41	39.0	24.4	36.6
Female	45	28.9	57.8	13.3
Rural (non farm)				
Total	138	32.6	49.3	18.1
Male	72	33.3	47.2	19.4
Female	66	31.8	51.5	16.7

occupational mobility of city males may be quite different from those of other groups within the population.[21] Among boys, the greatest occupational mobility occurred among those from rural non-farming backgrounds. Boys from towns showed an intermediate level of mobility while those from cities showed the least. City boys, in fact, had an occupational structure very similar to that of their fathers (almost 50% of them retained their fathers' occupational status). Among girls, those from cities also showed the least occupational mobility. Girls from other backgrounds (town and rural non-farming backgrounds) exhibited considerably more occupational mobility of an upward nature. Thus, occupational mobility for both boys and girls appears to be less prevalent in cities than in town or rural areas. This latter finding raises the interesting hypothesis that the greater occupational mobility of the non-city sample may stem from a lack of employment opportunities in rural and town areas; students, with fewer incentives to drop out of school, stay on to reach higher levels of educational attainment, which are subsequently reflected in higher status occupations.[22]

In an attempt to identify the factors which were associated with improvement and decline in socio-economic status, a comparison was made between the educational histories of students who had raised their status by two socio-economic levels over that of their fathers (classified as 'ascenders') and students whose status had decreased by a similar amount (described as 'descenders'). Altogether, 75 'ascending' students and 33 'descending' ones were identified. An examination of the scores of the two samples on the primary-school variables revealed that ascenders, by comparison with descenders, tended to have been ranked higher in their classes,[23] to have had less difficulty with Problem Arithmetic,[24] and to have received more positive satisfactory classroom behaviour ratings from their teachers.[25] Further, there were more girls (N:42) than boys (N:33) among the occupational status ascenders, while there were more than three times as many boys (N:25) as girls (N:8) among the descenders.

The performance on the Intermediate Certificate Examination (ICEX) of the ascenders (N:49) was compared with the performance of the descenders (N:21). The former group was found to have performed significantly better.[26] Similarly, a comparison between the performance of the groups on the Leaving Certificate Examination (LCEX) taken by 34 ascenders and 12 descenders revealed a significant difference in favour of the former.[27] However, despite the apparent differences in school achievement between the two groups, the difference between them in mean verbal reasoning ability was not significant.[28] The mean scores of both groups on the verbal reasoning test were relatively low; that of the ascenders was 99.87 (SD = 16.20) and that of the descenders, 94.88 (SD = 15.21).

Conclusion

Information on students' first occupations after leaving school was obtained for 95.6% of our sample. Occupations were classified according to the system which had been used to classify the occupations of students' fathers.

At virtually each level of school attainment, those who elected to remain in full-time education, by comparison with those who left school, tended to achieve a higher level occupational status. The difference in status reflects not alone differences between the persisters and terminal leavers on a variety of educational background variables, but also the bonuses or advantages that accrue to the persisters from further full-time attendance at school.

A comparison of the mean occupational status levels for different levels of school attainment indicates that level of occupational status tends to rise with the amount of education a student has received.[29] Separate individual comparisons show that primary-school terminal leavers differed significantly from junior-cycle terminal leavers and senior-cycle early leavers in terms of occupational status. Further, primary-school terminal leavers, junior-cycle early leavers and junior-cycle terminal leavers each differed significantly from senior-cycle terminal leavers and also from both higher-education attainment levels. Finally, significant occupational-status differences were recorded between higher-education graduates and senior-cycle dropouts and terminal leavers.

The occupational mobility exhibited by our sample appears low by international standards. In general, there was a slight increase in the occupational status levels of sons and daughters over those of their fathers. In comparison with students who experienced a decrease in occupational status, the more upwardly mobile members tended to have recorded better school achievement ratings. Among sons and daughters of non-farmers, pupil gender, verbal reasoning ability and location appear to be associated with occupational mobility. Given the rather crude nature of occupational classifications and our relatively small samples, this latter finding should be treated with some caution.

The correlation between fathers' occupation and students' first occupation was not very strong. First occupation was related to verbal reasoning ability and also to level of achievement at both the primary and post-primary levels. With the exception of private primary schools, attendance at a particular type of primary school was not related to occupational status. Attendance at a secondary school during the junior-cycle years as opposed to a vocational school was significantly related to subsequent occupational status, a finding which reflects the fact that most vocational students did not attempt senior cycle. Boarding-school students did better in terms of first occupational status than non-boarding school students. Students' level of performance on both the Intermediate Certificate and Leaving Certificate Examinations was related to first occupational status. The positive correlation between level of state examination performance and occupational status also applied to the ICE students who left school at the end of the junior cycle, but not to the LCE students who left school at the end of the senior cycle.

Level of attainment as measured by the highest grade level achieved was identified as the best predictor (.61) of level of first occupation.

FOOTNOTES

1 A total of four students left school to emigrate. Two of these left from primary school while the remaining two (one secondary, one vocational) emigrated from post-primary school shortly after commencing the junior cycle. A further 25 emigrated after leaving school. Of those who had attended vocational school, two failed to complete junior cycle, two were junior-cycle terminal leavers, one failed to complete senior cycle and two completed senior cycle. Among secondary-school dropouts, one failed to complete junior cycle, five were junior-cycle terminal leavers, one failed to complete senior cycle, and 11 were senior-cycle terminal leavers.

2 The number of students who became farmers was quite small (N:18), especially since 113 (22.5%) of the original sample were either sons or daughters of farmers. Half of these young farmers came from farms of 30 acres or more.

3 In these analyses, the higher- and intermediate-professional categories are grouped together, as are partly-skilled and unskilled categories. Hence there are only two degrees of freedom.

4 $\chi^2 = 48.43$; $df = 2$; $p < .001$

5 $\chi^2 = 16.65$; $df = 2$; $p < .001$

6 $\chi^2 = 15.95$; $df = 2$; $p < .001$

7 $\chi^2 = 7.46$; $df = 2$; $p < .05$

8 $\chi^2 = 37.73$; $df = 2$; $p < .001$

9 $\chi^2 = 0.55$; $df = 1$; N.S.

10 $\chi^2 = 2.03$; $df = 2$; N.S.

11 $\chi^2 = 74.94$; $df = 2$; $p < .001$

12 Given the relatively large size of the sample (N:478) for which data were obtained on occupations, statistical significance can be achieved with relatively low correlation values. Values greater than .09 are significant at the .05 level for all correlations based on the primary-school variables. The sample sizes for some of the post-primary measures are smaller, because some students left school before taking examinations.

13 The majority (N:341) had received average ratings (–0.99 to 0.99) for satisfactory classroom behaviour. Over half of these (54.8%) were in the skilled category with the remainder divided almost equally between the two higher and two lower occupational status categories.

14 $F = 3.29$; $df = 3{,}91$; $p < .05$

15 $F = 1.37$; $df = 3{,}142$; N.S.

16 t (for paired samples) $= 2.91$; $df = 485$, $p < .01$

17 The analysis relating to occupational structural mobility were carried out by Dr Adrian Raftery, Department of Statistics, Trinity College, Dublin. For the overall non-farm sample, the index of occupational structural mobility was 14. This index is lower than the corresponding indices for countries such as Scotland, Australia, England and Wales, U.S.A., and Canada, and higher than those reported for France, West Germany, Denmark and Italy (Raftery, in press). It should be borne in mind in making comparisons between countries that the years in which studies were carried out in other countries span approximately a 25-year period.

18 The indices of structural mobility were 18 and 9 for girls and boys respectively.

19 The indices of occupational structural mobility were as follows: Girls (108+), 6; Girls (–108), 27; Boys (108+), 18; Boys (–108), 18.

20 The results of a separate analysis showed that the extent of occupational mobility of the students in the present study is greater than that reported by Hutchinson (1969). The index of occupational structural mobility for the present non-farm sample was 14; the corresponding index for Hutchinson's Dublin male sample was 6.9.

21 The following indices of occupational structural mobility were computed: Boys (city), 6; Boys (town), 13; Boys (rural non-farmer), 23; Girls (city), 16; Girls (town), 50; Girls (rural non-farmer), 42.

22 The results of an additional analysis support this line of reasoning. They showed that the mean level of school attainment of the city sample (M:3.68; SD:1.74) was less than that of the town (M:4.17; SD:1.89) and rural (non-farm) (M:3.90; SD:1.70) samples. The addition of the sons and daughters of farmers to the rural sample raises the mean school attainment level of this latter sample to 3.95 (SD:1.68).

23 $F = 9.44$; $df = 1{,}106$; $p < .01$

24 $F = 4.27$; $df = 1{,}106$; $p < .05$

25 $F = 5.54$; $df = 1{,}106$; $p < .05$

26 $F = 8.75$; $df = 1{,}68$; $p < .01$

27 $F = 10.02$; $df = 1{,}44$; $p < .01$

28 $F = 2.25$; $df = 1{,}106$; N.S.

29 $F = 51.50$; $df = 6{,}471$; $p < .001$

11 Conclusion

In this book, we described the progress through the educational system and into their first occupation of a group of 500 students who had been identified when they were 11 years of age in 1967. We were aware, even before we commenced our study, that the educational careers of the students would vary greatly, both in terms of the length of time they would remain in the system (that is, in their level of educational attainment) and in terms of their actual educational achievements (for example, as evidenced by performance on examinations). The major purpose of the study was to attempt to identify factors which were associated with the differential attainments and achievements of the students.

Since our study was carried out at a time (in the 1960s and 1970s) when the attainment of equality of educational opportunity was being put forward as an objective of government policy, it seemed of particular interest to attempt to ascertain the extent to which a student's success in the system and his or her first occupational position after leaving school could, in equality terminology, be described as having been 'achieved' or 'ascribed'. We would regard success as having been 'achieved' if it were found to be dependent solely on educationally relevant variables, loosely defined as ability and effort. If, however, success seemed to depend primarily on what are generally regarded as educationally irrelevant variables, such as one's gender or social class or the geographical area of the country in which one resided, then such success would be regarded as 'ascribed'.[1] In monitoring the progress of our sample, we assessed at varying points in the system the relative influence on that progress of a number of educationally relevant variables (ability and scholastic achievement) and of a number of educationally irrelevant ones (gender, socio-economic status, location). Since students' progress may be a function of the structure of the educational system, as well as of the personal and background characteristics we have just outlined, we also included in our analyses characteristics of the system, such as the type of administration in the primary school which a student had attended and the type of post-primary school to which the student proceeded on completion of primary education.

Before considering how such factors were related to students' educational progress, we will briefly recapitulate the general statistics regarding perseverance in, and drop out from, the system. Over 92% of students entered a post-primary school on completing primary education. Over three quarters (76%) stayed at school to complete a junior-cycle course, while less than half (45%) completed a senior-cycle course. Thirteen percent continued their formal education in a third-level institution immediately after completing second-level education. These figures indicate that the largest numbers of students terminated their formal education at two points in the system — after the completion of junior cycle but before the completion of senior cycle (31%), or after the completion of senior cycle (32%). Though the number of students who left school before the completion of junior cycle was smaller, it was not inconsiderable; over 7% of students did not go to a post-primary school at all, while a further 16% did not complete a junior-cycle course in a post-primary school.

Personal and Background Factors Related to Educational and Occupational Performance

Of the primary-school factors which were related to persistence in or withdrawal from the educational system, the most important was the verbal reasoning ability of a student. In the case of secondary-school students, the mean level of verbal reasoning ability of those in the system rose consistently from the point of entry to post-primary school to the end of senior cycle. A similar trend, though not as strong, was also observable for a number of variables which described the educational history of students while they were still at primary school. These variables related to general scholastic behaviour and included teachers' ratings of a student's satisfactory classroom behaviour and general scholastic progress, place in class, the school grade the student had attained by the age of 12 years, and the student's school attendance record. On the other hand, students who were less able and had poorer records of educational progress in the primary school tended to drop out at varying points.

The situation in vocational schools was similar to that in secondary schools up to the end of junior cycle. As in the case of secondary-school students, the mean level of verbal reasoning ability of students in vocational schools and the mean ratings on the various indices of their scholastic achievement in primary school (particularly as represented by the satisfactory classroom behaviour rating and ratings of performance in Irish and Mathematics) tended to increase up to the beginning of senior cycle. Subsequently, students' scholastic performance in the primary school, but not their ability, assumed an increased importance.

Ability was again found to be important when we considered achievement as measured by public examinations. It correlated more highly with over-all performance on the Intermediate Certificate Examination (r = .52) than did any other variable. A number of indices of scholastic performance in primary school (a student's place in class and the teacher's appraisal of his or her classroom behaviour) also correlated relatively highly with ICE performance (r = .45 and r = .46 respectively).

At the Leaving Certificate level, students' verbal reasoning ability (measured some six years earlier) was again the best of the primary-school variables in predicting performance on the examination (r = .51). However, the student's over-all performance on the Intermediate Certificate Examination (taken two years earlier) was a much better predictor of Leaving Certificate Examination performance (.82). As at the Intermediate Certificate level, measures of students' earlier scholastic performance also predicted LCE performance.

When we come to consider entrance to third-level education, we see again the importance of previous scholastic achievement. Students who entered third-level institutions were most clearly distinguished from other students who completed second-level education by their superior performance on the Leaving Certificate Examination. Though not at all as important as previous public examination performance, verbal ability and a number of indices of students' scholastic progress while at primary school (school grade attained by the age of 12 and a student's rank in class) still served to distinguish between students who proceeded to third-level education and those who terminated their formal education at the end of post-primary school. The mean verbal reasoning score of third-level entrants was high — 115.63, a score which occurs at the 84th percentile. Among third-level students, those who went to university and colleges of education had higher levels of ability and achievement than the small number of students who went to regional technical colleges.

The best predictor of a student's occupational status on leaving school was the student's level of attainment, that is, the level of the educational system which the student had reached before leaving. The correlation between level of attainment and future occupational status (r = .61) was very close to those found in American studies.[2] Measures of the student's scholastic ability and achievement were also related to occupational status. Of the variables about which information was obtained when the student was still at primary school, the student's verbal reasoning ability had the highest correlation with future occupation (.40). Other relatively though less important variables, about which information was obtained at the same time, were socio-economic status and a teacher's rating of the student's classroom behaviour, both of which were positively and significantly related to future occupational status (r = .32 for SES and r = .33 for classroom behaviour). The correlation between fathers' occupations and those of their children was lower than ones reported for the United States.[3]

The correlations between students' performance on public examinations and future occupational status were slightly stronger than the correlation between verbal reasoning ability and future occupational status (.40). Occupational status had a correlation of .41 with Intermediate Certificate Examination performance and .47 with Leaving Certificate Examination performance. However, we cannot conclude that performance on these examinations was the critical factor in the achievement of that status. This may have been so for some students who left school after taking the Intermediate Certificate Examination; for these, better examination performance tended to be associated with higher occupational status. However, the relationship between Leaving Certificate Examination performance and occupational status was not significant when we confined our analysis to students who left school and did not proceed to third-level education. The fact that the relationship between LCE performance and occupational status was positive and significant when examinees who went on to third-level education were included in the analyses suggests that the higher-status occupations achieved by higher examination scorers should be attributed not to performance on the examination as such but to the additional education they received or to the higher ability of those students who went on to third-level education, or to a combination of these factors.

The relationship between the socio-economic status of a student's father and the student's own eventual occupational status, which we noted above as positive and significant, was also evident in analyses in which we examined occupational mobility, that is, the extent of intergenerational mobility in the occupations of parents and children. Almost two out of five children (39%) maintained the level of their fathers' occupation, while a slightly smaller number (37%) improved on it and just under one in four (almost 25%) dropped below it. It should be borne in mind that these data deal with the first occupation of the student and so are likely to underestimate somewhat final occupational status, though we may assume that the occupational status at which an individual begins his or her career will be substantially predictive of the level at which he or she will be found in later years (Duncan, Featherman, & Duncan, 1972).

Perhaps the most striking conclusion that emerges from this consideration of the variables which were related to the attainment and achievement of the students in our sample was the importance of students' scholastic ability and performance, both for survival in the system and for later scholastic performance.[4] Up to the Intermediate Certificate level, verbal reasoning ability was the best predictor of success in the system. Performance on the ICE examination was the best predictor of later survival in the system and of performance on the Leaving Certificate Examination. The effect of these relationships is that the educational system became increasingly more selective on the basis of scholastic ability and at later stages on the basis of scholastic performance as measured by public examinations.

None of the educationally irrelevant variables included in our study — socio-economic class, gender, or location — played as significant or consistent a role as ability and prior achievement in predicting the educational attainments and achievements of students. Of the educationally irrelevant variables, socio-economic status appeared to be the most important.

The first selection on the basis of socio-economic status was apparent when students completed their primary education. At this point, students proceeding to secondary schools, those proceeding to vocational schools, and those leaving school altogether, were distinguishable from one another in terms of their socio-economic backgrounds. Those of highest status tended to go to secondary school, those of next highest status to vocational school, and those of lowest status terminated their formal education. For example, the probability of a student from a professional home going to a secondary school was .87 and of going to a vocational school .11, while for the student from a non-professional home, the respective probabilities were .58 and .32. Within the non-professional category, chances varied with the degree of skill of the child's father. Children from skilled homes were more likely to go to a secondary school, those from unskilled homes to a vocational school.

In post-primary schools generally, the proportion of students from professional backgrounds increased as classes progressed through the system, while the proportion of students from non-professional backgrounds showed a corresponding decrease. In primary schools, students from professional families made up 31% of the school population. That percentage increased to 33% for post-primary entrants. By the end of junior cycle, students from professional backgrounds had increased their share by 4% and by the end of senior cycle by a further 9%, at which stage they made up 46% of the student body. On entry to third level, their proportion had increased to 58%, by which time the proportion of students from non-professional backgrounds had been reduced to 42% from 69% in primary school.

The role of socio-economic status as a discriminator between those who stayed in school and those who left was stronger in secondary than in vocational schools. In the former type of school, the mean socio-economic level of students rose consistently from the point of entry to the completion of senior cycle, indicating that students of lower socio-economic background were leaving school earlier than those of higher background. A similar trend occurred in vocational schools up to the end of junior cycle. After the commencement of senior cycle in vocational schools, however, there was not a further differential loss of students from lower socio-economic backgrounds. If anything, those of higher status tended to leave at this point. However, the numbers involved at this stage were very small. Socio-economic status did not discriminate between students who left school at the end of senior cycle and those who enrolled in a third-level educational institution.

In general, our findings on socio-economic background indicate that from the end of primary schooling up to third-level education, the representation of students from the lower socio-economic groups decreased, while the representation of those from the higher groups increased. The higher one goes in the educational system, the greater the disparity in participation by socio-economic status. This is not due to discrimination at the higher levels, but rather to the cumulative effect of disparities at earlier stages in the system. In fact, the role of a student's socio-economic status as a discriminator between persistence in and withdrawal from the education system diminished as students advanced through it. This conclusion is in accordance with the findings of studies in other European countries, which show that differences between persisters and drop-outs related to social class are much larger at earlier stages in the educational system (e.g., at the minimum school-leaving age) than at later stages (Halsey *et al.*, 1980; Shattock, 1981). Inequalities of opportunity, for the most part, have done their damage at earlier stages of schooling. For those who survive, inequalities are reduced, though not entirely eliminated.

Socio-economic status correlated more highly (r = .32) with the measure of a student's occupational status on leaving school than with other measures of achievement. Though substantially lower than the correlation between level of school attainment and future occupational status (r = .61), it was sufficiently high to indicate that for many students inter-generational occupational mobility did not operate.

Girls had a slight advantage over boys in representation in second-level education. The over-representation was confined to secondary schools and was more pronounced during the junior cycle than during the senior cycle. In vocational schools, girls were under-represented up to the end of senior cycle. The over-representation of girls in the system was reversed at third level. More boys than girls entered a third-level educational institution.

Location (i.e., whether the primary school the student had attended was situated in an urban or rural area or in a town) was of little relevance to perseverance in or drop-out from either secondary or vocational schools. There was only one case in which it was significantly related to drop-out: leavers from secondary schools at the end of junior cycle were more likely to have attended school in an urban than in a non-urban area. Those who went to a third-level institution and those who terminated their education at the end of second level did not differ from each other in the location of the primary school they had attended.

The educationally irrelevant variables of socio-economic status, gender, and location were less strongly related to scholastic achievement as measured by public examination performance than they were to retention in and drop out from the system. Socio-economic status did not correlate significantly with performance on the Intermediate Certificate Examination, with the one exception of performance on the Mathematics examination on which examination, students of higher socio-economic status tended to perform better (r = .17). There were no significant relationships between socio-economic status and performance on the Leaving Certificate Examination. The small contribution of family background variables to variation in achievement in public examinations has been documented in another study carried out in the 1970s (Madaus, Kellaghan, Rakow, & King, 1979). The lack of relationship is probably due, in part at any rate, to the selectivity of the system before the point at which students sit for public examinations.

Location was not related to performance on the Intermediate or

Leaving Certificate Examinations with two exceptions. Both exceptions concerned Irish. Students from schools in rural areas performed marginally better than students from other locations on the Irish examination at both Intermediate and Leaving Certificate levels. These findings support those of another investigation which concluded that achievement in Irish in primary schools was higher in rural than in other areas (Martin & Kellaghan, 1977).

Our findings on gender are perhaps among the most interesting of those which examined correlates of examination performance. Although among ICE candidates, boys had scored significantly higher than girls on the verbal reasoning test, this superiority was not reflected in ICE performance, except in the case of Mathematics. After initial differences in verbal ability were taken into account, there was no significant difference between boys and girls in their scores on the overall ICE index or on the Irish examination; girls did better on the English examination, while boys did better in Mathematics. Again, when differences in verbal ability are taken into account, girls scored higher than boys on the overall index for the Leaving Certificate Examination and also on the LCE English and Irish examinations. Together, these results indicate that girls tend to fare well under the present state-examination system, a finding that has been noted elsewhere (Greaney & Kelly, 1977).

Characteristics of the Educational System Related to Educational Performance

Do characteristics of the educational system affect students' educational and vocational chances? Is the type of school a student attends related to his or her survival in the system and the kind of educational qualifications he or she will obtain?

In our analyses of student attainment and achievement, the characteristics of the primary schools which students had attended did not figure strongly as being related to such attainment and achievement. While there were some characteristics of primary schools which appeared in analyses as significant correlates of students' scholastic progress, these always were less important than those relating to students' personal and background characteristics or other educational variables. The main effect of type of primary school was at the point of entry to post-primary school. Students from Catholic lay primary schools were under-represented in secondary schools and over-represented in vocational schools, while students who had attended Catholic religious, Protestant, and especially private schools, were over-represented in secondary schools and under-represented in vocational schools. Type of primary-school administration was not an important factor in analyses relating to drop-out or public-examination performance. It did, however, appear in our analyses of the occupational status achieved by students on leaving school; students who had attended Catholic lay-administered primary schools tended to achieve a slightly lower occupational status, while those who had attended private schools tended to achieve slightly higher status levels than those who had attended Protestant or Catholic religious-administered schools.

It is difficult to distinguish between the effects of attendance at a school as such and the effects of the characteristics of students who attend different kinds of schools. For example, the particular advantages associated with attendance at a private primary school may be the higher ability and socio-economic status of the students who go to such a school rather than to the education provided by the school.

That the characteristics of students interact with characteristics of the educational system is most obvious at the post-primary level. Secondary school was the more popular choice of students. Of those students who proceeded to post-primary education, 72% went to a secondary school,[5] while 28% went to a vocational school. There were considerable differences between the students who went to the two types of school. Firstly, the mean level of verbal reasoning ability of secondary-school entrants was superior to the mean level of vocational-school entrants. The mean verbal reasoning score (on a test with a mean of 100 and a standard deviation of 15) of students who went to secondary school was 104.65 (SD = 14.23), that of students proceeding to vocational school, 93.66 (SD = 13.31), while that of students who did not proceed to any type of post-primary school was 82.16 (SD = 11.71). It will be noted that there was considerable variance in the scores of students in the different types of school. For example, over one-third of secondary-school entrants scored below the national mean on the verbal reasoning test. Secondly, students who went to secondary school had higher scores than those who went to vocational school on a wide range of educational and personal variables (rank in class, grade achieved by age twelve, teachers' ratings of satisfactory school progress and of difficulty in specific subject areas). Thirdly, secondary-school entrants tended to come from homes of higher socio-economic status than did vocational-school entrants; they also came from smaller families. Fourthly, girls, by comparison with boys, were over-represented in secondary schools and under-represented in vocational schools. The probability of a girl going to a secondary school was .72; that for a boy .61. The probability of a girl going to a vocational school was only .21, while that for a boy was .31.

Given these differences between students in the two types of post-primary school, it is hardly surprising to find that the educational careers of students in the two types differed. For example, the likelihood of a student staying on in school was greater if he or she went to a secondary rather than to a vocational school. Almost nine out of ten entrants to secondary school completed junior cycle, most of them by taking the Intermediate Certificate Examination; two out of three entrants completed senior cycle by taking the Leaving Certificate Examination, and almost one in five went to a third-level institution. By contrast, less than two out of three entrants (including transfers) to vocational school completed junior cycle (somewhat over half of whom took the Intermediate Certificate Examination and the remainder the Day Group Certificate Examination). Only one in 14 completed senior cycle, while only one in 50 went on to third-level education.

Students in vocational schools who persisted in school did less well on public examinations (Intermediate and Leaving Certificate) than secondary-school students. However, if initial differences between students on the primary-school measures are taken into account, the performances of students in the two types of school were not significantly different from each other, with the one exception of ICE Mathematics, on which examination secondary-school students performed better.

The high drop-out rate from vocational schools should be interpreted in the context of the characteristics of the students who go to such schools and the constraints regarding academic courses under which vocational schools worked in the past. The vocational school, in its continuation education role, was essentially a junior-cycle school, and students (and/or parents and any others involved in the selection process) were obviously aware of this fact in selecting a post-primary school.

To the extent that the type of post-primary school which a student attended limited his or her prospects of staying in the system and of obtaining the qualifications conferred by the system, the traditional structure of post-primary education in Ireland must be regarded as an institutional constraint on the realization of equality of participation and achievement. The continual broadening of curricula in both vocational and secondary schools and the increase in the numbers of students enrolled in post-primary schools since the data for our study were obtained may be expected to have had a mitigating effect on that constraint.

Limitations of Study

It is obviously tempting to try to generalise the findings of this study to conditions in the educational system generally and, in particular, to try to assess the extent to which educational benefits are distributed on the basis of educationally relevant or educationally irrelevant variables. Before doing this, attention should be paid to certain limitations of the study.

Two considerations raise questions about the representativeness of the sample which was studied. In the first place, it will be noted that our sample was not a very large one. This creates problems especially when the sample is divided in analyses into smaller groups, such as students of differing socio-economic levels and students attending different types of school. In some of our analyses, we found it necessary to combine the professional and intermediate professional groups because of the small number of students in the former group. Similarly, the number of students attending vocational school at senior cycle and the number attending third-level institutions were so small that the results of analyses based on sub-groups of those students must obviously be treated with caution.

A second consideration relating to our sample is the fact that although our analyses are all concerned with students, our sampling unit was not the student but the primary school attended by students. This is a common practice in educational research and indeed, it is usually the only procedure that is feasible in terms of logistics and economics. However, it does mean that one cannot automatically assume that the sample, even if representative of schools in the country, also provides an accurate representation of students in the country. To examine this problem, we carried out a number of checks in which we compared statistics from our sample with published statistics which were available for the general population. These referred mainly to participation rates at various stages and in various types of school in the educational system as well as to participation and performance in examinations. We also carried out a rough check on the socio-economic composition of the sample. Almost all of these checks revealed that our sample statistics were very close to national ones, a finding that provides a basis for a certain amount of confidence in the representativeness of our sample.

Another major limitation of the study is that it was carried out during the late 1960s and through the 1970s. It might be argued that the educational system has changed so much since then that our findings may not be relevant today. While longitudinal studies have a number of advantages, particularly where it is possible as it was in our study to obtain follow-up data on practically all participants, they also have the disadvantage that while a cohort is being followed, conditions may be changing.

There is no doubt that the educational system has changed from the early 1970s in a number of respects. Firstly, the school-leaving age has been raised from 14 to 15 years. Secondly, the increasing participation at second and third levels, which was a feature of the 1970s, has continued into the 1980s. And thirdly, there has been a change in the structure of second-level education. When our study began, community schools did not exist and comprehensive schools were new and were attended by very few students (less than one percent of second-level students), so few that in our analyses we combined secondary and comprehensive-school students. That would not be necessary today when about nine percent of students attend community/comprehensive schools (Ireland: Department of Education, 1983). Further, we are aware that vocational schools have changed in character and students attending them are more likely to have the opportunity of sitting for public examinations than they had in the past.

If we were to carry out a similar study today, our figures for retention in the system would be greater than the ones we found, while our figures for drop-out would, of course, be correspondingly lower. However, we have little doubt that the general pattern of relationships which we described between success in the system and a variety of personal and background characteristics of students would still hold. For our findings bear a marked resemblance to findings of studies carried out elsewhere. In the United States, for example, where participation rates at second and third level are much higher than in this country, it has been shown that students who leave school early have lower levels of measured ability, particularly verbal ability, and of scholastic achievement than those who remain in school (Combs & Cooley, 1968; Duncan, 1968; Howell & Frese, 1982; Sewell, Palmo & Manni, 1981). In that country also, signs of impending drop-out are visible in elementary schools in grade retention and absenteeism (Stroup & Robins, 1972), while the influence of home background (socio-economic status, level of parental education, income, family structure) on educational attainment and achievement has been documented over and over again (e.g., Coleman *et al.*, 1966; Combs & Cooley, 1968; Duncan, 1968; Howell & Frese, 1982; Rumberger, 1983; Sewell & Hauser, 1975; Stroup & Robins, 1972). While the proportions of students who leave school early may differ over time in any given educational system, the characteristics of the students and their reasons for leaving seem fairly constant over time (Rumberger, 1983).

The Extent of Inequality in Irish Schools

Finally, we may ask to what extent can equality of opportunity be said to operate in Irish schools? Were the aspirations of the policy-makers in the 1960s and 1970s realized in the educational careers of the cohort of students who were the subject of this study in the 1970s? In particular, does the Irish system of education operate on meritocratic principles? Before attempting to answer these questions, we should recall the definitions of equality which we considered in Chapter 1. There we saw that equality may be defined in terms of access, participation, or achievement. All definitions are in agreement that a student's success in the system (whether that success is measured in terms of access, participation, or achievement) should not be based on ascribed characteristics such as gender, socio-economic status, or location. To what extent, we may ask, was the access, participation, and achievement of the students in our sample dependent on their gender, their socio-economic status, or their location?

Our study was not directed to the problem of equality of access. While inferences about access are often made on the basis of participation rates, we have no reason to believe that any discrimination on the basis of gender, socio-economic status, or place of residence existed which prevented students in our sample from attending school at least up to the end of post-primary school. However, factors which might have limited access to certain types of school and courses probably did exist. We know from other sources that all areas in the country are not equally well served by post-primary facilities.[6] We also know that the curriculum options available to girls in second-level schools differ from those available to boys (Hannan, Breen, Murray, Watson, Hardiman, & O'Higgins, 1983). Further, it is likely that financial considerations affected the ability of some students to remain at school. Since distance from a third-level institution (with its obvious financial implications) is related to participation in third-level education, we can conclude that access to education at this level is not uniform across the country (cf. Clancy, 1982; Kellaghan & Fontes, 1980). Since we did not address these issues in our study, we are not in a position to determine the extent to which students in our sample may have been affected by them in limiting their access to education.

The criterion of equality used in most studies of equality of opportunity has not been access, but participation. Furthermore, participation has usually been measured at the level of class membership. That is, the proportion of members of a gender, or socio-economic group living in a particular geographical location, which is found to participate in education at varying levels (most usually in Ireland at third level) is calculated, and only if that proportion matches the proportion in the general population is equality said to exist.

Taking participation as the criterion of equality in our study, location (that is whether the student went to school in an urban area, a town, or a rural area) was, in general, not an important factor. The only evidence that it might affect participation appeared in the tendency for students in urban areas to drop out of school at an earlier stage than students in other areas, a reflection perhaps of greater employment opportunities in cities. Gender was more closely related to participation than was location. The participation of girls in second-level education was greater than that of boys, while the position was reversed at third level.

The greatest discrepancies in participation occurred in the case of socio-economic class and it is to findings relating to these discrepancies that we must pay most attention. We have already noted the relationship between socio-economic background and early school leaving and its effect on the socio-economic composition of the student body. Despite these trends, we have to bear clearly in mind that of all the personal and background information which we obtained about students when they were in primary school, ability, and not social class, as some commentators (Bowles, 1972; Katz, 1971) might have led us to expect, was the factor that was most closely related to a student's progress through the system — how far the student went in the system and how well he or she did in it. As we have seen, this conclusion emerged from many of our analyses. For example, students of high ability (those who had a score at or above the mean level of verbal reasoning ability of students who passed the Leaving Certificate Examination) were more than twice as likely as students of low ability to complete the senior cycle in a post-primary school and more than five times as likely to enter a third-level educational institution.

The relationships between educationally irrelevant variables and achievement overtly manifested themselves most strongly in the early stages of students' educational careers and again when the student left school. As in the case of the participation index, of the educationally irrelevant variables, socio-economic status was the variable which was most closely related to indices of achievement. It correlated positively, though not very strongly, with several indicators of students' scholastic progress while in primary school (Greaney, 1972) and more strongly with the status of the first occupation achieved by the student after leaving school.

Performance on public examinations, with a few marginal exceptions, was not related to the socio-economic status of students. This was probably due, as we have already suggested, to the attrition that had taken place before students got to the point where they took a public examination. Since attrition was greater among students from lower socio-economic backgrounds, a greater proportion of such students than of ones of higher socio-economic status, did not have the opportunity of taking a public examination.

These relationships between socio-economic class and achievement at various stages, and particularly between socio-economic status and participation, strongly indicate that the educational system is not purely meritocratic. This conclusion receives added support from the evidence that not all students of high ability completed a senior-cycle course and sat for the Leaving Certificate Examination. Almost 30% of students who, according to our criterion, had the necessary ability to pass this examination, did not sit for it. Even allowing for the fact that our test of verbal ability was administered such a long time before the Leaving Certificate Examination and anyhow cannot be regarded as an entirely accurate measure of all the factors which are necessary for success in school, our findings point to a not inconsiderable loss of talent from the system.

Not only is the system not meritocratic in the sense that some more able students are lost from it at relatively early stages, it is also non-meritocratic in the sense that the loss of such students is proportionally greater among students from non-professional backgrounds (skilled, semi-skilled, and unskilled) than among students from professional backgrounds. For example, a student of high ability was just over 1.4 times more likely to complete a senior-cycle course if he or she came from a professional background than if he or she came from a non-professional background; again, a student of high ability from a professional background was almost 1.7 times more likely to enter a third-level institution than one from a non-professional background.[7] To the extent that loss from the system of high-ability students was not equally spread across students from different socio-economic backgrounds, we can infer that factors related to socio-economic background operated in the case of some students of high ability to deter them from continuing with their educational careers.

Differences in participation between socio-economic groups were even greater for less able students than for more able ones. Less able students (i.e., those who on the verbal reasoning test had scored below the mean of students who passed the LCE) were 2.1 times more likely to complete senior cycle in a post-primary school if they came from a professional home rather than from a non-professional home. Further, the chances of a less able student of entering a third-level institution, though slight, were 5.7 times greater if he/she came from a professional home rather than from a non-professional home.[8] A similar pattern of relationships between ability, social class, and entry to a third-level institution has been reported for students in the United States (Sewell & Hauser, 1976).

A consideration of the implications of a meritocratic system must inevitably raise deeper questions than we have been able to consider about the nature of ability and socio-economic background, and the relationship between them. It can be argued that the type of measure of ability which we used was biased or otherwise inappropriate as a measure of a student's ability to profit from education. For example, it has been said that a general measure of verbal ability is simply a surrogate for socio-economic status and that it, therefore, discriminates against children from non-middle class backgrounds (Carnoy, 1974). On the basis of our findings, it would be difficult to sustain such an argument, since the correlation between our measure of verbal ability and socio-economic status was only .3 (Kellaghan & Macnamara, 1972), a figure not dissimilar to that reported in other studies (White, 1982). However, at the same time, our findings also indicate that the application of meritocratic standards based on ability do tend to favour the student of high social status (cf. Karabel & Astin, 1975).

It is clear that by the age of eleven years, at the latest, ability is not distributed equally across socio-economic classes. Indeed, one of the most striking and perhaps disturbing conclusions that emerges from our consideration of the correlates of success and failure in the system is the early stage at which the patterns of future performance can be detected. The conditions which affect a student's future educational, and presumably life, chances are laid down relatively early in life and are clearly in evidence before the end of primary schooling.

Many studies of inequality have focussed on disparities in social-class participation at third level or, at any rate, during the period of non-compulsory education. While gross differences in participation at these stages may indicate that all is not well with the system, they may also be misleading on at least two counts. Firstly, they may suggest that the problem occurs only at that level and thus that solutions should be attempted at that stage, whereas it is clear from our findings, corroborated by findings elsewhere, that the origins of the problem have to be sought at a much earlier stage. Secondly, by focussing on social-class membership or socio-economic status of students in assessing inequality, one may be doing more to obscure than to elucidate the basic problems associated with the differential participation of groups of students. We regarded socio-economic status as an educationally 'irrelevant' variable. However, we also found that it correlated with scholastic progress. Does this mean that there is discrimination based on social class operating in the system? Or is it not more likely that educationally relevant variables correlate with socio-economic status? And if this is so, what is the logic of making judgments about inequality solely on the basis of statistics on social-class participation?

We cannot answer these questions unequivocally and studies which limit themselves to a consideration of socio-economic or social-class membership will never throw any real light on them. The use of a measure of ability, as was the case in our study, goes some way towards recognizing the variance that exists within classes, as well as being more faithful to the expressed objectives of government policy in this country. The fact that ability played such a dominant role in the educational progress of students in our study suggests that the meritocratic ideal is at least being approached if not quite being attained.

FOOTNOTES

1 Sometimes, variables such as gender and social class are regarded, in addition to being educationally irrelevant, as also being ones over which the individual has no control. The implication is that the variables involved in a success or status which is 'achieved' are ones over which an individual has control. The extent to which an individual has control over such factors as ability, effort, or even choice is, however, open to debate.

2 Blau & Duncan (1967) report a correlation of .60 between educational attainment and subsequent occupational status; Jencks *et al.* (1972) report one of .65.

3 For example, Blau & Duncan's (1967) correlation between fathers' occupation and that of their children was .40; that of Jencks *et al.* (1972), .50.

4 This finding is not unique to Ireland. For example, the findings of Rehberg & Rosenthal (1975) in the United States indicate that such factors as scholastic ability and academic performance were much more strongly associated with progress in school than was social class.

5 This figure includes the 1.4% who went to comprehensive school. In our analyses, these were combined with secondary-school students.

6 Areas such as counties or regions were not included in our study.

7 These figures are based on participation rates of more able students at the Leaving Certificate level of 86.4% for professional (professional and intermediate professional) students and of 61.3% for non-professional (skilled, semi-skilled, and unskilled) students. At the point of entry to third-level education, the participation rates of the two groups were 37.9% and 22.6% respectively. In calculating the percentages for the non-professional students, the data for the skilled, semi-skilled, and unskilled groups in Table 9.1 were combined.

8 These figures are based on participation rates of less able students at the Leaving Certificate level of 52.3% for professional (professional and intermediate professional) students and 25.1% for non-professional (skilled, semi-skilled, and unskilled) students. At the point of entry to third-level education, the participation rates of the two groups were 13.6% and 2.4% respectively. In calculating the percentages for the non-professional students the data for the skilled, semi-skilled, and unskilled groups in Table 9.1 were combined.

Glossary of Terms

This glossary is designed to provide an explanation of terms referred to in the text. It includes a brief description of some statistical concepts. The numbers in parentheses after some of the descriptions are the code values which were used in the data analysis.

Absenteeism: The number of days a student was absent during the 1967–68 school year.

Achievement: The student's level of knowledge and skills based on the school curriculum.

Aesthetic behaviour: A summary variable derived from a factor analysis of 20 personality characteristics of students. Appreciation of beauty is the most prominent characteristic of this rather poorly defined factor.

All-male primary school: Primary school in which all the students were boys (All male = 1; Other = -1).

All-female primary school: Primary school in which all the students were girls (All female = 1; Other = -1).

Analysis of variance: A statistical procedure used to determine whether the difference between two or more groups on a single variable is significant or whether the groups can be considered to have been drawn from the same population and the difference can be attributed to chance.

Attainment: The highest level in the educational system reached by an individual student. (Primary-school terminal leaver (1); Junior-cycle early leaver (2); Junior-cycle terminal leaver (3); Senior-cycle early leaver (4); Senior cycle terminal leaver (5); Higher-education early leaver (6); and Higher-education terminal leaver (7)).

Boarding school: School which has residential accommodation for students (Boarding = 1; Non-boarding = -1).

Catholic lay primary school: Primary school under Catholic management in which the principal teacher was a lay person.

Catholic religious (non-lay) primary school: Primary school under Catholic management in which the principal teacher was a member of a religious order or congregation.

Centroid: Mean score for a group on a particular discriminant function.

Class place: Student's rank position in class over all subjects as rated by the teacher (Top 10% = 5; Next highest 20% = 4; Middle 40% = 3; Next 20% = 2; and Lowest 10% = 1).

Class size: Number of pupils in a class (0–5 = 0; 6–15 = 1; 16–25 = 2; 26–35 = 3; 36–45 = 4; 46–50 = 5 and 50+ = 6).

College of Education Index: An index of student achievement in the Leaving Certificate Examination used in the selection of entrants to Colleges of Education. Letter grades are transformed into numerical values on the following basis: A = 72; B = 60; C = 48; D = 36. Numerical values for Irish and Mathematics are assigned a weight of 1.5. Values of grades scored on ordinary-level papers were reduced by one-third.

Common-level paper: An Intermediate Certificate Examination paper in which no distinction is made between Higher and Lower levels. Common level papers are offered in all subjects with the exception of English, Irish, and Mathematics.

Community school: Post-primary school which offers academic and technical subjects, as well as courses and facilities for local communities. New post-primary schools are usually community schools, rather than vocational or secondary. The school is like a comprehensive school in its curriculum but has a different management structure.

Comprehensive school: Post-primary school which offers academic and technical subjects. These schools have been built and financed by the Department of Education. The first comprehensive school opened in 1966. At present there are 15 such schools and no further ones are planned.

Correlation coefficient (r): A measure of the degree of relationship or the extent to which two sets of measures for the same individuals co-vary. Correlation coefficients vary from +1.00 (perfect positive relationship) through .00 (absence of a relationship) to -1.00 (perfect negative relationship). One would expect a positive correlation between student performance on verbal ability and reading tests (e.g., .60), no correlation between student height and examination grades (e.g., .03), and a negative correlation between students' scores on a Mathematics test and the number of days they had been absent from school (e.g., -.35).

Cross-sectional study: A study in which data are collected at one point in time (cf. Longitudinal study).

Dáil Éireann: Chamber of elected representatives in the legislature of the Republic of Ireland.

Day Group Certificate Examination: A state public examination for students who have followed an approved course for at least two years as a recognised student in a post-primary school. To obtain a pass in the examination, a candidate must pass one of the group of subjects described as Commerce (General), Commerce (Secretarial), Domestic Science, Manual Training and Rural Science. All students are required to take English and Irish as subjects.

Department of Education: The government department which has responsibility for the administration of primary, post-primary and special education. State subsidies for universities and colleges are chanelled through the Department.

Dependent variable: The variable which is predicted or explained. When the relationships between reading achievement and variables such as ability, gender, and teaching method are studied, reading achievement is the dependent variable. The other variables which are presumed to explain or predict reading achievement are termed independent variables. It is assumed that reading achievement 'depends on' the other factors which are isolated for study.

Deviation score: The amount by which a score differs from some reference value, such as the mean.

df (degrees of freedom): The number of changes that can be made to a group of figures (ratings, scores, etc.) while satisfying some external requirement. For example if five numbers total 20, the first four numbers can have various values, but the fifth is fixed. Thus four of the five numbers are free to vary. There are four degrees of freedom. Degrees of freedom have to be calculated for many tests of statistical significance.

Dichotomous variable: A variable which has only two possible values (e.g., gender).

Discriminant analysis: A statistical procedure which weights and linearly combines variables in such a fashion that predefined groups are forced to be as statistically distinct as possible.

Discriminant function: A linear combination of variables which emphasizes the nature of differences among groups.

Discriminatory power: The variability in the discriminant functions that is attributable to group differences. It indicates the extent to which a particular set of discriminant functions is effective.

Distribution: cf. frequency distribution.

Drumcondra Verbal Reasoning Test: A 110 item test designed by the Educational Research Centre as a measure of a student's ability to use and reason with verbal symbols. The test contains sections on analogies, the identification of words opposite in meaning to a given stimulus, the identification of concepts as belonging to a single category, and problems in inductive and deductive reasoning.

Educational-history variables: A group of variables which describe the school progress, progress in eight specific areas of the curriculum, attendance, and grade attained by students at the age of twelve.

English Reading: Teacher rating in response to question: 'Has the pupil any difficulty in English Reading?' (No = 1; Yes = -1).

Factor analysis: A mathematical procedure which attempts to identify a small number of underlying hypothetical constructs or 'factors' from a much larger number of variables.

Factor score: Score for an individual on a particular factor derived from factor analysis. Scores for a factor are derived from the factor loadings for that factor. In the present study, four factor scores were computed for each student.

F-ratio: Ratio yielded by analysis of variance, which is used to determine if the variability between means is statistically significant or is likely to have arisen by chance.

Frequency distribution: A tabulation of scores from low to high, or high to low showing the number of individuals that obtain each score or fall in each score interval or category.

Gender: Gender of student (girl = 1; boy = -1).

Goodness of fit test: A test which indicates if a particular sample is representative of some specified population.

Grade at age twelve: School grade attained by a student at the age of 12 years in the 1967–68 school year. (Fourth grade = 0; Fifth = 1; Sixth or seventh = 2; First year post-primary = 3; and Second year post-primary = 4).

Group leadership: A summary variable derived from a factor analysis of 20 personality characteristics of students. It reflects such characteristics as dominance, leadership and self-confidence.

Health/extroversion: A summary variable derived from a factor analysis of 20 personality characteristics of students. Health and physical energy and to a lesser extent popularity and gregariousness are the most prominent characteristics of this factor.

Higher-education early leaver (HIEDEL): A student who commences study in a higher-education institution but does not complete the course.

Higher-education terminal leaver (HIEDTL): A student who completes a course in a higher-education institution.

Higher-level paper: The upper of two levels at which Intermediate Certificate Examination papers are offered in English, Irish and Mathematics. Higher-level papers are also offered for almost all Leaving Certificate Examination subjects.

Home-background variables: A group of variables which describes the socio-economic status of the student's family (based on the occupation of the student's parent or guardian), the number of children in the student's family, the student's ordinal position in family, and whether or not the student's father or mother is alive.

ICEX: Index of student achievement on the Intermediate Certificate Examination. Letter grades were transformed into numerical values as follows: for higher and common-level papers, values ranging from 9 for an A to 3 for No Grade were assigned and for lower level papers, values ranging from 7 for an A to 1 for No Grade were assigned.

Intermediate Certificate Examination (ICE): A state public examination mainly of the essay type for students who have followed an approved course of not less than three years duration in a recognised post-primary school. The stated purpose of the course is to provide a well-balanced general education suitable for students who leave full-time education at about 16 years of age or alternatively, who wish to pursue more advanced courses of study.

Irish Reading: Teacher rating in response to question: 'Has the pupil any difficulty in Irish Reading?' (No = 1; Yes = -1).

Junior cycle: Initial years in post-primary school, normally three years in a secondary school (i.e., period up to the Intermediate Certificate Examination) and two years in a vocational school (i.e., up to Day Group Certificate Examination).

Junior-cycle early leaver (JCEL): Student who leaves a post-primary school without having taken either the Intermediate Certificate Examination or the Day Group Certificate Examination.

Junior-cycle terminal leaver (JCTL): Student who leaves post-primary school after taking the Intermediate or Day Group Certificate Examination.

Lay school: Primary school in which the principal teacher was a lay person.

LCEX: Index of student achievement on the Leaving Certificate Examination. Letter grades were transformed into numerical values as follows: for higher-level papers, values ranging from 9 for an A to 3 for No Grade were assigned and for ordinary-level papers, values ranged from 7 for an A to 1 for No Grade.

Leaving Certificate Examination (LCE): A state public examination mainly of the essay type for students who have followed an approved course for at least two years as a recognized senior student in a post-primary school. The results of the examination are widely used for selection purposes by third-level educational institutions and also by state, semi-state, and private organizations.

Level of final degree award: Categorized as either first-class honours (4), second-class honours, division one (3), second class honours, division two (2), and general or pass (1).

Longitudinal study: A study in which data on the same group of subjects is obtained at several points in time.

Lower-level paper: One of two levels at which the Intermediate Certificate Examination papers in English, Irish, and Mathematics are offered. Higher-level papers are also offered in these subjects.

Mean (M): The average or arithmetic mean of a set of scores or ratings.

Mechanical Arithmetic: Teacher rating in response to question: 'Has the pupil any difficulty in Mechanical Arithmetic?' (No = 1; Yes = -1).

Mixed-gender primary school: Primary school which catered for both boys and girls.

Modified ordinal position: Index created by dividing a student's ordinal position by the number of children in the family and multiplying this number by 100. For example, the third of four children has a modified ordinal position of 75.

Multivariate analysis of variance: A statistical procedure used to determine whether the differences between two or more groups on a set of variables considered together are likely to have arisen by chance.

Multiple regression analysis: A statistical technique based on correlational data designed to measure the relationship between a dependent or criterion variable (e.g., verbal ability) and a set of independent or predictor variables (e.g., home-background, reading achievement, and gender).

N: The symbol normally used to represent the number of cases in a group.

Oral English: Teacher rating in response to question: 'Has the pupil any difficulty in Oral English?' (No = 1; Yes = -1).

Oral Irish: Teacher rating in response to question: 'Has the pupil any difficulty in Oral Irish?' (No = 1; Yes = -1).

Ordinary-level paper: One of two levels at which Leaving Certificate examination papers are set. Higher-level papers are also offered.

Pearson product-moment correlation: A correlation coefficient credited to Karl Pearson (1857–1936). (cf. Correlation coefficient.)

Percentile rank: An index of test performance which indicates where a particular score lies in terms of its position within a group of 100 scores. A student who earns a percentile rank of 71 has achieved a score equal to or higher than those achieved by 71% of some reference group, such as a national sample.

Persister: Student who remains in school.

Personal characteristic variables: A group of variables which describes a student's verbal reasoning ability, gender and scores on each of four factor scores: satisfactory classroom behaviour, group leadership, health/extroversion, and aesthetic behaviour.

Personality variables: Teacher ratings on the following 20 personality characteristics: (1) keenness to get on, (2) enquiring mind, (3) achievement, (4) leadership, (5) concentration, (6) self-confidence, (7) dominance, (8) creativity, (9) dependence, (10) deference, (11) gregariousness, (12) common sense, (13) originality, (14) sense of humour, (15) popularity, (16) sensitivity, (17) appreciation of beauty, (18) intelligence, (19) health, and (20) physical energy. By means of factor analysis, these variables were reduced to four: satisfactory classroom behaviour, group leadership, health/extroversion, and aesthetic behaviour.

Points system: System for transforming Leaving Certificate Examination grades into numerical values for use in the selection of university entrants. (cf. University index.)

Primary Certificate Examination: A written test in Irish, English, and Arithmetic which all pupils in primary schools were expected to take at the end of sixth grade. The test was abolished in 1967.

Primary-school terminal leaver (PSTL): Student who after leaving primary school did not transfer to a post-primary school.

Primary-school type variables: A group of variables which describes the way schools were categorized in terms of administration (Catholic lay, Catholic religious, Protestant, Private), size, gender composition (all-female, all-male, mixed), and location (city, town, rural).

Private primary school: A primary school which was not in receipt of state funds.

Probability: A decimal fraction which expresses the ratio of actual occurrences to opportunities for occurrence. For example, a coin has a probability of .5 of landing with head facing upwards each time it is tossed.

Problem Arithmetic: Teacher rating in response to question: 'Has the pupil any difficulty in Problem Arithmetic?' (No = 1; Yes = -1).

Protestant primary school: A primary school under Protestant management.

Public examinations: Three examinations set by the state for post-primary students: Day Group Certificate Examination, Intermediate Certificate Examination, and Leaving Certificate Examination.

Questionnaire: A list of planned written questions relating to a particular topic.

Range: The difference between the highest and the lowest scores obtained. It provides a very rough measure of variability or spread.

Raw score: The number of correct answers on a particular test.

Reliability: The extent to which a measure is consistent in measuring whatever it measures.

Rural primary school: A primary school located in a centre of population of less than 1,500 people.

Satisfactory classroom behaviour: A summary variable derived from a factor analysis of teacher ratings of 20 personality characteristics of students. The factor reflects a number of characteristics normally associated with 'good' classroom behaviour. These include keenness to get on, enquiring mind, ability to work intently, determination to obtain high standards, as well as intelligence, common sense, and originality.

Scaled points index: A score derived from a transformation of Leaving Certificate Examination grades into points, based on a scaling of grades against scores on the Differential Aptitude Test. The scoring system was as follows: on a higher paper: A = 92, B = 77, C = 62, D = 47, E = 30, F = 17; on an ordinary paper. A=56, B=49, C = 41, D = 33, E = 25, F = 15; took paper but no grade awarded = 5 on both papers.

School location: Categorized as 'urban' if situated in one of the boroughs, Dublin, Dun Laoghaire, Cork, Limerick, or Waterford (1); as 'town' if in a town with a population of 1,500 or more (2) or as 'rural' if located in a centre of population of less than 1,500 people.

School progress: Teacher rating in response to question: 'Do you regard pupil's progress as satisfactory?' (Yes = 1; No = 0).

School size: Determined on the basis of number of teachers in the school (1 teacher = 1; 2 teachers = 2; 3 teachers = 3; 4 to 6 teachers = 4; 7+ teachers = 5).

SD: Standard deviation.

Secondary school: Post-primary school in which the emphasis is on classical academic type rather than technical education. These schools are private. Many are run by religious orders. They attract more pupils than all other types of post-primary school.

Senior-cycle: Normally a two-year period in post-primary school leading up to the Leaving Certificate Examination.

Senior-cycle early leaver (SCEL): Student who, after completing the junior cycle course, commences the two-year senior-cycle course but leaves post-primary school without sitting for the Leaving Certificate Examination.

Senior-cycle terminal leaver (SCTL): Student who leaves school after sitting for the Leaving Certificate Examination and does not proceed to a third-level educational institution.

Significant or statistically significant differences: A difference between two comparable statistics (e.g., M) from separate samples which is large enough so that the probability that the observed difference may be due to chance is less than some specified limit. Significance levels commonly specified are 5 times out of 100, once out of 100, and once out of 1,000. The notation $p < .05$ indicates that the perceived difference would be likely to occur by chance fewer than 5 times out of 100.

Socio-economic status: Home background assessed on the basis of the occupation of the student's parent or guardian. Occupations were classified as: higher professional, administrative, managerial, and farmers with over 150 acres (5); intermediate professional, administrative, managerial, and farmers with between 31 and 150 acres (4); skilled occupations (3); partly-skilled occupations and farmers with 30 or fewer acres (2); and unskilled occupations (1).

Standard deviation (SD): A measure of the extent to which scores or ratings vary. It is calculated by estimating how much each score or rating deviates from the mean. The more closely the scores cluster around the mean, the smaller is the standard deviation.

Standard deviation unit: A transformed score which expresses each score in terms of a positive or negative deviation from the mean. It is calculated by subtracting the score from the over-all mean and dividing by the over-all standard deviation.

Standardized mean: Mean score expressed in terms of standard deviation units from the over-all mean.

Standardization sample: The sample on which norms for a test are based. In the case of the Drumcondra Verbal Reasoning Test, the standardization sample was a sample of 6,000 children aged between 10 years 0 months and 12 years 11 months, selected so as to be representative of all schoolgoing children in that age range in the country.

Standard score: A score derived from a raw score and expressed on a uniform standard scale.

Statistic: A number used to represent some aspect of a sample (e.g., mean, standard deviation).

Structural mobility: A measure of the extent to which the occupations of a group differ from those of their fathers.

Terminal leaver: A person who terminates formal full-time attendance at school.

Town primary school: School located in a centre of population over 1,500, but excluding the boroughs of Dublin, Dun Laoghaire, Cork, Limerick and Waterford.

Undergraduate achievement: Three measures of undergraduate achievement were used: (1) rate of progress, i.e., the number of years taken above the minimum normally required to complete a course; (2) number of times a third-level examination was repeated; (3) level of final degree award (first-class honours; second-class honours, division one; second-class honours, division two; and general or pass).

Unique power (uniqueness): The variance attributable to a variable after the effects of other independent variables have been taken into account. It is calculated normally in conjunction with regression analysis.

University index: A score derived from a transformation of Leaving Certificate Examination grades into points for use in the selection of university entrants (Higher papers, grade A = 5 points; B = 4; C = 3; D = 2; on an ordinary paper, grade A = 2 and B = 1. A double score was awarded on the higher papers in Mathematics).

Urban primary school: School located in the boroughs of Dublin, Dun Laoghaire, Cork, Limerick, or Waterford.

Variable: A characteristic of a person or thing which varies, e.g., the number of children in a family or class, a person's age, height, or verbal ability.

Variance: A measure of the degree of spread in scores or ratings. Statistically, it is the mean of the squares of individual deviations from a mean. The more scores or ratings tend to differ from each other and from the mean, the larger the variance will be.

Verbal reasoning ability: The ability to reason with verbal symbols. In the present study, student ability was measured by the Drumcondra Verbal Reasoning Test.

Vocational school: Post-primary school owned and managed by a local vocational education committee. In the past, these schools provided technical and continuation education after primary school. Since 1963, they also provide Intermediate and Leaving Certificate Examination courses.

Written English: Teacher rating in response to question: 'Has the pupil any difficulty in Written English? (No = 1; Yes = -1).

Written Irish: Teacher rating in response to question: 'Has the pupil any difficulty in Written Irish?' (No = 1; Yes = -1).

References

Adamski, W. W. Social structure versus educational policy: Polish and European perspectives. In M. S. Archer (Ed.), *The sociology of educational expansion. Take-off, growth and inflation in educational systems.* London: Sage Publications, 1982.

Adamski, W. W., & Bialecki, I. Selection at school and access to higher education in Poland. *European Journal of Education*, 1981, *16*, 209-223.

Ainsworth, M. E., & Batten, E. J. *The effects of environmental factors on secondary educational attainment in Manchester: A Plowden follow-up.* London: Macmillan, 1974.

Airasian, P. W., Kellaghan, T., & Madaus, G. F. The stability of teachers' perceptions of pupil characteristics. *Irish Journal of Education*, 1977, *11*, 74-84.

Airasian, P. W., Kellaghan, T., & Madaus, G. F. *Concepts of school effectiveness.* Washington, DC: National Institute of Education, U.S. Department of Health, Education and Welfare, 1979.

Akenson, D. H. *The Irish education experiment. The national system of education in the nineteenth century.* London: Routledge & Kegan Paul, 1970.

Akenson, D. H. *A mirror to Kathleen's face. Education in independent Ireland 1922-1960.* Montreal: McGill-Queen's University Press, 1975.

Andrews, P. The influence of university entrance requirements on second level curricula and examinations. In J. Coolahan (Ed.), *University entrance requirements and their effect on second level curricula.* Dublin: Irish Federation of University Teachers, 1979.

Archer, M. S. *Social origins of educational systems.* London: Sage Publications, 1979.

Archer, M. S. The theoretical problem of educational expansion. In M. S. Archer (Ed.), *The sociology of educational expansion. Take-off, growth and inflation in educational systems.* London: Sage Publications, 1982.

Arundel, L. The effect of present selection procedures on the vocational sector. In J. Coolahan (Ed.), *University entrance requirements and their effect on second level curricula.* Dublin: Irish Federation of University Teachers, 1977.

Atkinson, N. The school structure in the Republic of Ireland. *Comparative Education Review*, 1964, *8*, 276-280.

Auchmuty, J. J. *Irish education. A historical survey.* London: Harrap, 1937.

Bamberg, M., Dickes, P., & Schaber, G. *Étude Magrip. Premier rapport de synthèse.* Luxembourg: Institut Pedagogique, 1977.

Barlow, A. C. *The financing of third-level education.* Dublin: Economic and Social Research Institute, 1981.

Baron, G. *Society, schools and progress in England.* Oxford: Pergamon, 1965.

Barrington, T. J. *The Irish administrative system.* Dublin: Institute of Public Administration, 1980.

Bell, D. *The coming of post-industrial society. A venture in social forecasting.* New York: Basic Books, 1973.

Blau, P. M., & Duncan, O. D. *The American occupational structure.* New York: Wiley, 1967.

Bloom, B. S. *Stability and change in human characteristics.* New York: Wiley, 1964.

Boudon, R. *Education, opportunity, and social inequality. Changing prospects in western society.* New York: Wiley, 1974.

Bourdieu, P. Cultural reproduction and social reproduction. In J. Karabel & A. H. Halsey (Eds.), *Power and ideology in education.* New York: Oxford University Press, 1977.

Bourdieu, P., & Passeron, J.-C. *Reproduction in education, society and culture.* (Trans. by Richard Nice). London: Sage Publications, 1977.

Bowles, S. Unequal education and the reproduction of the social division of labour. In M. Carnoy (Ed.), *Schooling in a corporate society.* New York: David McKay, 1972.

Bowles, S., & Gintis, H. *Schooling in capitalist America. Educational reform and the contradictions of economic life.* New York: Basic Books, 1976.

Brody, E. B., & Brody, N. *Intelligence. Nature, determinants, and consequences.* New York: Academic Press, 1976.

Butcher, H. J. *Human intelligence. Its nature and assessment.* London: Methuen, 1968.

Byrne, E. M. *Equality of education and training for girls (10–18 years).* Brussels: European Economic Community, 1979.

Carnoy, M. *Education as cultural imperialism.* New York: David McKay, 1974.

Clancy, P. *Participation in higher education: A national survey.* Dublin: Higher Education Authority, 1982.

Clancy, P., & Benson, C. *Higher education in Dublin: A study of some emerging trends.* Dublin: Higher Education Authority, 1979.

Coleman, J. S. The concept of equality of educational opportunity. *Harvard Educational Review*, 1968, *38*, 7–22.

Coleman, J. S. Equality of opportunity and equality of results. *Harvard Educational Review*, 1973, *43*, 129–137.

Coleman, J. S. What is meant by 'an equal educational opportunity'? *Oxford Review of Education*, 1975, *1*, 27–29.

Coleman, J. S., Campbell, E. Q., Hobson, C. J., McPartland, J., Mood, A. M., Weinfeld, F. D., & York, R. L. *Equality of educational opportunity.* Washington, DC: Office of Education, U.S. Department of Health, Education & Welfare, 1966.

Collins, R. *The credential society. An historical sociology of education and stratification.* New York: Academic Press, 1979.

Combs, J., & Cooley, W. W. Dropouts: In high school and after school. *American Educational Research Journal*, 1968, *5*, 343–363.

Conference of Convent Primary Schools in Ireland. *Evaluation of the new curriculum for primary schools.* Dublin: Conference of Convent Primary Schools in Ireland, 1975.

Coolahan, J. *Irish education: History and structure.* Dublin: Institute of Public Administration, 1981.

Craft, M. Economy, ideology and educational development in Ireland. *Administration*, 1970, *18*, 363–374.

Craft, M. Talent, family values and education in Ireland, In J. Eggleston (Ed.), *Contemporary research in the sociology of education.* London: Methuen, 1974.

Crooks, T. Research and development in curriculum and examinations at second level in the Republic of Ireland. *Compass*, 1977, *6*, 26–46.

Cullen, K. *School and family. Social factors in educational attainment.* Dublin: Gill & Macmillan, 1969.

Douglas, J. W. B., Ross, J. M., & Simpson, H. R. *All our future. A longitudinal study of secondary education.* London: Davies, 1968.

Duncan, B. Trends in output and distribution of schooling. In E. B. Sheldon & W. E. Moore (Eds.), *Indicators of social change: Concepts and measurements.* New York: Russell Sage Foundation, 1968.

Duncan, O. D., Featherman, D. L., & Duncan, B. *Socioeconomic background and achievement.* New York: Seminar Press, 1972.

EEC: Statistical Office of the European Communities. *Eurostat: Education and training.* Bruxelles: European Economic Community, 1980.

Egan, O. Informal teaching in the primary school: Effects on pupil achievement. *Irish Journal of Education,* 1982, *16,* 16–26.

Etzioni, A. *The active society.* New York: Free Press, 1968.

Floud, J., & Halsey, A. H. Social class, intelligence tests, and selection for secondary schools. In A. H. Halsey, J. Floud, & C. A. Anderson (Eds.), *Education, economy, and society.* London: Collier-Macmillan, 1961.

Floud, J. E., Halsey, A. H., & Martin, F. M. *Social class and educational opportunity.* London: Heinemann, 1956.

Foner, A. Ascribed and achieved bases of stratification. *Annual Review of Sociology,* 1979, *5,* 219–242.

Fontes, P. J., & Kellaghan, T. Incidence and correlates of illiteracy in Irish primary schools. *Irish Journal of Education,* 1977a, *11,* 5–20.

Fontes, P. J., & Kellaghan, T. *The new primary school curriculum: Its implementation and effects.* Dublin: Educational Research Centre, 1977b.

Fontes, P. J., Kellaghan, T., Madaus, G. F., & Airasian, P. W. Opinions of the Irish public on examinations. *Irish Journal of Education,* 1980, *14,* 53–74.

Frank, A. G. *Latin America: Underdevelopment or revolution?* London: Monthly Review Press, 1969.

Fraser, E. D. *Home environment and the school.* London: University of London Press, 1959.

Geary, R. C., & Henry, E. W. Education and socio-economic class: A statistical analysis of 1971 Irish census data. *Irish Journal of Education,* 1979, *13,* 5–23.

Geary, R. C., & Ó Muircheartaigh, F. S. *Equalization of opportunity in Ireland: Statistical aspects.* Dublin: Economic & Social Research Institute, 1974.

Gintis, H. Toward a political economy of education: A radical critique of Ivan Illich's *Deschooling society. Harvard Educational Review,* 1972, *42,* 70–96.

Girard, A. Selection for secondary education in France. In A. H. Halsey, J. Floud, & C. A. Anderson (Eds.), *Education, economy, and society.* London: Collier-Macmillan, 1961.

Girard, A., & Clerc, P. Nouvelles données sur l'orientation scolaire au moment de l'entrée en sixième. *Population,* 1964, *19,* 829–872.

Goldthorpe, J. H. *Social mobility and class structure in modern Britain.* Oxford: Clarendon Press, 1980.

Gorman, W. G. The construction and standardization of a verbal reasoning test for age range 10 years 0 months to 12 years 11 months in an Irish population. Unpublished Ph.D. thesis, University College, Dublin, 1968.

Gray, J., McPherson, A. F., & Raffe, D. *Reconstructions of secondary education. Theory, myth and practice since the War.* London: Routledge & Kegan Paul, 1983.

Greaney, V. A longitudinal study of Irish secondary school students, vocational school students and dropouts. Unpublished Ph.D. thesis, Boston College, 1972.

Greaney, V. A comparison of secondary school entrants, vocational school entrants and terminal leavers. *Irish Journal of Education,* 1973, *7,* 79–101.

Greaney, V. Teachers' perceptions of pupil personality. *Irish Journal of Education,* 1974, *8,* 89–101.

Greaney, V. The predictive validity of the Irish Leaving Certificate Examination. In J. Coolahan (Ed.), *University entrance requirements and their effects on second level curricula.* Dublin: Irish Federation of University Teachers, 1979.

Greaney, V., & Kellaghan, T. Cognitive and personality factors associated with the class placement of pupils. *Irish Journal of Education*, 1972, *6*, 93–104.

Greaney, V., & Kellaghan, T. School leaving examinations in Ireland. In F. Ottobre (Ed.), *Criteria for awarding school leaving certificates*. New York: Pergamon Press, 1979.

Greaney, V., & Kelly, P. Reading standards in Irish post-primary schools. In V. Greaney (Ed.), *Studies in reading*. Dublin: Educational Company, 1977.

Great Britain: Department of Education and Science. *Children and their primary schools. A report of the Central Advisory Council for Education (England)*. London: HMSO, 1967.

Great Britain: Ministry of Education. *Early leaving. A report of the Central Advisory Council for Education (England)*. London: HMSO, 1954.

Great Britain: Ministry of Education. *15 to 18. A report of the Central Advisory Council for Education (England)*. London: HMSO, 1959.

Great Britain: Registrar General. *Census 1951: Classification of occupations*. London: HMSO, 1956.

Green, T. F. *Predicting the behavior of the educational system*. Syracuse, NY: Syracuse University Press, 1980.

Hall, S. Schooling, state and society. In R. Dale, G. Esland, R. Fergusson, & M. MacDonald (Eds.), *Schooling and the national interest* Vol. 1. Lewes, Sussex: Falmer Press, 1981.

Halsey, A. H. (Ed.) *Educational priority, Volume I: EPA problems and policies*. London: HMSO, 1972.

Halsey, A. H. Sociology and the equality debate. *Oxford Review of Education*, 1975, *1*, 9–23.

Halsey, A. H. *Change in British society*. Oxford: Oxford University Press, 1978.

Halsey, A. H., Heath, A. F., & Ridge, J. M. *Origins and destinations. Family, class, and education in modern Britain*. Oxford: Clarendon Press, 1980.

Halsey, A. H., Sheehan, J., & Vaizey, J. Schools. In A. H. Halsey (Ed.), *Trends in British society since 1900. A guide to the changing structure of Britain*. London: Macmillan, 1972.

Hannan, D., Breen, R., Murray, B., Watson, D., Hardiman, N., & O'Higgins, K. *Schooling and sex roles: Sex differences in subject provision and student choice in Irish post-primary schools*. Dublin: Economic and Social Research Institute, 1983.

Herrnstein, R. J. *IQ in the meritocracy*. London: Allen Lane, 1973.

Holland, S. *Rutland street*. The Hague: Bernard van Leer Foundation, and Oxford: Pergamon Press, 1979.

Hopper, E. I. A typology for the classification of educational systems. In J. Karabel & A. H. Halsey (Eds.), *Power and ideology in education*. New York: Oxford University Press, 1977.

Howell, F. M., & Frese, W. Early transition into adult roles: Some antecedents and outcomes. *American Educational Research Journal*, 1982, *19*, 51–73.

Husén, T. *Talent, opportunity and career*. Stockholm: Almqvist & Wiksell, 1969.

Hutchinson, B. *Social status and inter-generational social mobility in Dublin*. Dublin: Economic and Social Research Institute, 1969.

ICE report. Final report of the Committee on the form and function of the Intermediate Certificate Examination. Dublin: Stationery Office, 1975.

Investment in education. Report of the Survey Team appointed by the Minister for Education in October 1962. Dublin: Stationery Office, 1966.

Ireland. *Acht oideachais ghairme beatha, 1930. Vocational education act, 1930*. Dublin: Stationery Office, 1930.

Ireland. *Second programme for economic expansion*. Part II. Laid by the Government before each House of the Oireachtas, July, 1964. Dublin: Stationery Office, 1964.

Ireland. *White paper on educational development.* Laid by the Government before each House of the Oireachtas, December, 1980. Dublin: Stationery Office, 1980.

Ireland: Central Statistics Office. *Census of population of Ireland, 1971. Volume V. Occupations and industries, classified by ages and conjugal conditions.* Dublin: Stationery Office, 1975.

Ireland: Department of Education. *Tuarasgabháil. Report 1942/43.* Dublin: Stationery Office, 1944.

Ireland: Department of Education. *Report of the Council of Education as presented to the Minister for Education. (1) The function of the primary school. (2) The curriculum to be pursued in the primary school from the infant age up to 12 years of age.* Dublin: Stationery Office, 1954.

Ireland: Department of Education. *Report of the Council of Education: The curriculum of the secondary school.* Dublin: Stationery Office, 1960.

Ireland: Department of Education. *Tuarascáil 1962-63.* Dublin: Stationery Office, 1964.

Ireland: Department of Education. *Rules for national schools under the Department of Education.* Dublin: Stationery Office, 1965.

Ireland: Department of Education. *Tuarascáil. Tablaí staitistic 1964-65.* Dublin: Stationery Office, 1966.

Ireland: Department of Education. *Rules and programme for secondary schools 1968-69.* Dublin: Stationery Office, 1968.

Ireland: Department of Education. *Ár ndaltaí uile. All our children.* Dublin: Department of Education, 1969.

Ireland: Department of Education. *Rules and programme for secondary schools, 1970-71.* Dublin: Stationery Office, 1970.

Ireland: Department of Education. *Primary school curriculum. Teacher's handbook.* Part 1. Dublin: Department of Education, 1971.

Ireland: Department of Education. *Rules and programme for secondary schools 1973/74.* Dublin: Stationery Office, 1973.

Ireland: Department of Education. *Tuarascáil. Táblaí staitistic 1968/69-1971/72.* Dublin: Stationery Office, 1974.

Ireland: Department of Education. *Rules and programme for secondary schools, 1975-76.* Dublin: Stationery Office, 1975a.

Ireland: Department of Education. *Tuarascáil Staitistiúil (Statistical report) 1972/73-1973/74.* Dublin: Stationery Office, 1975b.

Ireland: Department of Education. *Tuarascáil staitistiúil (Statistical Report) 1974/75-1975/76.* Dublin: Stationery Office, 1977.

Ireland: Department of Education. Rules and programme for the Day Vocational Certificate Examinations. Dublin: Department of Education, 1979.

Ireland: Department of Education. *Tuarascáil staitistiúil (Statistical report) 1979-80.* Dublin: Stationery Office, 1981.

Ireland: Department of Education. *Tuarascáil staitistiúil (Statistical report) 1980-81.* Dublin: Stationery Office, 1983.

Ireland: Department of Finance. *Economic development.* Dublin: Stationery Office, 1958.

Ireland: Higher Education Authority. *Accounts 1978 and student statistics 1978/1979.* Dublin: Higher Education Authority, 1980.

Ireland: Higher Education Authority. *Accounts 1979 and student statistics 1979/80.* Dublin: Higher Education Authority, 1981.

Ireland: Higher Education Authority. *Accounts 1980 and student statistics 1980/81.* Dublin: Higher Education Authority, 1982a.

Ireland: Higher Education Authority. *Accounts 1981 and student statistics 1981/82.* Dublin: Higher Education Authority, 1982b.

Irish National Teachers Organisation: Education Committee. *Primary school curriculum. Curriculum questionnaire analysis.* Dublin: Irish National Teachers Organisation, 1976.

Jencks, C., Smith, M., Acland, H., Bane, M. J., Cohen, D., Gintis, H., Heyns, B., & Michelson, S. *Inequality. A reassessment of the effect of family and schooling in America.* New York: Basic Books, 1972.

Jensen, A. R. How much can we boost IQ and scholastic achievement? *Harvard Educational Review*, 1969, *39*, 1-123.

Jensen, A. R. *Bias in mental testing.* New York: Free Press, 1980.

Karabel, J. & Astin, A. Social class, academic ability, and college 'quality'. *Social Forces*, 1975, *53*, 381-398.

Karstanje, P. Selection for higher education in the Netherlands. *European Journal of Education*, 1981, *16*, 197-208.

Katz, M. B. *Class, bureaucracy, and schools.* New York: Praeger, 1971.

Kellaghan, T. Relationships between home environment and scholastic behavior in a disadvantaged population. *Journal of Educational Psychology*, 1977a, *69*, 754-760.

Kellaghan, T. *The evaluation of an intervention programme for disadvantaged children.* Slough, Berks.: NFER Publishing Co., 1977b.

Kellaghan, T. The child and the school. In V. Greaney (Ed.), *The rights of children.* New York: Irvington, in press a.

Kellaghan, T. The educational system in the Republic of Ireland. In T. Husén & T. N. Postlethwaite (Eds.), *International encyclopedia of education: Research and studies.* Oxford: Pergamon Press, in press b.

Kellaghan, T., & Fontes, P. J. Participation in university education by gender and geographical location. *Irish Journal of Education*, 1980, *14*, 3-18.

Kellaghan, T., & Greaney, V. Factors related to choice of post-primary school in Ireland. *Irish Journal of Education*, 1970, *4*, 69-83.

Kellaghan, T., & Macnamara, J. Family correlates of verbal reasoning ability. *Developmental Psychology*, 1972, *7*, 49-53.

Kellaghan, T., Macnamara, J., & Neuman, E. Teachers' assessments of the scholastic progress of pupils. *Irish Journal of Education*, 1969, *3*, 95-104.

Kellaghan, T., Madaus, G. F., Airasian, P. W., & Fontes, P. J. The mathematical attainments of post-primary school entrants. *Irish Journal of Education*, 1976, *10*, 3-17.

Kellaghan, T., Madaus, G. F., Airasian, P. W., & Fontes, P. J. Opinions of the Irish public on innovations in education. *Irish Journal of Education*, 1981, *15*, 23-40.

Kennedy, F. *Public social expenditure in Ireland.* Dublin: Economic & Social Research Institute, 1975.

Lazar, I., & Darlington, R. Lasting effects of early education: A report from the Consortium for Longitudinal Studies. *Monographs of the Society for Research in Child Development*, 1982, 47 (2-3, Serial No. 195).

Levin, H. A taxonomy of educational reform. In M. Carnoy (Ed.), *The limits of educational reform.* New York: McKay, 1976.

Lightfoot, G. F. *Personality characteristics of bright and dull children.* New York: Teachers' College Press, Columbia University, 1951.

Linton, R. *The study of man.* New York: Appleton Century, 1936.

Lipset, S. M., & Bendix, R. *Social mobility in industrial societies.* Berkeley, CA.: University of California Press, 1959.

Litton, F. (Ed.) *Unequal achievement. The Irish experience 1957-1982.* Dublin: Institute of Public Administration, 1982.

MacDonald, K., & Ridge, J. Social mobility. In A. H. Halsey (Ed.), *Trends in British society since 1900. A guide to the changing structure of Britain.* London: Macmillan, 1972.

MacGleannáin, S. S. Internal organization of primary education in Ireland. In L. Legrand (Ed.), *Educational research on new developments in primary education.* Windsor, Berks.: NFER Publishing Co., 1979.

MacGréil, M. *Educational opportunity in Dublin.* Dublin: Catholic Communications Institute of Ireland, 1974.

MacHale, J. P. The socio-economic background of students in Irish universities. *Studies*, 1979, *68*, 213-221.

Macnamara, J. *Bilingualism and primary education.* Edinburgh: University Press, 1966.

Madaus, G. F., Airasian, P. W., & Kellaghan, T. *School effectiveness: A reassessment of the evidence.* New York: McGraw Hill, 1980.

Madaus, G. F., Fontes, P. J., Kellaghan, T., & Airasian, P. W. Opinions of the Irish public on the goals and adequacy of education. *Irish Journal of Education*, 1979, *13*, 87-125.

Madaus, G. F., & Greaney, V. Competency testing: A case study of the Irish Primary Certificate Examination. National Consortium on Testing Staff Circular No. 10. Cambridge, MA.: Huron Institute, 1982.

Madaus, G. F., Kellaghan, T., & Rakow, E. A. A study of the sensitivity of measures of school effectiveness. Report submitted to the Carnegie Corporation of New York, 1975.

Madaus, G. F., Kellaghan, T., Rakow, E. A., & King, D. J. The sensitivity of measures of school effectiveness. *Harvard Educational Review*, 1979, *49*, 207-230.

Madaus, G. F., & Macnamara, J. *Public examinations. A study of the Irish Leaving Certificate.* Dublin: Educational Research Centre, 1970.

Marjoribanks, K. (Ed.). *Environments for learning.* Slough, Bucks.: NFER Publishing Co., 1974.

Marjoribanks, K. Family environments. In H. J. Walberg (Ed.), *Educational environments and effects. Evaluation, policy, and productivity.* Berkeley, CA.: McCutchan, 1979.

Martin, M. Reading and socio-economic background: A progressive achievement gap? *Irish Journal of Education*, 1979, *13*, 62-78.

Martin, M., & Kellaghan, T. Factors affecting reading attainment in Irish primary schools. In V. Greaney (Ed.), *Studies in reading.* Dublin: Educational Company, 1977.

Matthews, M. R. *The marxist theory of schooling. A study of epistemology and education.* Brighton: Harvester Press, 1980.

McCluskey, D. Access to secondary education. Abridged report. Dublin: Secretariat of Secondary Schools, 1977.

McDonagh, K. The way the money goes. *Oideas*, 1977, *17*, 5-102.

McElligott, T. J. *Education in Ireland.* Dublin: Institute of Public Administration, 1966.

McElligott, T. J. *Secondary education in Ireland 1870-1921.* Dublin: Irish Academic Press, 1981.

McIntosh, D. M. *Educational guidance and the pool of ability.* London: University of London Press, 1959.

McNemar, Q. *Psychological statistics* (4th ed.). New York: Wiley, 1969.

Meyer, J. W., & Hannan, M. T. (Eds.). *National development and the world system: Educational, economic, and political change, 1950-1970.* Chicago: University of Chicago Press, 1979.

Moran, M. A., & Crowley, M. J. The Leaving Certificate and first year university performance. *Journal of the Statistical and Social Inquiry Society of Ireland*, 1978/79, *24*, 231-266.

Morton-Williams, R., & Finch, S. *Young school leavers.* London: HMSO, 1968.

Mosteller, F., & Moynihan, D. P. (Eds.). *On equality of educational opportunity.* New York: Vintage Books, 1972.

Mulcahy, D. G. *Curriculum and policy in Irish post-primary education.* Dublin: Institute of Public Administration, 1981.

Murphy, C. *School report. A guide for parents, teachers and students.* Dublin: Ward River Press, 1980.

Murphy, T. Statement made at Seminar organized by Irish Federation of University Teachers on University Entrance Requirements and their effect on second level curricula, 1978.

Musgrove, F. *School and the social order.* Chichester: Wiley, 1979.

National Economic & Social Council. *Economic and social policy 1982. Aims and recommendations.* Dublin: National Economic & Social Council, 1983.

Neuman, E. A study of social and personality characteristics of children of high verbal ability. Unpublished M.Psych.Sc. thesis, University College, Dublin, 1970.

Nevin, M. A study of the social background of students in the Irish universities. *Journal of the Statistical and Social Inquiry Society of Ireland*, 1967/68, *21*, 201–225.

Nie, N. H., Hull, C. H., Jenkins, J. G., Steinbrenner, K., & Bent, D. H. *SPSS: Statistical package for the social sciences (2nd ed.).* New York: McGraw-Hill, 1975.

Ó Catháin, S. *Secondary education in Ireland.* Dublin: Talbot Press, 1958.

O Connor, S. Post-primary education: Now and in the future. *Studies*, 1968, *57*, 233–249.

O Connor, S. The future for third level education. In J. Coolahan (Ed.), *University entrance requirements and their effect on second level curricula.* Dublin: Irish Federation of University Teachers, 1979.

Ó Domhnalláin, T. An Ghaeilge san oideachas: Fás nó meath? *Teangeolas*, 1978, *7*, 12–16.

O Donoghue, M. *Economic dimensions in education.* Dublin: Gill & Macmillan, 1971.

OECD. *Reviews of national policies for education. Ireland.* Paris: Organisation for Economic Co-operation and Development, 1969.

O Leary, P. K. The development of post-primary education in Eire since 1922, with special reference to vocational education. Unpublished Ph.D. thesis, Queen's University, Belfast, 1962.

Ó Raifeartaigh, T. The state's administration of education. *Administration*, 1954, *2*, 67–77.

Ó Raifeartaigh, T. Some impressions of education in the USA. *Studies*, 1961, *50*, 57–74.

Ó Súilleabháin, S. V. Secondary education. In P. J. Corish (Ed.), *A history of Irish Catholicism, Vol. 6.* Dublin: Gill & Macmillan, 1971.

O'Sullivan, D. Teacher profiles, school organization, and teaching styles in contrasting socio-economic contexts. *Irish Journal of Education*, 1980, *14*, 75–87.

Parkyn, G. W. *Children of high intelligence. A New Zealand study.* London: Oxford University Press, 1948.

Parsons, T. The school class as a social system: Some of its functions in American society. *Harvard Educational Review*, 1959, *29*, 297–318.

Paul, J.-J. Education and employment: A survey of French research. *European Journal of Education*, 1981, *16*, 95–119.

Raftery, A. E. Social mobility measures for cross-national comparisons. *Quality and Quantity*, in press.

Randles, Sister Eileen. *Post-primary education in Ireland 1957–1970.* Dublin: Veritas Publications, 1975.

Raven, J., Handy, R., Benson, C., Hannon, B., & Henry, E. A survey of attitudes of post-primary teachers and pupils. Volume 1. Teachers' perception of educational objectives and examinations. Dublin: Irish Association for Curriculum Development, n.d.

Rehberg, R. A., & Rosenthal, E. Social class and merit in the high school: A multi-study analysis. Research Paper 27. Center for Comparative Political Research, State University of New York at Binghamton, 1975.

Resnick, L. B. (Ed.), *The nature of intelligence*. Hillsdale, N.J.: Lawrence Erlbaum, 1976.

Roseingrave, T. A. *Early school leaving and subsequent employment*. Dublin: Irish National Productivity Committee, 1971.

Rottman, D., Hannan, D., Hardiman, N., & Wiley, M. *The distribution of income in the Republic of Ireland: A study of social class and family cycle inequalities*. Dublin: Economic and Social Research Institute, 1982.

Rottman, D. B., & O Connell, P. J. The changing social structure. In F. Litton (Ed.), *Unequal achievement. The Irish experience 1957–1982*. Dublin: Institute of Public Administration, 1982.

Rudd, J. A survey of national school terminal leavers. *Social Studies*, 1972, *1*, 61–72.

Rumberger, R. W. Dropping out of high school: The influence of race, sex, and family background. *American Educational Research Journal*, 1983, *20*, 199–220.

Ryan, L. University education and social class in Ireland. *Christus Rex*, 1966, *20*, 108–124.

Ryan, L. Social dynamite: A study of early school-leavers. *Christus Rex*, 1967, *21*, 7–44.

Seidman, R. H. The logic and behavioural principles of educational systems: Social independence or dependence. In M. S. Archer (Ed.), *The sociology of educational expansion. Take-off, growth and inflation in educational systems*. London: Sage Publications, 1982.

Sewell, T. S., Palmo, A. J., & Manni, J. L. High school dropout: Psychological, academic, and vocational factors. *Urban Education*, 1981, *66*, 65–76.

Sewell, W. H. Inequality of opportunity for higher education. *American Sociological Review*, 1971, *36*, 793–809.

Sewell, W. H., & Hauser, R. M. *Education, occupation, and earnings*. New York: Academic Press, 1975.

Sewell, W. H., & Hauser, R. M. Causes and consequences of higher education: Models of the status attainment process. In W. H. Sewell, R. M. Hauser, & D. L. Featherman, (Eds.), *Schooling and achievement in American society*. New York: Academic Press, 1976.

Sewell, W. H., & Hauser, R. M. The Wisconsin longitudinal study of social and psychological factors in aspirations and achievements. In A. C. Kerckhoff (Ed.), *Research in sociology of education and socialization*. Volume 1. Greenwich, CT.: Jai Press, 1980.

Sewell, W. H., Hauser, R. M., & Featherman, D. L. *Schooling and achievement in American society*. New York: Academic Press, 1976.

Shattock, M. Demography and social class: The fluctuating demand for higher education in Britain. *European Journal of Education*, 1981, *16*, 381–392.

Sheehan, J. Educational expenditure in Ireland. In National Economic and Social Council, *Educational expenditure in Ireland*. Dublin: Stationery Office, 1975.

Shipman, M. The limits of positive discrimination. In M. Marland (Ed.), *Education for the inner city*. London: Heinemann, 1980.

Sjöstrand, W. *Freedom and equality*. Stockholm: Almqvist & Wiksell, 1973.

Sorokin, P. A. *Social mobility*. New York: Harper, 1927.

Spelman, B. Principles and organisation of comprehensive education in the Republic of Ireland, 1963-70. Unpublished M.A. thesis, New University of Ulster, 1970.

Spring, J. *The sorting machine. National educational development since 1945.* New York: David McKay, 1976.

Stroup, A. L., & Robins, L. N. Elementary school predictors of high school dropout among black males. *Sociology of Education*, 1972, *45*, 212-222.

Sussman, L. Summary review by the rapporteur. In OECD: Study Group in the Economics of Education. *Social objectives in educational planning.* Paris: Organisation for Economic Co-operation and Development, 1967.

Swan, T. D. *Reading standards in Irish schools.* Dublin: Educational Company, 1978.

Tatsuoka, M. M. *Discriminant analysis: The study of group differences.* Champaign, IL.: Institute for Personality and Ability Testing, 1970.

Tawney, R. H. *Secondary education for all: A policy for Labour.* London: Allen & Unwin, 1922.

Tawney, R. H. *Equality.* London: Allen & Unwin, 1931.

Taylor, B. W. Jeremy Bentham and the education of the Irish people. *Irish Journal of Education*, 1980, *14*, 19-32.

Terman, L. M., *et al. Genetic studies of genius. Vol. 1. Mental and physical traits of a thousand gifted children.* Stanford, CA.: Stanford University Press, 1926.

Thernstrom, S. *Poverty and progress: Social mobility in a nineteenth century city.* Cambridge, MA.: Harvard University Press, 1964.

Turner, B. *Industrialism.* London: Longmans, 1975.

Tussing, A. D. *Irish educational expenditures – past present and future.* Dublin: Economic and Social Research Institute, 1978.

Tyack, D. B., Kirst, M. W., & Hansot, E. Educational reform: Retrospect and prospect. *Teachers College Record*, 1980, *81*, 253-269.

Vaizey, J. Review of *Investment in education. Irish Journal of Education*, 1967, *1*, 71-74.

Warner, W. L., Havighurst, R. J., & Loeb, M. B. *Who shall be educated? The challenge of unequal opportunities.* London: Kegan Paul, Trench, & Trubner, 1946.

Westergaard, J., & Little, A. Educational opportunity and social selection in England and Wales: Trends and policy implications. In OECD: Study Group in the Economics of Education. *Social objectives in educational planning.* Paris: Organisation for Economic Co-operation and Development, 1967.

Westinghouse Learning Corporation/Ohio University. *The impact of Head Start. An evaluation of the effects of Head Start on children's cognitive and affective development.* 2 volumes. Washington, D.C.: Office of Economic Opportunity, 1969.

White, K. R. The relation between socio-economic status and academic achievement. *Psychological Bulletin*, 1982, *91*, 461-481.

Whyte, J. H. *Church and state in modern Ireland 1923-70.* Dublin: Gill & Macmillan, 1971.

Wickham, A. National education systems and the international context: The case of Ireland. *Comparative Education Review*, 1980, *24*, 323-337.

Willmott, A. S. *CSE and GCE grading standards: The 1973 comparability study.* London: Macmillan Education, 1977.

Wiseman, S. *Education and environment.* Manchester: University Press, 1964.

World Bank. Education: Sector working paper. Washington, DC: World Bank, 1974.

Young, M. *Labour's plan for plenty.* London: Gollancz, 1947.

Young, M. *The rise of the meritocracy 1870-2033.* London: Pelican Books, 1961.

Zweig, F. *The new acquisitive society.* Chichester, West Sussex: Rose, 1976.

Name Index

Subject Index